PASSING
THROUGH

PASSING THROUGH

PILGRIM LIFE IN THE WILDERNESS

Jeremy Walker

Reformation Heritage Books
Grand Rapids, Michigan

Reformation Heritage Books
2965 Leonard St. NE
Grand Rapids, MI 49525
616-977-0889 / Fax 616-285-3246
orders@heritagebooks.org
www.heritagebooks.org

Printed in the United States of America
15 16 17 18 19 20/10 9 8 7 6 5 4 3 2 1

Library of Congress Cataloging-in-Publication Data

Walker, Jeremy (Jeremy R.), 1975-
  Passing through : pilgrim life in the wilderness / Jeremy Walker.
     pages cm
  ISBN 978-1-60178-387-5 (pbk. : alk. paper) 1. Identification (Religion) 2. Christian life. 3. Christianity and culture. I. Title.
   BV4509.5.W346 2015
   248.4—dc23
                              2015013768

For additional Reformed literature, request a free book list from Reformation Heritage Books at the above regular or e-mail address.

CONTENTS

PASSING THROUGH

I walk as one who knows that he is treading
   A stranger soil;
As one round whom a serpent-world is spreading
   Its subtle coil.

I walk as one but yesterday delivered
   From a sharp chain;
Who trembles lest the bond so newly severed
   Be bound again.

I walk as one who feels that he is breathing
   Ungenial air;
For whom as wiles, the tempter still is wreathing
   The bright and fair.

My steps, I know, are on the plains of danger,
   For sin is near;
But looking up, I pass along, a stranger,
   In haste and fear.

This earth has lost its power to drag me downward;
   Its spell is gone;
My course is now right upward, and right onward,
   To yonder throne.

Hour after hour of time's dark night is stealing
   In gloom away;
Speed thy fair dawn of light, and joy, and healing
   Thou Star of day!

For thee its God, its King, the long-rejected,
   Earth groans and cries;
For thee the long-beloved, the long-expected,
   Thy bride still sighs!

—HORATIUS BONAR

1

A WAY IN THE WORLD

Who are you? What are you? The answers to these questions will effectively establish the way you live, because your sense of identity substantially governs your modes of activity. Being precedes and determines doing. So, for example, if you are a king, then the way that you think of yourself and of others in relation to you is going to be very different from your expectations and relationships if you are a servant. Your whole demeanor and every part of your conduct will shift in accordance with your sense of yourself.

So it is with Christians in relationship to God in Christ and to the world around them. Our sense of who and what we are will substantially determine our attitudes, affections, appetites, and actions as we make our way in the world. In brief, if you do not know who and what you are, you will not know how to behave in your various relationships to the world around you.

Sadly, too many believers barely consider their identity, if at all. Some think about it carelessly or misguidedly, out of a position of ignorance or negligence. Some do so under the influence of false or foolish teachers, and go badly awry. The result is wrong and often, ultimately, very damaging conclusions. These have an impact on the individual, on the church, and on the character and reputation of the triune God as He is known in the earth through the testimony of His saints.

I was once asked to preach on the question of the Christian's relationship to the world. The question was posed this way: Should we relate to the twenty-first-century world? You will appreciate immediately the issue that the question intends to raise, and yet—as I pointed out at the time—the question itself can be badly misinterpreted. It at least implies that Christians have a choice as to whether or not they relate to the world. Of course, we have no choice in the matter. All of us, by very definition, are relating to the world around us. All our attitudes, affections, appetites, and actions are manifestations of that relationship. If we immerse ourselves in the world, we are relating to the world. If we attempt to cut ourselves off from the world, the very desire to have no relationship is a way of relating. The key question is not so much whether we should, must, or need to relate to the world. The concern is, *how* are we relating to the world? As professing disciples of Jesus Christ and followers of "the Way" (Acts 9:2), are we relating to the world around us foolishly and sinfully, or wisely and righteously? If we have not grasped our identity and our calling, we will not be able to answer that key question accurately and righteously. As a consequence, we will not live as we ought to as we make our way in the world.

We need, therefore, to consider our identity and our activity in the light of Scripture. This is especially necessary because the issue of worldliness—the implied dangers of a too-close walk with the world in its opposition to God—is a topic much neglected and often reinterpreted, even twisted, in the church today. Exegesis is strained and applications are contorted to provide believers with strange counsels and to direct them in dangerous ways. Under such influences sincere Christians can undermine not only their own gospel comforts but also damage the church's reputation and dishonor God in the eyes of men. By and large, the church and her members, especially in the modern West, seem to be losing sight of who and what they are. The Puritan preacher Jeremiah Burroughs suggested that there are no men upon the face of the earth who darken the glory of God so much as those who profess to be followers of Jesus and yet live carelessly. He claimed, "If our forefathers who were godly and holy and maintained a strict walk with God were alive again, they would spit in the faces of many who think themselves eminent professors of religion, because of the looseness of their conversations [carelessness of their conduct]. And this is the worst, that they can all put it upon Christ and the doctrine of Christ."[1] Confusion, carelessness, and

---

1. Jeremiah Burroughs, *Gospel Conversation* (Morgan, Pa.: Soli Deo Gloria, 1995), 22–23.

even outright carnality—sometimes in the very name of Christ—are great enemies of the gospel and the souls of men, a screeching brake on the progress of true religion.

So how does a believer relate to the world? Our Lord Jesus Himself puts us on the right track when He made intercession for His disciples, as recorded in John's gospel. Considering His people, He prayed in this way to His Father and to ours:

> "I have given them Your word; and the world has hated them because they are not of the world, just as I am not of the world. I do not pray that You should take them out of the world, but that You should keep them from the evil one. They are not of the world, just as I am not of the world. Sanctify them by Your truth. Your word is truth. As You sent Me into the world, I also have sent them into the world. And for their sakes I sanctify Myself, that they also may be sanctified by the truth." (John 17:14–19)

Our Lord self-consciously identifies Himself as the determining factor and the abiding paradigm for our relationship to the world in which He has put us. Our union with Him, our saving relationship to Him in accordance with the sovereign grace of God, determines and sets the tone for all other relationships. He Himself models our relationship to the world.

Here in John 17 the Lord speaks of Christians as those who, having been given His world, now sustain a relationship to the world that is conditioned by their likeness to and connection with Him: "They are not of the world, just as I am not of the world." But notice further that the Lord does not pray that the world would be taken away or that we would be taken out of the world. Instead, He pleads that we would be protected and preserved from the evil one as we make our way in the world. Our relationship to the world is conditioned by and patterned after His own. So the Savior prays that we would be holy in the world—living distinctively and increasingly as those who belong to and are set apart by and for God—under the influence of the truth of God. He desires that we should conduct ourselves in accordance with the purposes for which we have been sent in just the same way that the Son was sent by the Father. To this end and for this purpose, on our behalf the Son sanctified Himself: He consecrated Himself entirely and without reserve, committing

Himself entirely to His duty before God in such a way as to secure the same end for His people.

If this is so, then we come back to the question, Who and what am I as a follower of this Christ in my relationship to the world? In addressing this matter of identity and activity, we must define our terms and recognize that Scripture has at least three broad categories, linguistically or conceptually, for defining or describing *the world*.

What Is "the World"?

First, sometimes the Word of God speaks of the world in a *creative* sense. So we find Elihu asking of the Lord, "Who gave Him charge over the earth? Or who appointed Him over the whole world?" (Job 34:13). The Psalms employ the language in this sense repeatedly. Consider Psalm 8, for instance:

> O LORD, our Lord,
> How excellent is Your name in all the earth,
> Who have set Your glory above the heavens!...
> When I consider Your heavens, the work of Your fingers,
> The moon and the stars, which You have ordained,
> What is man that You are mindful of him,
> And the son of man that You visit him?...
> You have made him to have dominion over the works of
>   Your hands;
> You have put all things under his feet. (vv. 1, 3–4, 6)

The psalmist considers the realm of the whole cosmos, and—more specifically—the habitable earth where mankind dwells and in which he has been given responsibility. The Psalter continues to express this sense:

> The earth is the LORD's, and all its fullness,
> The world and those who dwell therein. (Ps. 24:1)

> "If I were hungry, I would not tell you;
> For the world is Mine, and all its fullness." (Ps. 50:12)

> Before the mountains were brought forth,
> Or ever You had formed the earth and the world,
> Even from everlasting to everlasting, You are God. (Ps. 90:2)

Let the sea roar, and all its fullness,
The world and those who dwell in it. (Ps. 98:7)

The New Testament employs the same concept. For example, the Lord asks, "For what profit is it to a man if he gains the whole world, and loses his own soul? Or what will a man give in exchange for his soul?" (Matt. 16:26). Here the primary sense has to do with all the riches of the created world. Also, Paul on Mars Hill proclaims to the Athenians the God they do not know, the one "who made the world and everything in it, since He is Lord of heaven and earth" (Acts 17:24).

In this sense the general idea of the world covers the whole created order of things, all that the Lord has made and sustains. Sometimes it is the heavens and the earth, the cosmos as a whole, sometimes more specifically the earth as the realm in which mankind dwells and governs, a place populated by creatures and things, animate and inanimate.

Secondly, the Bible sometimes describes and discusses the world in an *extensive* sense, dealing with the human inhabitants of the earth, the nations of the world. This concept takes account of mankind as a race. Often it means all peoples in all places simultaneously. In Romans 3 the apostle uses it to describe the whole human race, asking, "How will God judge the world?" (v. 6), and demonstrates his broad sense of this by going on to declare that

we have previously charged both Jews and Greeks that they are all under sin. As it is written:
"There is none righteous, no, not one;
There is none who understands;
There is none who seeks after God.
They have all turned aside;
They have together become unprofitable;
There is none who does good, no, not one." (vv. 9–12)

The same essential idea is captured in Matthew 28:18–20: "'All authority has been given to Me in heaven and on earth. Go therefore and make disciples of all the nations, baptizing them in the name of the Father and of the Son and of the Holy Spirit, teaching them to observe all things that I have commanded you; and lo, I am with you always, even to the end of the age.' Amen." Christ's cosmic authority entitles Him to send the disciples to all the nations of the earth. A slightly different but related sense is found in Luke 2:1, where the historian records that "it came to pass in those days that a decree went out from Caesar Augustus that all the world should be registered." Here it is used to designate the Roman world, all those under the particular authority of Caesar. So, in this category, the notion of the world is most often used comprehensively and even universally, without making any contrast or distinction, to identify the peoples of the earth. Within this, it can also be used comparatively and relatively restrictively, comparing or distinguishing between the Jewish people and the other peoples of the world, for example, or vice versa.

Thirdly, and finally, the Scriptures speak of the world in a *moral or ethical* sense. This is a particular favorite of the apostle John, quoting or following the Lord Jesus:

> "The world cannot hate you, but it hates Me because I testify of it that its works are evil." (John 7:7)

> "Now is the judgment of this world; now the ruler of this world will be cast out." (John 12:31)

> "I will no longer talk much with you, for the ruler of this world is coming, and he has nothing in Me. But that the world may know that I love the Father, and as the Father gave Me commandment, so I do. Arise, let us go from here." (John 14:30–31)

> You are of God, little children, and have overcome them, because He who is in you is greater than he who is in the world. They are of the world. Therefore they speak as of the world, and the world hears them. (1 John 4:4–5)

> We know that we are of God, and the whole world lies under the sway of the wicked one. (1 John 5:19)

Also, Paul uses the concept in this sense when he speaks of the Lord, "who gave Himself for our sins, that He might deliver us from this present evil age,[2] according to the will of our God and Father" (Gal. 1:4). Again he testifies, "But God forbid that I should boast except in the cross of our Lord Jesus Christ, by whom the

---

2. The idea of the world in this sense lies beneath the language of "this present evil age."

world has been crucified to me, and I to the world" (Gal. 6:14). He writes to the Ephesians of the work of God in them: "And you He made alive, who were dead in trespasses and sins, in which you once walked according to the course of this world, according to the prince of the power of the air, the spirit who now works in the sons of disobedience" (Eph. 2:1–2). He warns these same Christians that "we do not wrestle against flesh and blood, but against principalities, against powers, against the rulers of the darkness of this age, against spiritual hosts of wickedness in the heavenly places" (Eph. 6:12). James employs it, too, when he asks believers, "Do you not know that friendship with the world is enmity with God? Whoever therefore wants to be a friend of the world makes himself an enemy of God" (4:4).

Here we are clearly speaking of creation as fallen, considered in its systemic corruption and systematic opposition to God, often explicitly contending against the kingdom of heaven to which disciples belong. It designates those who are antagonistic to God and to His reign. It regularly involves an identification of Satan as "ruler of this world," the great and chief adversary of God and His people. This fierce enemy leads the rebellion against the Lord, driving on his slaves in their senseless and self-destructive campaign against the righteous authority of the Most High God. The Scottish theologian George Smeaton captures the sense when he speaks of Satan as "the head of all who attach themselves to that natural life which lies in estrangement from God, or who set themselves in banded opposition to the Christ of God. How fitly the name applies to the world in its moral and intellectual condition under ungodly influences that come from the evil one, the first cause and father of corruption, scarcely requires to be pointed out."[3]

It should also be noted that these various usages, or shades of usage, are often in close connection with one another, in combination or even with a degree of overlap. So, for example, consider Psalm 2:

> Why do the nations rage,
> And the people plot a vain thing?
> The kings of the earth set themselves,

---

3. George Smeaton, *Christ's Doctrine of the Atonement* (Edinburgh: Banner of Truth, 1991), 307.

And the rulers take counsel together,
Against the LORD and against His Anointed, saying,
"Let us break Their bonds in pieces
And cast away Their cords from us."

"He who sits in the heavens shall laugh;
The Lord shall hold them in derision.
Then He shall speak to them in His wrath,
And distress them in His deep displeasure:
"Yet I have set My King On My holy hill of Zion."

"I will declare the decree:
The LORD has said to Me,
'You are My Son,
Today I have begotten You.
Ask of Me, and I will give You
The nations for Your inheritance,
And the ends of the earth for Your possession.
You shall break them with a rod of iron;
You shall dash them to pieces like a potter's vessel.'"

Now therefore, be wise, O kings;
Be instructed, you judges of the earth.
Serve the LORD with fear,
And rejoice with trembling.
Kiss the Son, lest He be angry,
And you perish in the way,
When His wrath is kindled but a little.
Blessed are all those who put their trust in Him.

Here there is an extensive sense, in which the whole world is encompassed within the designators of "the people" (the Jews) and "the peoples" (the other nations). And yet it is quite clear that this is a world that is considered in its essential hostility to God the Lord, the moral or ethical sense. The great and the not-so-good of all the earth are uniting to express a shared antagonism to the rule of "the LORD and...His Anointed," a deep-rooted antipathy to the one "who sits in the heavens" (vv. 2, 4). This rebellion among the world extensively is an expression of its antagonism morally to the rule of God. But again,

God's promise to Messiah concerns the nations and the ends of the earth, bringing in the extensive and the creative senses together.

Or take John 1:9–10: "That was the true Light which gives light to every man coming into the world. He was in the world, and the world was made through Him, and the world did not know Him." When the apostle speaks of "every man coming into the world," he uses a word that speaks to us of the creative sense, but "every man" points us also to the extensive notion. Christ "in the world" and "making the world" probably refer almost exclusively to the world as created, but how much of the moral and ethical sense is there in the declaration that "the world did not know Him"?

Or, finally, what of our Lord's words in John 16:33? "These things I have spoken to you, that in Me you may have peace. In the world you will have tribulation; but be of good cheer, I have overcome the world." Almost certainly the primary meaning of overcoming the world has in view the world opposing God and His Christ. Even so, the warning that "in the world you will have tribulation" hints at both the creative sense and the moral sense. As we make our way through this created world we will have the tribulation that arises from being "children of God without fault in the midst of a crooked and perverse generation, among whom you shine as lights in the world" (Phil. 2:15), to draw in a little of Paul. We are reminded that tribulations will often come through the men who inhabit the earth. There is an implication, too, that when we leave this fallen world or it is renewed, there will be no more tribulation.

These shades, nuances, and combinations of meaning are important to note because one of the right and proper rules of biblical interpretation is that, generally speaking, the same word is used in the same way in the same context. And yet, as so often, exceptions exist, and these shades of the concept can lurk in various linguistic forms and different phrases. It is important that we ask how and to what purpose these various shades of sense are employed.

Flawed Relationships to the World

Christians must appreciate that they are called to relate to the world in a certain way in each of these different spheres in accordance with their different definitions. What happens if we fail to distinguish between them or to cultivate a properly nuanced understanding with an unwillingness to discern and direct our responses accordingly? We may be bewildered and betrayed, confused and compromised, indecisive and ineffective.

One result of such a failure will be the likely adoption of a lazy, blanket approach to the whole matter. In such a case, the child of God might—for various reasons and perhaps because of a too absolute rigidity or a too careless fluidity—be betrayed into one of three flawed approaches.

The first flawed approach is *isolation*. We might describe this as the bunker mentality, when a church or a Christian seeks to back off or simply to cut themselves off from all contact with the world in any form. Some might adopt it as an offensive strategy, often sincerely seeking to promote a high degree of holiness. Though perhaps rooted in a right desire to show distinctiveness as the people of God, this often degenerates into a crass "them and us" attitude. It can be a breeding ground for the kind of pride that—like the Pharisee in the temple—begins to thank God that we are not like other men (particularly those dreadful sinners *outside*) but are rather well endowed with the kinds of good works with which God is obliged to be pleased. Others adopt this approach as a defensive maneuver, attempting to shut out everything that is unholy, making the walls high, the ditches deep, the doors thick, and the bars strong. They persist in their notion that they can create some kind of spiritual hermetic seal around a church, a family, or a person and so keep everything spiritually contaminating at a distance. The assumption seems to be that if they can establish and maintain such a seal, eventually the world might just go away and they will not have to deal with it.

There may be some degree of truth and wisdom in elements of this approach. However, the problem with isolation is that no matter how many others I might be able to keep out, I am left inside. But I know that "from within, out of the heart of men, proceed evil thoughts, adulteries, fornications, murders, thefts, covetousness, wickedness, deceit, lewdness, an evil eye, blasphemy, pride, foolishness. All these evil things come from within and defile a man" (Mark 7:21–23). Anyone who invites and shuts me into that community or space has shut in a man who carries sin in him. Furthermore, even our Lord did not pray that we would be taken out of the world, but that we would be kept from the evil one (John 17:15), preserved in the world and maintained in godliness despite the environment into which He has sent us. We should remember the apostle Paul's words to the Corinthian church: "I wrote to you in my epistle not to keep company with sexually immoral people. Yet I certainly did not mean with the sexually immoral people of this world, or with the covetous, or extortioners, or idolaters, since then you would need to go out of the world" (1 Cor. 5:9–10). In the context, Paul is explaining that there is a righteous distance that must be maintained between the church and a professing Christian who commits such sins without repentance. However, to attempt to cut ourselves off from all such people would require that we remove from the world entirely. This is not only unreasonable to attempt or expect, but it would also sever our contact with the very people for whose benefit the church has been entrusted with the gospel.

The monastic tendency ultimately fails. This miserable truth has been discovered whenever men and women have tried to cloister themselves, imagining that everything unholy can be excluded and that this will ensure the holiness of God's people (for these offensive and defensive postures often coexist). Martin Luther, for example, discovered it in an Augustinian cloister. Tragically, this failure also betrays one of the very purposes for which Christ has called us, commanding us to "let your light so shine before men, that they may see your good works and glorify your Father in heaven" (Matt. 5:16).

A second flawed attitude is *inattention*. This is the congregation or saint who maintains a kind of distant ignorance, perhaps with something of a sneer. To such people the world is irrelevant, the object of casual neglect and carelessness. Perhaps there is pride here, or ignorance of how to handle the world, or fear that they are not equipped to do so. It may be that the language of holiness is used to put a veneer on what is actually a thoughtless disregard for the world and the things in it. This is cultivated not in the sense of esteeming and holding such things lightly for Christ's sake, but is the absence of any genuine concern, legitimate interest, sincere compassion, and real care. Have we forgotten that in Iconium Paul and Barnabas "went together to the synagogue of the Jews, and so spoke that a great multitude both of the Jews and of the Greeks believed" (Acts 14:1)? How could they speak so as to catch the ears and win the hearts of the people of Iconium without considering them and desiring to do them good? Or again, Paul in Athens is righteously provoked not because he has been trying to ignore the world around him but because he has been observing it. He is able to say, "Men of Athens, I perceive that in all things you are very religious" (Acts 17:22). As he engages with them, he goes on to quote their own poets to prove the correctness of some of his fundamental assertions, truths which ought to be—and are, in measure—evident to clear-thinking men in the world. And if not Paul, what of Christ Himself, who clearly did not go through the world with his eyes half shut, but was able to ask His hearers to consider the birds of the air and the flowers of the field, the sower at his work and the children at their play?

The church and the world often drift along side by side in a strange relationship, neither one really acknowledging the other. The church can even become something of a parasite. It exists among the people of the world and feeds off the profits and processes of society and the culture at large, but makes no genuine and righteous investments and seeks no gospel influence. Again, there may be something of an appropriate and righteous disregard—the absence of any obsession—with the world, but there is also a grand mistake being made. In the beginning, before sin entered the world, the Lord gave a charge to our first parents: "Then God blessed them, and God said to them, 'Be fruitful and multiply; fill the earth and subdue it; have dominion over the fish of the sea, over the birds of the air, and over every living thing that moves on the earth'" (Gen. 1:28). The entrance of sin may have altered the circumstances under which that charge is to be obeyed as seen in the curses that fall upon sinful mankind, but the charge itself has not been suspended or revoked. What is called the "dominion mandate" remains as a binding obligation upon men and women made in God's image.

Furthermore, while we should not ignore the specific context of the people to whom Jeremiah spoke, there is a principle in his words that those who are in exile in a fallen world might still embrace: "And seek the peace of the city where I have caused you to be carried away captive, and pray to the LORD for it; for in its peace you will have peace" (Jer. 29:7). This disposition is not simply to be one of remote concern. The apostle Peter wrote in this way to the Christians of his day: "Beloved, I beg you as sojourners and pilgrims, abstain from fleshly lusts which war against the soul, having your conduct honorable among the Gentiles, that when they speak against you as evildoers, they may, by your good works which they observe, glorify God in the day of visitation" (1 Peter 2:11–12). The way in which such a child of God lived before and among the Gentiles might not remove the slur of his attachment to the Lord. It should, though, demand—eventually—some measure of recognition for the good works carried out on behalf of those Gentiles who might still despise him. So David is able to testify this way in Psalm 35:11–16:

> Fierce witnesses rise up;
> They ask me things that I do not know.
> They reward me evil for good,
> To the sorrow of my soul.
> But as for me, when they were sick,
> My clothing was sackcloth;
> I humbled myself with fasting;
> And my prayer would return to my own heart.
> I paced about as though he were my friend or brother;
> I bowed down heavily, as one who mourns for his mother.
>
> But in my adversity they rejoiced
> And gathered together;
> Attackers gathered against me,
> And I did not know it;
> They tore at me and did not cease;
> With ungodly mockers at feasts
> They gnashed at me with their teeth.

That is not the testimony of a man who is ignoring the world even while being assaulted by it.

The third flawed outlook might be described as *emulation*. This is the church or believer who ends up seeking to be (or, in some cases, deliberately sets out to be) like the world. Often this begins with the desire, legitimate in itself, of doing genuine good to those around her. However, it can result in a church immersed in the world's culture, adopting its patterns, mimicking its behavior, imbibing its priorities, and mirroring its movements. These Christians ape what they see around them and simply meld into the environment, perfectly camouflaged. In some cases, the mantra "in it to win it" might

be used to justify such a principle. Others will twist Paul's statement that "I have become all things to all men, that I might by all
means save some" (1 Cor. 9:22). In itself, it is an individual's simple
testimony to his readiness to accommodate himself to substantially
neutral norms around him. Warped, it becomes a mandate for corporate contextualization—all too often and too quickly nothing less
than compromise—in which the church adapts its nature, forms, and
functions to suit the spirit of the age, floating adrift on the current
of present carnality. Sadly, this often happens thoughtlessly where it
has not been undertaken deliberately.

Under such circumstances, the church ceases to be a thermo-
stat that regulates the moral temperature of society and becomes
a thermometer that merely registers and reflects that temperature.
There is no doubt that the church must have points of contact—must
make points of contact—with those around her if she is to have an
impact upon the souls of men and women. However, the Scriptures
are perfectly clear that "friendship with the world is enmity with
God" (James 4:4). Paul exhorts the saints in Rome—the very center
of the mighty empire, where the temptation to ape the world might
be particularly potent—"do not be conformed to this world, but be
transformed by the renewing of your mind, that you may prove what
is that good and acceptable and perfect will of God" (Rom. 12:2).

Again, all of these approaches might be undertaken instinctively,
ignorantly, thoughtlessly, or deliberately. But all are flawed in that
they fail to root our activity in our identity, taking into account the
various nuances of relationship demanded by the shades of meaning
that lie behind the idea of "the world."

Each one, as we have seen, abuses or neglects some element of
biblical revelation considered as a whole. None of them answers the
distinctive demands of the relationship that the church must sustain
to the world considered in all its various manifestations and guises.
None of them is an option for the church seeking to be faithful to
God and fruitful among men. Indeed, to live like this—individually
or corporately—would be to fail in our responsibilities, privileges,
and duties. They have the virtue of relative simplicity, providing
a sort of catch-all approach by means of which it is then possible
to relieve one's conscience, avoid combat, suspend thoughtfulness,

make less effort, give in to temptation, or take some other apparently easy way out.

Our flesh—considered either in the absolute sense of our humanity, so weak and easily wearied, or in the more particular sense of our remaining sinfulness, so quick to salivate over passing pleasures— might demand an easy way out. We are not at liberty to seek such a way or to take one.

Rather, our thoughts, words, and deeds must be governed by the Word of God. We cannot fall back on the mere rationalism that would raise man's thoughts and opinions to the highest authority, leaving the church to be directed by the judgment of the one (the guru), the few (the council or committee), or the many (the coalition or the mob). Traditionalism will not answer, whether it be the unthinking adoption of some old rule without consideration of the application of principle to the here and now or the embrace of some new model churned out by the great and the good for this brave new world. Pragmatism will not do, with its obsession with apparent but often temporary effectiveness. This too often leads to a desperation for an impact, resulting in a faddishness, a church that skips from program to program, abandoning each one successively as it wears out and becomes old, thoughtlessly adopting whatever happens to be popular in the time and place in which God has situated us. We do not need to jump on bandwagons. We need not put ourselves in hock to personalities on a local, national, or global scale, slavishly following those with fame, charisma, wealth, eloquence, aggression, or whatever else it may be that gives them a platform and an authority to be heard in the eyes of many. Neither do we need to default to a kind of confused fatalism in which we are not even sure if an answer exists or whether it really matters, an attitude in which the best we can do is keep our heads down, remaining faithless, fruitless, and frozen. We need not hope merely for survival and trust that things might brighten up somewhere down the road while we drift along on the current of circumstances about which we feel we can do nothing.

Guided by Scripture

Instead, if we are to be guided and guarded on our way through this life, it is to our Bibles, in reliance upon the Holy Spirit, that we must

turn: "The Holy Scriptures…are able to make you wise for salvation through faith which is in Christ Jesus. All Scripture is given by
inspiration of God, and is profitable for doctrine, for reproof, for cor-
rection, for instruction in righteousness, that the man of God may be
complete, thoroughly equipped for every good work" (2 Tim. 3:15–17).

How is a child of wrath to be saved? What is it that changes our
fundamental relationship to the world? What brings us out of the
way of death and puts us onto the way of life, delivering us from the
power of darkness and conveying us into the kingdom of the Son of
God's love (Col. 1:13)? It is through the Scriptures, which make us
wise for salvation through faith in Jesus Christ.

And how is the child of God to be kept from the evil one? How
will you make your way in the world, knowing "how you ought to
walk and to please God" (1 Thess. 4:1)? It is the Scriptures that equip
us for the road.

What relief there is here for the determined-though-sometimes-
bewildered, willing-but-often-exposed disciple of Christ! Here is
realism about the persecutions we must endure and about the decep-
tions that will abound: "All who desire to live godly in Christ Jesus
will suffer persecution. But evil men and impostors will grow worse
and worse, deceiving and being deceived" (2 Tim. 3:12–13). But here
also is a firm anchor, a source of divine wisdom for salvation in its
complete scope, a means for our entering in and our going on in
the kingdom of God. Its quality—the breathed-out word of the living God—gives us confidence. Its utility for bringing wisdom for
salvation to those who are lost in darkness and who require a Savior
(2 Tim. 3:15) and for enabling the "man of God"[4] to be "complete,
thoroughly equipped for every good work" (2 Tim. 3:17) assures us
that it will answer our needs. Its sufficiency, answering every phase
of Christian experience and every sphere of Christian need, makes
us entirely fit for purpose. John Murray reminds us that

> there is no situation in which we are placed, no demand that
> arises, for which Scripture as the deposit of the manifold

---

4. In the context, "man of God" probably has primary reference to those
appointed for the care of the flock of God, but if in principle the Scriptures are sufficient for them to do their work, which involves ministering to all the saints, then
in practice that sufficiency provides for every member of the church.

wisdom of God is not adequate and sufficient. It is the Scripture that provides the equipment, the furnishings, the investments, that prepare us for the kingdom of God, "till we all come in the unity of the faith and of the knowledge of the Son of God unto a perfect man, unto the measure of the stature of the fulness of Christ" and are "filled unto all the fulness of God."[5]

But we cannot forget that we are utterly dependent on the Holy Spirit to enable us to grasp the truth that saves and embrace the truth that sanctifies: "The natural man does not receive the things of the Spirit of God, for they are foolishness to him; nor can he know them, because they are spiritually discerned" (1 Cor. 2:14). Without the illumination of the Holy Spirit we are blind men in a dark room. Even if that room is filled with the treasures of divine revelation we cannot see them until the lights are turned on and our eyes are opened. He opens the truth to us (John 16:12–15), and us to the truth (Acts 16:14). Without Him, we will miss our way. When He is at work in and with and through the Word of God, then we find answered that great prayer-declaration of our Lord and Savior: "Sanctify them by Your truth. Your word is truth" (John 17:17).

Our Bibles, given through and illuminated by the Holy Spirit, are a safe and sufficient guide for us. The Scriptures expose and condemn certain attitudes and approaches, putting them distinctly and definitely out of bounds for the child of God seeking to live in this present age in fulfillment of his calling and God's will. The same Bible also provides precepts, principles, and practices by means of which we may discern our duty as disciples, pursuing that duty in dependence on the Spirit of the risen Christ. John Calvin described this relationship between Word and Spirit, telling us that

> the Holy Spirit so inheres in his truth, which He expresses in Scripture, that only when its proper reverence and dignity are given to the Word does the Holy Spirit show forth his power.... For by a kind of mutual bond the Lord has joined together the certainty of his Word and of his Spirit so that the perfect religion of the Word may abide in our minds when the Spirit, who causes us to contemplate God's face, shines; and that we in turn

---

5. John Murray, "Holy Scripture," in *Collected Writings* (Edinburgh: Banner of Truth, 1977), 3:261.

may embrace the Spirit with no fear of being deceived when we recognize him in his own image, namely, in the Word. So indeed it is. God did not bring forth his Word among men for the sake of a momentary display, intending at the coming of his Spirit to abolish it. Rather, he sent down the same Spirit by whose power he had dispensed the Word, to complete his work by the efficacious confirmation of the Word.[6]

With the Word of God as our map and the Spirit of Christ as our compass, we are equipped to navigate this world, to make our way in the world so as to bring honor and glory to God. By means of the Scriptures and with the light of the Spirit we can establish and embrace our identity and direct and pursue our activity to the praise of the glory of our God and Savior.

---

6. John Calvin, *Institutes of the Christian Religion*, ed. John T. McNeill, trans. Ford Lewis Battles (Philadelphia: Westminster Press, 1960), 1.9.3.

2
STRANGERS AND PILGRIMS

If the Word of God is our map and the Spirit of God our compass, and if we need to grasp our identity accurately if we are to govern our activity righteously as we make our way in the world, then how do we answer the question, Who and what are you? We should acknowledge, in all fairness, that there are a good number of right answers to the question of our identity. Many of those answers substantially overlap. For example, you could answer, "I am a disciple of the Lord Jesus"; or, "I am a son of the Most High God"; or, "I am a sheep belonging to the Good Shepherd"; or, "I am a servant of the best of masters"; or, "I am a crossbearer following in the Lord's footsteps." Any of those answers is accurate and could be profitably developed.

Nevertheless, the answer I wish to give is one I believe is often neglected today. It is related to all of these suggested answers, but is perhaps considered outmoded and irrelevant by some. I am persuaded that it provides the modern church with an anchor point and a perspective that is sadly lacking in too many saints, especially in the West.

The identity in question is that of the pilgrim. This motif is prominent throughout the whole Bible, found in both the Old and the New Testaments. It is used as a means of describing, characterizing, encouraging, and directing the saints. Homer's epic poem *The Odyssey* tells of the hero navigating his ship between two monsters called Scylla and Charybdis, in which steering away from one usually meant falling prey to the other. The Christian in the world faces a similar challenge. A sense of our identity as pilgrims will help us to navigate between the Scylla of isolation and the Charybdis of emulation, as well as the aimless drift of inattention. And these are present dangers. In some circles, a more fundamentalist viewpoint—often in reaction to professing believers appearing to pursue or actually pursuing friendship with the world—will promote a more absolute isolation from the world in all its aspects. In other spheres, an undiscerning approach—certainly seen among many in the emerging and emergent church movement, but far from absent in certain expressions of evangelicalism—seems to advocate a thoughtless embrace of the world in some of its more dangerous aspects. Around them swirls a host of others who simply do not consider the issue.

This is where the notion of the pilgrim provides a scriptural perspective, a solid point from which to assess and act. It enables us to approach the world, taking account of the various nuances of the pilgrim identity in such a way as to "walk worthy of the Lord, fully pleasing Him, being fruitful in every good work and increasing in the knowledge of God" (Col. 1:10).

The Bible's Pilgrims

We find this motif in Psalm 119:19: "I am a stranger in the earth; do not hide Your commandments from me." This is a seminal statement in this psalm, helping to establish the whole framework by which the psalmist—and, by extension, those who seek to know and follow God as he does—perceives and interprets the world and his place in it. Here is his situation: "I am a stranger"—an alien, a temporary resident, one who does not belong here. Here is his location: "in the earth"—traveling through this world. Here is his supplication: "do not hide Your commandments from me"—that is, provide me with all the revelation of Your will that is in keeping with what is needful given this character and its demands. William Plumer summarizes the sense:

> All God's people have been strangers and pilgrims on the earth. They had here no continuing city, but sought one to come. They confessed that earth was a wilderness, through which they were hastily passing. That which guided and cheered them in their journey was the word of God, every part of it, including his whole preceptive will. To *hide* his word from us is to leave us

to our natural blindness without saving knowledge, or spiritual illumination.... "The pilgrim spirit is the pulse of the soul."[1]

That last phrase is a quote from Charles Bridges, who in his commentary goes on, "All of us are travelling to eternity. The worldling"—today that is not only a strange word but a barely known idea—"is at home *in the earth*—the pilgrim only by restraint."[2] Instructive for us is that the psalmist's sense of things answers to our Lord's in His prayer in John 17:14–19. Notice the common ground: His people are in the world, but not of the world; they need to be sanctified by the truth, and God's Word is the truth they need.

David used this language when speaking to the Lord at the accession of Solomon:

> For we are aliens and pilgrims before You,
> As were all our fathers;
> Our days on earth are as a shadow,
> And without hope. (1 Chron. 29:15)

Peter calls new covenant believers to grasp it when he begs them to "abstain from fleshly lusts which war against the soul" as those who are and ought to consider themselves "sojourners and pilgrims" (1 Peter 2:11).

Paul employs the same basic notion in writing to the Philippians:

> Brethren, join in following my example, and note those who so walk, as you have us for a pattern. For many walk, of whom I have told you often, and now tell you even weeping, that they are the enemies of the cross of Christ: whose end is destruction, whose god is their belly, and whose glory is in their shame—who set their mind on earthly things. For our citizenship is in heaven, from which we also eagerly wait for the Savior, the Lord Jesus Christ, who will transform our lowly body that it may be conformed to His glorious body, according to the working by which He is able even to subdue all things to Himself. Therefore, my beloved and longed-for brethren, my joy and crown, so stand fast in the Lord, beloved. (Phil. 3:17–4:1)

---

1. William S. Plumer, *Psalms* (Edinburgh: Banner of Truth, 1975), 1029, 1031.
2. Charles Bridges, *Psalm 119* (Edinburgh: Banner of Truth, 1974), 41.

His point here is that the saints are a celestial colony, an outpost of heaven, living here but belonging elsewhere. We derive our character from our citizenship in heaven, but our temporary residence is on earth, and this is where we display our character in anticipation of the return of the King.

The controlling factor, the great event that divides the believer from the world, is the cross of Christ: "But God forbid that I should boast except in the cross of our Lord Jesus Christ, by whom the world has been crucified to me, and I to the world" (Gal. 6:14). We must remember this from both sides: the world looks at the believer as under the shadow of death, and the believer returns the favor. That should help us not just in our perceptions of ourselves and of the world, but as a reminder of how we are perceived when we are standing with Christ.

Perhaps the clearest emphasis comes in the letter to the Hebrews, particularly in the account of Abraham, the father of the faithful (Rom. 4:12; Gal. 3:29). When Abraham was called to leave his home in Ur of the Chaldees, he went in faith, traveling to a place he did not know. He and his heirs lived in that land as if it were a foreign country, "for he waited for the city which has foundations, whose builder and maker is God" (Heb. 11:10). By faith Sarah was given strength to conceive a child and bore Isaac at an old age so that from this one man, Abraham, were born as many people as there are stars in the sky and sand by the sea. As the writer to the Hebrews explains, believing Abraham and his children were seeking that city whose builder is God, and they

> died in faith, not having received the promises, but having seen them afar off were assured of them, embraced them and confessed that they were strangers and pilgrims on the earth. For those who say such things declare plainly that they seek a homeland. And truly if they had called to mind that country from which they had come out, they would have had opportunity to return. But now they desire a better, that is, a heavenly country. Therefore God is not ashamed to be called their God, for He has prepared a city for them. (Heb. 11:13–16)

The abiding validity of this character and its perspectives is later pressed home for all believers in the same language: "For here we have no continuing city, but we seek the one to come" (Heb. 13:14). All believers have always been present in but passing through the world.

Mentioning Abraham brings us from the realm of straightforward instruction to that of example. I will be brief because wise readers are able to see this for themselves from the Bible. Even if we restrict ourselves substantially to the book of Hebrews, we find Abraham and the patriarchs, who are waiting for their inheritance. They are living in tents as they hang upon the promises of God, and there could hardly be a more potent reminder of their status than that. Joseph was a man whose wisdom made him a great blessing to the whole nation of Egypt and who was used to preserve and protect the fledgling nation of Israel. However, by faith "when he was dying," Joseph "made mention of the departure of the children of Israel, and gave instructions concerning his bones" (Heb. 11:22). Joseph knew that Egypt, however much he had been involved in it during his sojourn, was not his home. Moses, brought fully into the wealth and wisdom of Egypt as a prince in the nation, chose "rather to suffer affliction with the people of God than to enjoy the passing pleasures of sin, esteeming the reproach of Christ greater riches than the treasures in Egypt; for he looked to the reward" (Heb. 11:25–26). The whole Exodus generation provides a spectrum of instruction: in Hebrews 3, drawing extensively on Psalm 95, they are used to remind us that there is a need to persevere in order to enter into the rest that is to come. In their wilderness journey, many of them lusted after evil things, became idolaters, committed sexual immorality, tempted Christ, and complained. Paul uses them in 1 Corinthians to warn those believers about their way in the world:

> Moreover, brethren, I do not want you to be unaware that all our fathers were under the cloud, all passed through the sea, all were baptized into Moses in the cloud and in the sea, all ate the same spiritual food, and all drank the same spiritual drink. For they drank of that spiritual Rock that followed them, and that Rock was Christ. But with most of them God was not well pleased, for their bodies were scattered in the wilderness.... Now all these things happened to them as examples, and they were written for our admonition, upon whom the ends of the ages have come. Therefore let him who thinks he stands take heed lest he fall. (1 Cor. 10:1–5, 11–12)

We might cite Daniel, whose indoctrination into Babylonian modes of thought and behavior could not eradicate his convictions concerning obedience to the living God. Daniel was an exile from Jerusalem who lived and labored in Babylon but loved and longed for Zion. We could consider others "of whom the world was not worthy," who "wandered in deserts and mountains, in dens and caves of the earth. And all these, having obtained a good testimony through faith, did not receive the promise, God having provided something better for us, that they should not be made perfect apart from us" (Heb. 11:38–40). In addition, Paul, Peter, John, James, Jude, and the other New Testament authors repeatedly emphasize the same concept, using more or less the same language.

And of whom are all these faint reflections? Surely they point us toward Christ Jesus, the great Pilgrim, the Pioneer and Perfecter of our faith (Heb. 12:1–2), the Prophet who reveals God's will as we make our journey, the King who rules and defends us as we travel, and the Priest who—having purchased us with His own blood— intercedes for us that we might safely arrive at home:

> "Father, I desire that they also whom You gave Me may be with Me where I am, that they may behold My glory which You have given Me; for You loved Me before the foundation of the world. O righteous Father! The world has not known You, but I have known You; and these have known that You sent Me. And I have declared to them Your name, and will declare it, that the love with which You loved Me may be in them, and I in them." (John 17:24–26)

Here is the perfect and perpetual paradigm of One who—though not belonging to this world—nevertheless came into it. He was neither isolated from the world, nor neglectful of it, nor consumed by it. He was preeminently in the world but not of it, rejected by it but dying for it.

All those who in this matter imitate Christ grasp that identity by faith: faith lays hold of what is not seen and acts in accordance with it. Confusion and compromise increase where faith struggles (think of Abraham with Abimelech or Abraham and Sarah with Hagar and Ishmael, using man's means to try to preserve or progress God's plans in accordance with divine promises) and diminish where faith grasps the truth. When the saints grasp their identity, it governs their activity—their being informs their doing.

Church History's Pilgrims

And so it is through the ages, as we turn to an illustration from church history. Consider, for example, Augustine's great book *City of God*, in which he is contending with the fallout from the Constantinian settlement[3] and that the realm of Rome is collapsing under the assaults of the barbarians. Many believers in his day were fearfully persuaded that the kingdom of God would collapse with the empire of Rome. Here, in his "mature reflection on God's purposes in the realm of history,"[4] Augustine rejects the high Eusebian view of Roman history. He sets out to demonstrate that the two kingdoms are not yoked together and that the kingdom of God is marked out by a pilgrim mentality. Michael Haykin summarizes Augustine, who tells us that "the city of God is a pilgrim city that is not at home in this world." Augustine makes clear that the city of the saints is on high, although its citizens are produced here below. In the persons of believers, the whole city of God is on a pilgrimage until the time its kingdom comes. "Given the repetitive way in which Augustine describes the City of God in these terms," says Haykin, "there is little doubt that the state of being a pilgrim in this world is an essential aspect of the City of God. This City has no home here in this world, but is on its way to its true home in the world to come."[5] The city of God will outlast any empires of the world. Though the saints in the world suffer through the same circumstances as any others, the City of God will find "its true home in the unending glory of God's presence and the felicity of the beatific vision."[6]

We will skip some centuries to other well-known figures and think of the life and ministry of John Calvin. When the five-hundredth anniversary of his birth was celebrated in 2009, a number of biographies

---

3. This was the time when the Emperor Constantine made Christianity the dominant religion of the Roman Empire during his reign of AD 306–337.

4. Michael Haykin, "'The Most Glorious City of God': Augustine of Hippo and *The City of God*," in *The Power of God in the Life of Man: Papers Read at the 2005 Westminster Conference* ([London]: Westminster Conference, 2005), 46.

5. Haykin, "'Most Glorious City of God,'" 51.

6. Haykin, "'Most Glorious City of God,'" 52.

were published. Several of them drew attention to this theme in the Reformer's life, such as Robert Godfrey's *John Calvin: Pilgrim and Pastor*[7] and Herman Selderhuis's *John Calvin: A Pilgrim's Life*.[8] It is no accident that they chose this motif to decorate their work. Selderhuis writes:

> "We are always on the road." With these words Calvin not only expressed his view of life in general but unconsciously summed up the story of his own life as well. The same is true of his spiritual offspring, since *on the road* can be understood both literally and spiritually. Over the centuries, Reformed Christians have often lived as sojourners, refugees and emigrants, but they have also seen themselves as being "on the road" spiritually since heaven has become their new homeland—the journey will finally end only when they have arrived there. Believers are "just sojourners on this earth, so that with hope and patience they strive toward a better life." If heaven is one's homeland, one can, at one and the same time, feel at home both anywhere and nowhere.[9]

Calvin himself writes, "It is clear to us that all that is said and done in the church goes back to the main point, that we, withdrawn from the world, are raised up to heaven with our Head and Savior."[10]

Other Reformers on the Continent and on the British mainland found many of their comforts in the fact that they were pilgrims and strangers. Following them, the Puritans cultivated a pilgrim mentality, allowing Joel Beeke and Mark Jones to conclude, "The Puritan mentality was biblically based, pietistic, churchly, wayfaring, methodical, and two-worldly. In these ways, the Puritans were pilgrims, heavenly visionaries who traveled through this world to a land they could see only in the Scriptures with the eyes of faith.... They can teach us, as no other group of writers in church history,

---

7. W. Robert Godfrey, *John Calvin: Pilgrim and Pastor* (Wheaton, Ill.: Crossway, 2009).

8. Herman J. Selderhuis, *John Calvin: A Pilgrim's Life*, trans. Albert Gootjes (Downers Grove, Ill.: IVP Academic, 2009).

9. Selderhuis, *John Calvin*, 35.

10. Quoted in Selderhuis, *John Calvin*, 60. For a more complete study of this motif in some of Calvin's thought, see Gopalswamy Jacob, *The Motif of Stranger in Calvin's Old Testament Commentaries* (Apeldoorn: Instituut voor Reformatieonderzoek, 2008).

how to live a disciplined life to God's glory without falling into dead orthodoxy or deadly legalism."[11]

Moving on, we might consider Andrew Fuller, who, in the sermon "The Choice of Moses," challenges us:

> The people of God in our day [may not] lie under such reproaches and afflictions as in the time of Moses. But this only proves that our temptations are not so strong as his; and, consequently, that if the world conquer us, we shall be the less excusable. But the world and Christ are in competition for our choice, and we are required to give a decisive and immediate answer. Choose ye this day who ye will serve. There are many who can and do say as Joshua did, "As for me and my house, we will serve the Lord." His people shall be our people, and his cause our cause. If any refuse, and prefer the present world before him, be it known to them that, as if their choice in this world, such will be their portion in that which is to come.[12]

And Spurgeon, in a sermon on Hebrews 11:15–16, writes,

> As many of us as have believed in Christ have been called out. The very meaning of a church is, "called out by Christ." We have been separated. I trust we know what it is to have gone without the camp, bearing Christ's reproach. Henceforth, in this world we have no home, no true home for our spirits; our home is beyond the flood; we are looking for it amongst the unseen things; we are strangers and sojourners as all our fathers were, dwellers in this wilderness, passing through it to reach the Canaan which is to be the land of our perpetual inheritance.[13]

It is no accident that, bridging some of these years, Marcus Loane writes of David Brainerd, Henry Martyn, Robert Murray M'Cheyne, and Ion Keith-Falconer under the title *They Were Pilgrims*.[14]

---

11. Joel R. Beeke and Mark Jones, *A Puritan Theology: Doctrine for Life* (Grand Rapids: Reformation Heritage Books, 2012), 858.

12. Andrew Fuller, "The Choice of Moses," in *The Complete Works of the Rev. Andrew Fuller* (Harrisonburg, Va.: Sprinkle Publications, 1988), 1:428.

13. Charles H. Spurgeon, "The Pilgrim's Longings," in *Metropolitan Tabernacle Pulpit* (Pasadena, Tex.: Pilgrim Publications, 1984), 18:26.

14. Marcus L. Loane, *They Were Pilgrims* (Edinburgh: Banner of Truth, 2006).

Bunyan's Pilgrim

But perhaps the finest and most sustained treatment of this theme is found in John Bunyan's ageless book *The Pilgrim's Progress*. In this volume as a whole, the structure is governed by the journey of a man we come to know as Christian—a kind of redeemed Everyman—who has set out from the City of Destruction and is making his way toward the Celestial City, the Mount Zion above. The broad sweep, therefore, is of the Christian life as a pilgrimage, with its many dangers, toils, and snares to be overcome along the way. Sometimes the pilgrim is helped by true friends and companions, and sometimes hindered by deceivers, hypocrites, and destroyers.

However, the focus on the pilgrim's relationship to the world intensifies in a particular episode. Bunyan describes Christian and his first close companion, Faithful, arriving in a town named Vanity, known for its perpetual fair: "It is kept all the year long; it beareth the name of Vanity Fair, because the town where it is kept is lighter than vanity; and also because all that is there sold, or that cometh thither, is vanity. As is the saying of the wise, 'All that cometh is vanity.' This fair is no new-erected business, but a thing of ancient standing."[15]

Bunyan then describes the origin of the fair, a place established by the enemies of pilgrims "wherein should be sold all sorts of vanity, and that it should last all the year long." It is a place of much commerce:

> At this fair are all such merchandise sold, as houses, lands, trades, places, honours, preferments, titles, countries, kingdoms, lusts, pleasures, and delights of all sorts, as whores, bawds, wives, husbands, children, masters, servants, lives, blood, bodies, souls, silver, gold, pearls, precious stones, and what not.
>
> And moreover, at this fair there is at all times to be seen juggling, cheats, games, plays, fools, apes, knaves, and rogues, and that of every kind.
>
> Here are to be seen too, and that for nothing, thefts, murders, adulteries, false swearers, and that of a blood-red colour.[16]

---

15. John Bunyan, *The Pilgrim's Progress*, in *The Works of John Bunyan*, ed. George Offor (Edinburgh: Banner of Truth, 1991), 3:127.

16. Bunyan, *Pilgrim's Progress*, 3:127.

Having provided us with such a painfully accurate view, not just of his own time and place but of our own, Bunyan then gets to the nub of the matter:

> The way to the Celestial City lies just through this town where this lusty fair is kept; and he that will go to the City, and yet not go through this town, must needs "go out of the world."
>
> The Prince of princes himself, when here, went through this town to his own country, and that upon a fair day too; yea, and as I think, it was Beelzebub, the chief lord of this fair, that invited him to buy of his vanities; yea, would have made him lord of the fair, would he but have done him reverence as he went through the town.[17]

The author describes how Beelzebub gave the Lord a guided tour of Vanity, showing and offering all that it had to display, but the "Blessed One" rejected it root and branch, leaving the town "without laying out so much as one farthing upon these vanities."[18] It is through this same place that Bunyan's pilgrims must travel. Even before they arrive, there is a considerable stir about them. First, the pilgrims wear clothing different from that sold at the fair. It attracts much staring and speculation that these are "bedlams" (madmen) or "outlandish men" (distant strangers). Secondly, they speak differently from the people at the fair, so that few can understand them. "They naturally spoke the language of Canaan; but they that kept the fair were the men of this world…so…they seemed barbarians each to the other."[19] Finally, the pilgrims have little regard for the merchandise at the fair, and they put their fingers in their ears when the sellers cry out to them and say,

> "Turn away mine eyes from beholding vanity," and look upwards, signifying that their trade and traffic was in heaven….
>
> One chanced mockingly, beholding the carriage of the men, to say unto them, What will ye buy? But they, looking gravely upon him, answered, "We buy the truth." At that there was an occasion taken to despise the men the more: some mocking,

---

17. Bunyan, *Pilgrim's Progress*, 3:127.
18. Bunyan, *Pilgrim's Progress*, 3:128.
19. Bunyan, *Pilgrim's Progress*, 3:128.

some taunting, some speaking reproachfully, and some calling upon others to smite them.[20]

When things get out of hand, the pilgrims are taken and asked where they come from and where they are going and why they are dressed so strangely. They answer that "they were pilgrims and strangers in the world, and that they were going to their own country, which was the heavenly Jerusalem," making plain "that they had given no occasion to the men of the town, nor yet to the merchandisers, thus to abuse them, and to let them in their journey, except it was, for that, when one asked them what they would buy, they said they would buy the truth."[21] This testimony brings a beating and imprisonment, as men so strange are made objects of entertainment, malice, and revenge, much to the glee of the fair's cruel ruler. The pilgrims' gracious and patient behavior stirs up sympathy and interest among some of Vanity's inhabitants, which causes further strife among the townspeople. In language clearly intended to communicate something of the apostolic experience, the pilgrims are blamed for the uproar and so are further abused as a discouragement to any who might be tempted to join them. This strategy sufficiently backfires so that their wisdom and meekness actually win several people to their side. So the antagonism heightens again, with the wicked men of Vanity determining now to put the pilgrims to death. Then Christian and Faithful "called again to mind what they had heard from their faithful friend Evangelist, and were the more confirmed in their way and sufferings by what he told them would happen to them." Finally, after all this prolonged suffering, they are brought to trial. The hostility, cruelty, and injustice of the town are made quite clear by Bunyan's narrative.

> The judge's name was Lord Hate-good. Their indictment was one and the same in substance, though somewhat varying in form; the contents whereof were this:
> "That they were enemies to, and disturbers of their trade; that they had made commotions and divisions in the town, and had won a party to their own most dangerous opinions, in contempt of the law of their prince."

---

20. Bunyan, *Pilgrim's Progress*, 3:128.
21. Bunyan, *Pilgrim's Progress*, 3:128.

Then Faithful began to answer, that he had only set himself against that which had set itself against Him that is higher than the highest. And, said he, as for disturbance, I make none, being myself a man of peace; the parties that were won to us, were won by beholding our truth and innocence, and they are only turned from the worse to the better. And as to the king you talk of, since he is Beelzebub, the enemy of our Lord, I defy him and all his angels.[22]

There follows an extended trial scene, in which three witnesses—Envy, Superstition, and Pickthank—give their evidence before Lord Hate-good and the jury, who eventually bring in their verdict against Faithful:

> And first, among themselves, Mr. Blind-man, the foreman, said, I see clearly that this man is a heretic. Then said Mr. No-good, Away with such a fellow from the earth. Ay, said Mr. Malice, for I hate the very looks of him. Then said Mr. Love-lust, I could never endure him. Nor I, said Mr. Live-loose, for he would always be condemning my way. Hang him, hang him, said Mr. Heady. A sorry scrub, said Mr. High-mind. My heart riseth against him, said Mr. Enmity. He is a rogue, said Mr. Liar. Hanging is too good for him, said Mr. Cruelty. Let us dispatch him out of the way, said Mr. Hate-light. Then said Mr. Implacable, Might I have all the world given me, I could not be reconciled to him; therefore, let us forthwith bring him in guilty of death.[23]

Sentenced to "the most cruel death that can be invented,"[24] Faithful is scourged, buffeted, cut with knives, stoned, and pricked with swords. Finally, he is burned at the stake and taken straight to the gates of heaven at the very moment of his death, while Christian is remanded in custody. By the Lord's kindness, he finds a way of escape and travels on, singing of the joys and sorrows that Faithful's testimony has worked in his heart.

There are many things to draw from Bunyan's vivid scenes that help us to begin to answer our questions about our relationship to the world. What do we see? The general character of the fair and

---

22. Bunyan, *Pilgrim's Progress*, 3:129.
23. Bunyan, *Pilgrim's Progress*, 3:131.
24. Bunyan, *Pilgrim's Progress*, 3:131.

its merchandise as "vanity"—emptiness—helps us to understand the nature of the world in various aspects. We are reminded that the Master and His servants must of necessity pass through this town if they are to arrive at the Celestial City. We observe that as they go through the fair, the pilgrims' appearance, speech, and appetites mark them out as distinctive. The pilgrims are not permitted to be at peace in the fair, and their behavior has two results. First, those who are inveterately antagonistic become only more enraged. Secondly, though, some—among whom, it should be noted, is one called Hopeful, who becomes Christian's later and noble companion on the road—are won to their position by their testimony. A mock trial is conducted with all the appearance and none of the reality of reason and justice. During this trial, the malice of Vanity's inhabitants is voiced by their representatives on the jury. This results in Faithful's cruel death, his immediate translation to glory, and the unexpected escape of Christian, who continues on his way.

In sum, these pilgrims—like Christ before them—could not avoid going through the town. They knew that the way to the Celestial City lay through the town, so they did not turn back. They were not ashamed to be in the town, though they did not pander to its character. They had a distinctive testimony in the town and took a righteous stand when the issue of their appearance, speech, and appetites was raised. By the end of the episode, one has been slain, one has survived, and one—Hopeful—is saved and sets out on the road.

This missing motif is the Bible's vision. It is Bunyan's vision, as it has been the vision of countless faithful men and women before him. It ought to be our vision. We must get hold of our identity as *pilgrims*. The testimony of Scripture and history tells us that we neglect, despise, or overlook this character at our peril. It is an integral part of faithful discipleship. If we fail to grasp that we are passing through, we will settle down, make ourselves at home, and lose our savor.

Separation and Engagement

Like pilgrims past, the present new covenant church must pass through this world, must hold fast, press on, speak out, win some, suffer much, and triumph at last. She finds in herself some equivalence to the Old Testament congregation (*qahal*), gathered for the work of worship and warfare, separate from the world yet engaging with it. She maintains a distinctive identity as she stands before her God and engages with the world. In the words of William Still:

> The Church's first task, it seems to me, is to *keep being herself* in a changing world, and thus to build herself up and fortify herself against the growing onslaughts of evil, as prophesied in history and in each successive generation. This she can only do by being, not evangelically minded, devotionally or convention minded, socially minded, ecumenically minded, or politically minded; but by taking the whole Word of God as her diet, and feeding and building herself up on that. Thus she preserves her strength for every heroic task, including all these, and makes impact, often painful impact, upon all the life of her day. To this end I think we all, without respect of denomination, need to dismantle our churches, congregation by congregation, right down to the stocks. Then we must build them up again upon a more severe pattern, and strictly on the one unchangeable foundation of Jesus Christ, in order to meet the challenge of our day.[25]

"To keep being herself"—that is the calling of the pilgrim body and her pilgrim members. We need to grasp that we are both present in but passing through this world, taking into account the various conceptions hidden in the word. We are to be properly separate from the world and yet sincerely engaged with it. We must not err on either side. Again, some professing and genuine Christians seem to have missed the principle of holy separation, while others appear to have missed the principle of holy engagement. Some have forgotten that we are in the real world, while others have overemphasized our expectations in this world. Some have neglected the "not yet" of our existence. They try to bring forward experiences and actualities that belong to the glorified state or live as if we were already out of the world and there was no one else to bother with. Others take no account of the "already" of our existence, the distinctive character and holy calling of the church militant (and there is a reason why she is called that).

We need to grasp afresh our identity as pilgrims, with its consequences of holy separation and therefore holy interaction, standing

---

25. William Still, *Letters* (Edinburgh: Banner of Truth, 1984), 75–76.

before God as those belonging to Him and then dealing with men as those who belong to God.

But, we might ask, does one need to reconcile separation and engagement? Can they be held together? What is their relationship?

Let us ask a soldier. He wears the uniform of his brothers-in-arms and has sworn allegiance to his country. He has an absolute commitment to his fellows, existing in a relationship of mutual inter-dependence in which he must be able entirely to trust the men to his left and to his right. At their best, such warriors are bound by an absolute kind of loyalty to one another and to the higher cause in which they are united, serving their monarch or their country. Different attitudes, different convictions, different principles bring one nation into conflict with another, and the soldiers go to war with competing strategies and opposing tactics. Soldiers go into battle bound by certain rules of engagement, for engagement there is. Those rules dictate how they are to go about their business. And here, on the single battlefield, two sides clash, each seeking the supremacy. It is vitally important to know whose side you are on and who is on your side. In the various fields of combat, from a distance it may at times be hard to distinguish between the two forces, so bound up are they with each other. Utterly separate from one another, they remain entirely engaged with each other.

Or let us ask a sportsman. The game is about to begin, and the two teams line up opposite each other, clad in their distinctive uniforms. Before the competition even starts, some teams have what is, in effect, a war dance, complete with some elaborate and often bloodthirsty challenge bellowed out alongside of it. Watch the confrontation between the two teams at this point, and there would be no debate concerning the absolute separation between the two sides, as they go eyeball to eyeball. There is no question whose side each player is on. When the whistle blows, that separation is maintained— each player lines up with his team. There is simultaneous and wholehearted engagement because there is a no-holds-barred confrontation. They are on the same field, subject to the same ultimate government, and handling the same objects. Each team is contending for a victory that cannot be achieved without the opponents—for whom, if he has any sense, the player has a great deal of respect and even some degree of appreciation and at times affection—being properly overcome. To that end, there will be times when the two opposing sides are thoroughly intertwined, although that is a rather delicate word to describe the blood-and-thunder, "Whose body part is this?," give-and-take of the various aspects of some games. After certain episodes, you might see one player pick up another and point him back to his position, where he will need to be run over again. Competing strategies and thunderous collisions combine to render the whole thing quite splendid and sometimes appalling, as the two teams lock together head to head, eye to eye, shoulder to shoulder, without ever forgetting who they are and to whose side they belong.

But, lest we think that this is all about aggression, however righteous, and lose sight cf those various aspects of the world, let us also ask the aid worker. Th s person enters a hostile environment in order to serve. He sees all around him the abject misery of the people to whom he has come. Perhaps they are the victims of war, perhaps oppressed by cruel and selfish leaders, perhaps afflicted by sickness or famine. For whatever reason, they are desperately in need, and the aid worker is determined to meet that need. This man of compassion goes out among them. He is undoubtedly separate from them in many distinctive ways. He belongs outside, and yet he enters in and cares for them. Maintaining a strict impartiality, he may be in danger from all factions, and yet he seeks to treat all factions alike. He ministers equally to all who have any need. Sometimes, perhaps, he shows medical care to the wounded soldiers of some particular party while their comrades stand around with loaded guns. At another time he will be found supplying food and medicine to the victims of those very soldiers. He returns often to the compound where his supplies are stored, loading them up and bringing them out for the sake of those around him. In order to care in this way, the worker must maintain a degree of distance, not compromising himself by an attachment to some other group or cause in the place where he serves. His skin color, training, clothing, demeanor, his own national allegiance, his resources, his attitude—all these put him very much on the outside, separate in many ways, and yet no one could question his full-orbed engagement with the people in the environment he shares with them.

To be sure, in each of these examples there will be times when questions arise, when there are challenges to a person's maintaining his or her identity and the code of conduct bound up in it. There will be painful hardships and particular trials. Nevertheless, you can see that there is no inherent tension in being both wholly separate and wholly engaged, the one building on the other. In each case, identity firmly grasped governs activity readily carried out. All of these people understand who they are and what they are called to do in relationship to the environment in which they are placed and the various people around them. They simultaneously maintain a genuine separation while pursuing a wholehearted engagement and are enabled to do so by this clear and fixed sense of their identity.

Followers of the Way

So it is with the saints in the church of Christ in the world as created, populated, and corrupted. As disciples of Christ, as fellow pilgrims, they are—in the little-used phrase employed of God's people before they came to be known as Christians—"followers of the Way" (Acts 9:2; 19:9, 23; 24:14, 22), with its delightful echoes of the pilgrim path. We must get hold of the fact that we are followers of the Way, strangers on the earth, strangers and pilgrims who desire a better—that is, a heavenly—country, and that this Scripture-directed, Spirit-enabled combination of holy separation and holy engagement is the biblical norm.

So each one must ask, Whose side am I on? Where do I belong? What is my hope? Where is my home? The fact is that our lives tell the truth about us. Just as identity governs activity, so activity reveals identity. Look at the way a man lives, and you will be able to tell where he belongs. There is no neutrality here, no middle ground. If there is no holy separation to God, your engagement with the world will be unholy, demonstrating your commitment to and condemnation with a fading world. You either belong to the world, or you are passing through the world. You are dwelling in Destruction, or traveling to Zion. You are at ease under the shadow, or pressing on toward the light.

Remember the words of James: "Do you not know that friendship with the world is enmity with God? Whoever therefore wants to be a friend of the world makes himself an enemy of God" (James 4:4). Consider that by nature we are "without Christ, being aliens from the commonwealth of Israel and strangers from the covenants of promise, having no hope and without God in the world" (Eph. 2:12). Consider, too, that in Christ Jesus, those who once were far off can be brought near by the blood of Christ (Eph. 2:13). There can be no shared allegiance. We must turn from the world, and to trust in Christ is to find and follow the Way.

Are you truly a part of the church of Jesus Christ? We either belong to this present evil age, or we are set apart to God, and no amount of dressing up, even in religious clothes, makes the former healthy or happy. Though we may stand in rank with the soldiers of God on the display ground, having somehow cobbled together a uniform that enables us to fit in, when the time for battle comes our attitudes, affections, appetites, and actions will quickly make plain whose side we are on.

Let every reader, therefore, "be even more diligent to make your call and election sure" (2 Peter 1:10). All else is irrelevant apart from this. No amount of coaching or behavior will change the heart, and no pretense or effort will hide our allegiance forever: "Do not lay up for yourselves treasures on earth, where moth and rust destroy and where thieves break in and steal; but lay up for yourselves treasures in heaven, where neither moth nor rust destroys and where thieves do not break in and steal. For where your treasure is, there your heart will be also" (Matt. 6:19–21; cf. 7:24–29).

If our treasure is in heaven, then let us live like it. If we are strangers and pilgrims, then that ought to be our clear and fixed identity, manifest in appearance, speech, and appetites. God "has saved us and called us with a holy calling" (2 Tim. 1:9). It is only when we grasp that we are strangers on the earth that we can, as citizens of heaven, pursue and maintain the principles of holy separation and holy engagement in our relationship to the world.

We like to speak of death as "going home," and so it is to every child of God, but why do we then live as if we are already home? Such confusion betrays us. It makes plain that we have not understood or grasped our identity, and therefore we are not able to govern our activity. As a result, the church is compromised, the saints are disheartened, the Lord is dishonored, and all the while the world laughs and the devil applauds.

We must think on these things, and we must return to our Bibles in dependence on the Spirit of the Lord to discern the will of God for His people as we make our way in the world. We must learn to consider, to watch, to pray, and to live to the praise of our God.

You may have heard of a Puritan called Richard Sibbes. One of his contemporaries, a man called Izaak Walton, wrote of Sibbes: "Of this blest man, let this just praise be given: / heaven was in him, before he was in heaven." Can anyone speak of you in that way? Would anyone think to describe you thus—"heaven was in him, before he was in heaven"? Your attitudes, affections, appetites, and actions will reveal your allegiance. You may determine your present spiritual affiliation and eternal destination by the behavior you manifest, the desires you pursue, the life you live, and the company you love.

We must know to whom and with whom we belong and to whom and where we are going. Only when the issue of our identity is decided and demonstrated in our attachment to Christ and His church are we in a position to consider the principles that govern our separation to God and interaction with the world.

Christian, in *The Pilgrim's Progress*, was able to say, "I have come from the City of Destruction and I am going to Mount Zion." So can every clear-thinking child of God. And as we increasingly grasp that pilgrim identity, so we can increasingly demonstrate our pilgrim activity:

> Therefore, my beloved, as you have always obeyed, not as in my presence only, but now much more in my absence, work out your own salvation with fear and trembling; for it is God who works in you both to will and to do for His good pleasure. Do all things without complaining and disputing, that you may become blameless and harmless, children of God without fault in the midst of a crooked and perverse generation, among whom you shine as lights in the world, holding fast the word of life, so that I may rejoice in the day of Christ that I have not run in vain or labored in vain. (Phil. 2:12–16)

3

UNDERSTAND THE ENVIRONMENT

I trust you are persuaded that it is good and valuable for us, the people of God, to see ourselves—among other proper, legitimate notions of our identity—as pilgrims passing through this world. In addition, we must understand this world in biblical categories as created, populated, and corrupted. All that being so, none of us can take the seemingly easy ways out of icy isolation, thoughtless inattention, or crass emulation. We are required to cultivate that holy separation and holy engagement by which we will bring glory to our God as we travel from the City of Destruction to the Celestial City.

As we make that journey, following the footsteps of many who have walked this way before us, chief among them our Lord Himself, I want to offer some guidance for the road. First and foremost, as we have already made plain, is the need to get off the broad road that leads to destruction and to enter through the narrow gate onto the difficult but straight way that leads to life (Matt. 7:13–14). Our Lord says that there is an apparently easy way that leads downward to hell and a difficult path that leads to life, taking us upward to glory. The Word of God is the map that brings us to the path of salvation, and the Spirit of God is the guide who brings us to and puts us on that right way (2 Tim. 3:15). The Word and the Spirit remain the helps we need for our continued navigation.

My aim is to bring the Word of God to bear in a series of principles for pilgrims that I trust the Spirit will bless to your heart and so equip you for the journey that you must make. These are, however, principles. Though I hope to offer applications, I will not give a series of minute prescriptions, for part of the genius of Scripture is that it provides what is necessary for wisdom for all saints in all times and places. This is often accomplished by means of broad directives that we must then apply to our lives in the situations into which God leads us, seeking the help of the Spirit to do so.

In considering each principle my aim will be to identify a scriptural framework, building up the weight of biblical evidence by turning to key passages or epitomizing texts. Then I will attempt some summary thoughts, drawing together the primary teaching, and then offer some specific applications and counsels.

As these principles are brought to light and explained, I hope you will see that a balance develops across the whole. I will take each in its own turn and deal with it independently, for it stands in its own right, and the full weight of it must be felt. As we work through each one in turn, we will find that, while we cannot shave the edges off any, there are some that we must hold in tension. I hope that by the end of the sequence we will have a set of anchor points that—if we cling to each with equal tenacity—will help us make our way through this world in the right way. That said by way of introduction, our first concern as pilgrims passing through the world must be to understand our environment, and so we begin by identifying certain relevant Scriptures.

Understand the Environment: Scriptural Framework

The World's Hatred

> "If the world hates you, you know that it hated Me before it hated you. If you were of the world, the world would love its own. Yet because you are not of the world, but I chose you out of the world, therefore the world hates you. Remember the word that I said to you, 'A servant is not greater than his master.' If they persecuted Me, they will also persecute you. If they kept My word, they will keep yours also. But all these things they will do to you for My name's sake, because they do not know Him who sent Me." (John 15:18–21)

The "if" with which our Lord begins this declaration does not offer a possibility but establishes a reality. If we are separated to the Lord from the world, chosen out by Him, we belong to God. If we express that allegiance to Christ in our lives, we will be hated. Hatred is the characteristic disposition of Satan and his kingdom to all those who oppose him. That hatred will be directed toward God and His Christ and toward the body of Christ as well as the Head of the body. Just as the risen Lord Jesus could ask Saul of Tarsus, "Why are you persecuting Me?" so we will find that association with Christ will bring persecutions to us.

As we make our way through the world we will find that those who argue on almost everything else will manage to agree on this point. In Christ's experience, the Pharisees, the Herodians, and the Romans found a common cause in seeking to destroy Him. In the same way, we will find that the exclusiveness of the Christian message and the distinctiveness of the Christian life will receive a negative reaction from the world as it stands in opposition to God. Here various parties and factions will find a reason to unite against the people of God.

The Christian faith and life is a standing rebuke to the world. If we are full of faith, hope, and love, our speech and behavior will set up a sharp contrast between the church and the world. Our conviction and conduct expose the futility of the world and its pursuits. They condemn the carnality of the world and its appetites. They highlight the folly of the world and its delights. They agitate the conscience of the world in its love of darkness. A pilgrim mentality makes plain that we are living for a world to come and that those who do not live for this are missing their way.

If Christians were "of the world," then it is possible that we might obtain its admiration and commendation because we would fit in and go with the flow. But, belonging to God, we share in the response of the world to our God. This world is fundamentally hostile to God and to godliness.

Please appreciate that this is not a sort of McCarthyite Christianity in which we constantly search for imaginary (or real) spiritual "reds under the beds." It does not mean that when you put this book down you will see a mob gathered outside wherever you are reading, or that you will hear the gnashing of teeth as you appear in your workplace, or that you must watch out for snipers on the rooftops when you next walk through the streets. It does not mean that there is constant and open aggression toward all Christians at all times or that there is no common grace in the world or that we are reinterpreting the doctrine of total depravity to mean that all people are as bad as they possibly could be.

It *does* mean that there is ingrained opposition that will manifest itself by aggression as there is more or less common grace in a society, more or less righteous restraint imposed upon the actions of the ungodly, more or less legislative programming against the freedoms of Christians to express their convictions in what they say and how they act.

You need to spend only a few minutes listening to faithful preaching in a public place to see and hear how quickly this antagonism bubbles up from beneath the surface of polite society. By faithful preaching I do not mean picking a fight or selecting the most offensive themes and making the most aggressive points. I refer to the simple declaration of the sinfulness of mankind by nature and the exclusive sufficiency of Christ as Savior, with the need for sinners to turn from sin and trust in the Lord lest they go down to the pit. The British still have some kind of reputation for politeness, but they would swiftly lose it if the world perceived their response to the preaching of Christ. All kinds of vulgarity, dismissive and sneering statements, and outright anger or scornful pity are on display. Generally speaking, the vast majority of those who bother responding express an antagonism to God and the preaching of the truth without even listening to what is actually being said; it is a knee-jerk spiritual reaction.

The world, in this sense, is not your friend. The way we walk is narrow and difficult. You will find no encouragements in the world to enter that way or to stay on it. You will not find in the systems, practices, pursuits, assumptions, and currents of this world any aids to genuine holiness. That is because the world is not a neutral environment. You will find in this life that your soul is diverted from the road, that your heart is a tinderbox and that this is a world of sparks, and that you are in some measure a marked man or woman. The more evidently like the Lord Jesus Christ we are, the more evident will be the world's antagonism toward us, and it was always so. Sadly, one of the reasons why we so often "get away with" our Christianity is that we avoid distinctive allegiance to Christ and thereby avoid the open hatred of the world.

Abel found it so:

And the LORD respected Abel and his offering, but He did not respect Cain and his offering. And Cain was very angry, and his countenance fell. So the LORD said to Cain, "Why are you angry? And why has your countenance fallen? If you do well, will you not be accepted? And if you do not do well, sin lies at the door. And its desire is for you, but you should rule over it." Now Cain talked with Abel his brother; and it came to pass, when they were in the field, that Cain rose up against Abel his brother and killed him. (Gen. 4:4–8)

David, the man after God's own heart (1 Sam 13:14; Acts 13:22), found it so when Saul became his bitter enemy. Micaiah found it so when he maintained a faithful witness in Israel during the days of King Ahab and exposed the king's wickedness. Ahab testified regarding Micaiah, "There is still one man…by whom we may inquire of the LORD; but I hate him, because he does not prophesy good concerning me, but evil" (1 Kings 22:8). Daniel found it so when his testimony as a follower of the living God won the hatred of his peers, who knew his character and perceived what they saw as a weak spot:

Then this Daniel distinguished himself above the governors and satraps, because an excellent spirit was in him; and the king gave thought to setting him over the whole realm. So the governors and satraps sought to find some charge against Daniel concerning the kingdom; but they could find no charge or fault, because he was faithful; nor was there any error or fault found in him. Then these men said, "We shall not find any charge against this Daniel unless we find it against him concerning the law of his God." (Dan. 6:3–5)

We might consider our Lord Christ Himself. He came to His own, but His own did not receive Him. He came to the temple at which He should have been worshiped and there He was hated and despised. Ask Stephen as he stands before the Sanhedrin with his face shining like the Moses they profess to love, condemned by men who gnash their teeth at him and cannot contain their physical anger. Ask Paul as he drags his battered body from city to city preaching the gospel, picking up a phenomenal catalog of wounds and scars of mind and flesh from those who cannot abide the messenger or his message.

Ask John, an old man on a dry rock in the middle of the sea, in exile because of his faith.

This is the hatred of the world for those who plainly belong to God, and it has been present ever since God said to the serpent,

> "I will put enmity
> Between you and the woman,
> And between your seed and her Seed;
> He shall bruise your head,
> And you shall bruise His heel." (Gen. 3:15)

Walking Warily

See then that you walk circumspectly, not as fools but as wise, redeeming the time, because the days are evil. Therefore do not be unwise, but understand what the will of the Lord is. (Eph. 5:15–17)

"The days are evil." The context for Paul's assertion is the uncleanness of the world at large and the commandment that the saints must walk as children of light, "finding out what is acceptable to the Lord. And have no fellowship with the unfruitful works of darkness, but rather expose them" (Eph. 5:8–11). He means by this description of "the days" that wickedness will swirl about and trouble will come upon the saints in their lives in this world. In such an environment, we need to walk circumspectly, placing our feet carefully, stepping out on the right way. I remember standing on moorland during a school trip many years ago, listening to the instructions of a competent guide. It was a boggy area, a region of moss and mud with thick, wiry grass springing up from the ground in tussocks. It all looked similarly uninviting. We were strictly warned only to place our feet where the guide or the person in front of us had last put his. As the guide set off across the muck, I was next in line. The place where he put his foot looked, to me, exactly like any other number of clumps of grass he might have chosen, but that was the place that I had to step, and so on, only able to see the next step by the fact that his foot had been there moments before. Carelessness up and down the line led to many false moves and resulted in much clinging filth and soggy misery.

So it is with the child of God in this world. We must walk circumspectly rather than carelessly and ignorantly, remembering that John Newton was not simply looking for a line that scanned and rhymed when he wrote in his hymn "Amazing Grace" of "many dangers, toils, and snares." We must watch where we put our feet, for there are few solid points, and the rest is mire and morass.

We must walk as wise men, redeeming the time—buying back every opportunity to make some spiritual gains in this world, finding and using every such opening. To do this, not being deceived or enticed by the siren cries of the world, we need to understand what the will of the Lord is. We must obtain insight into the plans and purposes of God for His people because only in this way can we put our feet down safely. Only then can we "be imitators of God as dear children" (Eph. 5:1), remembering that Christ "gave Himself for our sins, that He might deliver us from this present evil age, according to the will of our God and Father, to whom be glory forever and ever" (Gal. 1:4–5).

Understand the Times

> These…came to David at Hebron to turn over the kingdom of Saul to him, according to the word of the LORD:…of the sons of Issachar who had understanding of the times, to know what Israel ought to do, their chiefs were two hundred; and all their brethren were at their command. (1 Chron. 12:23, 32)

Among those who came to David at Hebron were the sons of Issachar. These men could see that the Lord was passing Saul's crown and kingdom to David, who was the Lord's anointed, and so they rallied to him. These Israelites "had understanding of the times": they knew the tone, temper, tendencies, trends, and trajectories of the time and place in which they lived. They had skill to gauge and discern the spirit of the age and were blessed with a corresponding ability to determine, from observation and experience, the way in which they and others should go for duty and for blessing. This distinctive capacity for discernment enabled them to consider, identify, and pursue the course of action demanded by a particular situation. Significantly, the Chronicler makes clear that they knew how to rule and to be ruled: the sons of Issachar had wise leaders who directed responsible and responsive followers.

Friendship with the World

> Adulterers and adulteresses! Do you not know that friendship with the world is enmity with God? Whoever therefore wants to be a friend of the world makes himself an enemy of God. (James 4:4)

James makes clear that there is no middle ground for the child of God. We cannot love the world, with its characteristic disposition of antagonism to God. To pursue the world is to reject and betray the God who saves us. If you are married, how would you feel if you arrived home one day to find your husband or your wife locked in a passionate embrace with some other person, let alone one identifiable as a wicked individual who has continually and deliberately opposed and dishonored you in all things? How does God feel when He sees His church locked in a passionate embrace with a world in rebellion against Him?

Affection to the world is rejection of and aggression against God; to befriend this evil age is to betray Christ as Savior. James says that friendship with the world is spiritual adultery, and we probably do not feel the force of that language in the way that we should. The collapse of marriage and the dismissal of faithfulness as quaint and outmoded in the modern West robs us of the impact. There is a covenant made between God and His people, and James draws on the prophetic imagery and language of unfaithful Israel turning its back upon God and running after its lovers and applies it to professing Christians who seek their fulfillment and pleasure in the world.

The world's friend is God's enemy; the spirit of the world is contrary to the Spirit of God; the kingdoms of darkness and light are implacably opposed, being governed by different principles, practices, and ends. To set your heart on this world and the things that belong to it will eventually result in your turning your back upon God and abandoning His people. It happens repeatedly: "Demas has forsaken me, having loved this present world, and has departed for Thessalonica" (2 Tim. 4:10). The world calls to us like a seductress, and her enticements must be resisted. Consider the commendation of Lady Wisdom in the book of Proverbs and the contrasting warning given to the son about the enticing woman. This counsel applies as much to unfaithful Mistress World—who promises much and delivers only grief and pain—as it does to any particular adulteress:

> My son, pay attention to my wisdom;
> Lend your ear to my understanding,
> That you may preserve discretion,
> And your lips may keep knowledge.
> For the lips of an immoral woman drip honey,
> And her mouth is smoother than oil;
> But in the end she is bitter as wormwood,
> Sharp as a two-edged sword.
> Her feet go down to death,
> Her steps lay hold of hell. (Prov. 5:1–5)

The world says, in effect, "Everything is prepared: come and enjoy me." It is no accident that another image Bunyan employs to describe "this vain world" is the loose-living Madam Bubble, who waylays faithful Standfast. He reports the experience:

> As I was thus musing, as I said, there was one, in very pleasant attire, but old, who presented herself unto me, and offered me three things; to wit, her body, her purse, and her bed. Now the truth is, I was both a-weary and sleepy; I am also as poor as an owlet, and that, perhaps, the witch knew. Well, I repulsed her once and twice, but she put by my repulses, and smiled. Then I began to be angry; but she mattered that nothing at all. Then she made offers again, and said, if I would be ruled by her, she would make me great and happy; for, said she, I am the mistress of the world, and men are made happy by me. Then I asked her name, and she told me it was Madam Bubble.[1]

Madam Bubble continues to follow and entice Standfast, who explains to his companions that eventually he fell to his knees and prayed, with hands lifted up, to the One who said He would help. Defeated, Madam Bubble goes on her way, and Standfast thanks the Lord for deliverance from her.

---

1. Bunyan, *Pilgrim's Progress*, 3:239.

Greatheart responds with a telling description of Madam Bubble, a seductress who speaks very smoothly and smiles at the end of each sentence, and issues a warning:

> This woman is a witch, and it is by virtue of her sorceries that this ground is enchanted. Whoever doth lay his head down in her lap, had as good lay it down on that block over which the axe doth hang; and whoever lay their eyes upon her beauty are counted the enemies of God. This is she that maintaineth in their splendour all those that are the enemies of pilgrims. Yea, this is she that has bought off many a man from a pilgrim's life.

The faithful man of God goes on to speak of her as a gossiper, dogging the heels of pilgrims and always hymning the good things of this present world. She is shameless and vindictive and greedy, offering much and delivering nothing. She is willing to be worshiped; she loves praise; she is utterly unreliable and unfaithful. She tears apart the best of friends and the closest of families:

> It was she that set Absalom against his father, and Jeroboam against his master. It was she that persuaded Judas to sell his Lord, and that prevailed with Demas to forsake the godly pilgrims' life; none can tell of the mischief that she doth. She makes variance betwixt rulers and subjects, betwixt parents and children, betwixt neighbour and neighbour, betwixt a man and his wife, betwixt a man and himself, betwixt the flesh and the spirit.[2]

If you make a friend of Madam Bubble, you make an enemy of God, for the two are opposed. No wonder that the faithful father gives his son this counsel:

> Keep my commands and live,
> And my law as the apple of your eye.
> Bind them on your fingers;
> Write them on the tablet of your heart.
> Say to wisdom, "You are my sister,"
> And call understanding your nearest kin,
> That they may keep you from the immoral woman,
> From the seductress who flatters with her words. (Prov. 7:2–5)

---

2. Bunyan, *Pilgrim's Progress*, 3:239.

The seductress has slain many strong men, and her "house is the way to hell" and death (vv. 26–27). So is the world to those who listen to her honeyed lips and enter her poisonous embrace and, in doing so, commit adultery against God.

Craving Understanding

> Give me understanding, and I shall keep Your law;
> Indeed, I shall observe it with my whole heart.
> Make me walk in the path of Your commandments,
> For I delight in it. (Ps. 119:34–35)

This pilgrim cry compares with the psalmist's self-identification earlier in the psalm: "I am a stranger in the earth; do not hide Your commandments from me" (Ps. 11):19). It is a typical cry of the pilgrim who recognizes that he needs divine illumination if he is to walk in cheerful obedience. Where the Lord grants understanding, there is a person who observes God's law with his whole heart. When the Lord gives someone an appetite for godliness, there will be delight along the way. To be taught of God's Spirit is to be on the way to constant and cheerful submission to God's will, wholehearted subscription to all His direction.

The Fear of the Lord

> The fear of the LORD is the beginning of knowledge,
> But fools despise wisdom and instruction....
> Wisdom is the principal thing;
> Therefore get wisdom.
> And in all your getting, get understanding....
> The wisdom of the prudent is to understand his way,
> But the folly of fools is deceit. (Prov. 1:7; 4:7; 14:8)

At the core of wisdom, its chief part, its central element and unassailable foundation, is the fear of the Lord. Without this, all other knowledge is essentially pointless. We will not profit from what we learn nor rightly employ it without the direction of a reverent and obedient heart conditioned by God's majestic holiness and constraining grace. You cannot direct your steps without the powerful impulses of the love of the God who has loved us and called us to be manifestly His own. The fear of the Lord is that awareness of living before God that gives rise to a love of pleasing Him and a hatred and horror of offending Him. This is the wisdom we need, and it ought to be a priority for the child of God. It is most excellent and ought to be pursued before anything else that the world has to offer, and it ought to be employed by us as we make our way in the world. What do we so often grasp after in this world? Wealth, reputation, ease, peace? But without understanding all else will fall to the ground. True wisdom is wisdom for living. Considering Proverbs 14:8, Matthew Henry calls us to think about

> the good conduct of a wise and good man; he manages himself well. it is not the wisdom of the learned, which consists only in speculation, that is here recommended, but *the wisdom of the prudent*, which is practical, and is of use to direct our counsels and actions. Christian prudence consists in a right *understanding of our way*; for we are travellers, whose concern it is, not to spy wonders, but to get forward towards their journey's end. It *is to understand our own way*, not to be critics and busybodies in other men's matters, but to look well to ourselves and *ponder the path of our feet*, to understand the directions of our way, that we may observe them, the dangers of our way, that we may avoid them, the difficulties of our way, that we may break through them, and the advantages of our way, that we may improve them—to understand the rules we are to walk by and the ends we are to walk towards, and walk accordingly.[3]

Understand the Environment: Summary Thoughts

The Word of God calls us to understand the environment through which we pass and our relationship to it. As we shall see later, there are beauties to be enjoyed and blessings to be received with thankfulness in this world, but we must understand that, as Christians, we live in a fundamentally hostile spiritual environment. Even the created, physical world—taking into account those beauties and blessings—has a voice with which it cries out under the burden of sin, waiting for that moment when corruptions finally will be undone and there will be a restoration of all things:

---

3. Matthew Henry, *Matthew Henry's Commentary on the Whole Bible* (Peabody, Mass.: Hendrickson, 1991), 3:712.

For the earnest expectation of the creation eagerly waits for the revealing of the sons of God. For the creation was subjected to futility, not willingly, but because of Him who subjected it in hope; because the creation itself also will be delivered from the bondage of corruption into the glorious liberty of the children of God. For we know that the whole creation groans and labors with birth pangs together until now. (Rom. 8:19–22)

This is a "present evil age" (Gal. 1:4) and "the days are evil" (Eph. 5:16). The saints dwell "in the midst of a crooked and perverse generation" (Phil. 2:15). This world is not our home and cannot be our friend if we are to be faithful to God. It is a wilderness, not a garden. It is an obstacle course, not a park through which we stroll. It is a battleground, not a playground. The world, fallen from God, is an arena in which there is a general atmosphere of hostility to Christ and His people, with particular pressures directed against the saints in specific times and places, expressions of underlying hostility and antagonism. The world hates you, and you will find it so and feel it so at particular times and places.

So do we panic and run for the hills? Do we find a hole to hide in? Our reaction to this reality need be neither paranoia nor despair. British readers might be aware of a classic long-running British sitcom called *Dad's Army*, about the Home Guard in the fictional British village of Walmington-on-Sea during the Second World War. This character comedy focused on the efforts of a mismatched group of old men, invalids, and slackers to prepare for a German invasion, facing various challenges and crises. Among the members of the platoon was Private Frazer, a Scots undertaker who would invariably declare, "We're doomed!" from whichever corner he was lurking in when a crisis approached. Corporal Jones would run back and forth like a headless chicken, bellowing, "Don't panic!" Private Godfrey would lose control of his bodily functions and gently approach someone in authority with a request for the bathroom: "I say, old boy, may I be excused?" Captain Mainwaring, the very embodiment of pompous incompetence, would blame the youngest member of the platoon for the problem, usually issuing a withering, "You stupid boy!" Meanwhile, in the background the vicar and the verger (a minor functionary in the Anglican Church) would flap about accomplishing absolutely nothing.

Sadly, when faced with the reality of a world that opposes us, the church might seem to degenerate into a kind of Dad's Army of ill-equipped incompetents, each with his own catchphrase communicating a complete inability to respond rightly to the demands of the hour, with the spiritual leaders blathering and arguing in the background.

What we need is wisdom—what someone has described as skill for righteous living. This is the only way to understand and to negotiate—to watch, listen, discern, interpret, and respond to—the environment and circumstances in which God has put us. Like the sons of Issachar, we must know the times in which we live. We must watch and listen, like our Lord Christ, to understand the currents of the world, the spirit of the age. Remember how He condemned the Pharisees and Sadducees who came to test Him: "When it is evening you say, 'It will be fair weather, for the sky is red'; and in the morning, 'It will be foul weather today, for the sky is red and threatening.' Hypocrites! You know how to discern the face of the sky, but you cannot discern the signs of the times" (Matt. 16:2–3). Christ says, "You should be able to look around—in the same way you predict the weather from the sky—and work out what is happening, but you are ignorant of what should be evident from the events taking place around you." How is it that we live without any sense of what is going on around us, the characteristic temper of the time and place in which we have been put and the parallels with biblical promises and warnings?

We need to understand the place in which we dwell while we maintain our distinctive character within it, like Daniel's necessary insights into and mastery of Babylonian learning and culture while he maintained a proverbial godliness within it (Ezek. 14:14, 20). We need to know the men in these times and places with an insight not unlike that of our Lord, who knew men's thoughts (Matt. 9:4) and rebuked His disciples when they manifested an ungodly spirit (Luke 9:55). I do not think it in any way undermines our Savior's divinity nor dismisses His heavenly wisdom or supernatural knowledge to suggest that such discernment might have been, in large measure, the product of the training of a godly home and the cultivation of an alert ear and penetrating eye. He had been taught to observe, think, and deduce, and He did so as He watched men. Above all, we need to know the will of God if we are to walk circumspectly in these evil days (Eph. 5:17).

Understand the Environment: Specific Counsels

Taking all this into account, what do we pilgrims need to grasp as we seek to understand the environment and our relationship to it?

First, we must *fear the Lord*. This is the chief part of wisdom. You will lose your way and your soul unless you are governed by a deep and constraining consciousness of living before a holy and redeeming God. We need to know His character and respond to that revelation of His being as sons who love to honor their heavenly Father and loathe to grieve Him. Without this to orient us, without this spiritual sensitivity, without this controlling reality of the living God, we will wander aimlessly rather than travel purposefully as pilgrims "whose concern it is, not to spy wonders, but to get forward towards their journey's end."[4]

Remember that mere biblical literacy is no substitute for genuine spiritual maturity. The fear of the Lord is what carries us from knowing what is right to doing what is right. You might hear people complaining that they need guidance on some matter. Too often their quandary is that they are not yet willing to do what the guidance they already have is directing them to do. Their problem is not that they do not know but that they have no appetite to do. The will of God is already clearly revealed in the Word of God. All that is lacking is the readiness to obey that flows from a reverence to the God who speaks.

The fear of the Lord will give us a way of going and a direction to go in. This disposition is a fruit of conversion and growing maturity as a saint. It is the attitude of the child of God, born again from above and learning the character of God's family. It ought to be earnestly cultivated by every saint. Do you have it? All those who name the name of Christ should ask whether the truth that the God of Scripture is, and is their God, and has become their Redeemer is having the conditioning impact upon their life that ought to be the case. If it is, it will increasingly be your desire to be holy as God is holy. Your worst fear will be to put a frown on the face of the God

---

4. Henry, *Commentary*, 3:712.

who has loved you. The sweetest thing you can imagine is to know and do His holy will.

Furthermore, we must *face the facts*. We must stop denying that the world hates us, and we must stop playing here as if it were a safe place. The world hates Christlike Christians (and that adjective ought to be unnecessary, by definition). We can draw a little of the sting by camouflaging ourselves so that we do not stand out, but that is to deny the Lord who bought us. We must understand that "all who desire to live godly in Christ Jesus will suffer persecution" (2 Tim. 3:12). Indeed, the more Christlike we are, the more open and evident will be the hatred. Have we been tempted to navigate through this world by avoiding all those times and places in which we fear or predict persecution will come upon us? It may be that we have avoided tensions, backed down from battles, and blustered our way through situations without ever taking a distinctive stand for God and being willing to suffer the reproach of Christ. We are afraid, perhaps, that our children will not love us, so we bend to their will rather than bowing to God's, forgetting that "'a man's enemies will be those of his own household'" (Matt. 10:36, quoting Mic. 7:6). We are afraid that our colleagues will laugh at us, so we retreat when the honor of God is at stake. We are afraid that we will be mocked and scorned by the mass of mankind, so we do everything within our power to make sure nobody knows that we belong to Jesus Christ. We privatize our faith, we listen to the message that was sent to many of the New Testament churches: "Get back in your box. Wind in your neck. Don't rock the boat. Be like the rest of us, especially in public." We have listened to the world's threats and promises, and we have sunk into spiritual anonymity, willing to have the world applaud us for our worldly "wisdom" rather than honor God by our distinctive lives. If we strive to make the world our friend, we are being unfaithful to our sovereign King. If we are faithful to Him, the world will hate us. The more clearly we plant our flag, the more rapidly we will be assaulted. The sooner you realize that and come to grips with it, the healthier your soul will be, the purer the church will be, and the more exalted God in Christ will be.

The world is not and cannot be your friend if you are to be faithful to God in Christ. What a relief it is to know it! It liberates us from the vain hope that for us it might be different. It saves us the hassle of trying to avoid it. What a comfort to be prepared! We will not be taken unaware if we put our house in order now. I do not suggest for one instant that this is pleasant, but at least we know what we face and why we face it. We do not need to start a fight; faithfulness will bring us one. We do not need to look for trouble; trouble will come upon us.

We must remember that the crises we face will not form our character but will reveal it. If we have not understood what is coming and decided and determined in advance that—by God's grace—we will do what God's will requires, when that crisis comes we will drift with the spirit of the age. When the storm comes, you and I must know already whose we are and where we stand and in what direction we intend to go; otherwise, we will be driven about.

The hatred of the world is, in many ways, a badge of honor, for it is a testimony to God's ownership of us. It is a mark of our separation to God that the world wants nothing of us. Satan's hosts mainly fire at those who wear the King's uniform openly. It is time we stopped trying to relax and get comfortable in this world. It is time to stop trying to please and pacify a hostile world and to get on with the business of pilgrimage, counting the cost of what it means to follow Christ, taking up our cross and walking in His footsteps.

Then, we must *heed the warnings*. This is more than simply hearing them. It is paying attention to them, so that when the battle begins we are not unprepared and ill-equipped, like a man who was repeatedly told that he lived on a flood plain and that the rains were coming, yet faced the mounting waves with no plans, no preparations, and no defenses. Remember that you have been told these things so that you can be ready, steeled for the moment. Otherwise, when a crisis comes you might scream, "Don't panic!" or gloomily confirm what you have always long suspected: "We're doomed!" There is no need for a child of God to hide from the world or to head out into the world ill-equipped and careless.

What would you think of a soldier in a war zone who went out on patrol and neglected all the counsels given about snipers on the rooftops, Improvised Explosive Devices (IEDs) on the sides of the road, the mines laid down the centers of the roads, and the obstacles designed to slow down him and his comrades? What will happen to the men who neglect the counsels given about the danger of the environment and the preparations for defense that they should make? They will lose their limbs, if not their lives, and go limping because they refused to take the warnings to heart.

If you are so careless, heedless, or arrogant as to imagine that you are the one who will make your way through the world soaring above all dangers and difficulties, you will get caught in the blast. There are traps and snares that the Scriptures warn us about. For the saint, as for the soldier in a war zone, the path to glory is littered with IEDs, the fields we traverse are sown with mines. There are obstacles to negotiate and enemies with whom to contend. The blasé, careless, overconfident traveler will get injured and be hindered. One of the reasons why so many saints go limping is because they thought they knew better than anyone else and so neglected the warnings and equipment issued to them. They walked into the firefight and trod on the tripwire. They did not hide themselves when they had the chance to do so. We may reach our destination, though too many of us will go slowly and painfully if we neglect the warnings provided.

Therefore, we must *open our eyes and ears.* Too many Christians go through the world with blinkers raised and earplugs firmly installed. To be sure, there are occasions when a blind eye and a deaf ear are well advised, but to cultivate ignorance of our environment will leave us helpless. This is one of the dangers of isolation and inattention in the church. We can neither be safe nor useful if we do not know our environment. We must look at and listen to the world around us, seeking to understand and gauge the way of the world so that we will know how to pass through it righteously. We must learn to identify the tone, discern the temper, observe the tendencies, plot the trends, and trace the trajectories of the time and place in which God has put us. We are to bring all to the touchstone of Scripture as illuminated by Christ's Spirit. We need field intelligence if we are to fight our battles. We need to understand what is going on in our communities, towns, nations, and in the world at large so that we can see the dangers and plot our course. We must understand what is taking place. When we hear the world's songs, read her articles, see her popular media, and watch the individuals elevated for adoration and imitation, and when we interpret those things in the light of God's Word, we will begin to understand the challenges, opportunities, obstacles, and assaults that we will face. We will hear the

world's view of love, forgiveness, repentance, faith, obedience, goodness, compassion, redemption, and mercy. We must then compare
it to the Scriptures and neither be sucked in by the lie nor ashamed
of the truth. Unless we look and listen and discern, we will be ill-
equipped to make our way in the world.

How much, then, should we also *seek for wisdom*? "If any of you
lacks wisdom, let him ask of God, who gives to all liberally and
without reproach, and it will be given to him" (James 1:5). What an
encouragement to the child of God! Seek your wisdom at the fountain of wisdom. Pray for God to teach you by His Word and Spirit
how to live righteously in an unrighteous environment. Open your
map and rely on your compass. Too often we get lost because we
never consult the map or check the compass, and then we complain
that we have been left without guidance. Of course you will get lost
in the wilderness if you neglect the means of staying on the path!
Christians often wander aimlessly through the world, confused and
exposed, because their map is abandoned at the bottom of their bag
and their compass is left in the far reaches of their pocket.

The Bible is the Word of God that makes us wise for salvation
and equips us for every good work. How can we expect to walk
by the map if we have not studied its contours, considered the key,
employed the compass to set our direction, and prepared to walk
by means of constant reference to the accurate representation of
the landscape through which we must pass? Scripture contains the
divine deposit of wisdom supplied by God and necessary for the
living of a godly life in a fallen world: "in all your getting, get understanding." Get it by asking the Spirit of God to make the truth of God
abundantly plain to you as you kneel over it, asking for light from
heaven for discernment of the truth in faith and life.

In addition, the Lord has given us other helpers and counselors.
Most churches have mature saints who have been on the way for a
long time. (Bear in mind that by mature saints I do not merely mean
older Christians, but those who have a proven track record of faithful and fruitful living.) Those mature believers should have a deposit
of wisdom to pass on to others willing to learn from them—think of
the trickle-down of experience and insight in Titus 2 from the older
to the younger. In addition, while the elders of the church do not
have a monopoly on wisdom, they are those who have been sent by

Christ, given to the church, and equipped by the Spirit for the purpose of leading and guiding His sheep: "And He Himself gave some to be apostles, some prophets, some evangelists, and some pastors and teachers, for the equipping of the saints for the work of ministry, for the edifying of the body of Christ, till we all come to the unity of the faith and of the knowledge of the Son of God, to a perfect man, to the measure of the stature of the fullness of Christ" (Eph. 4:11–13).

Again, many are wounded because, neglecting the Scripture and despising the Spirit, ignoring all counsels, they are determined to find their own way, and often and sadly it is a hard one. They might have been spared much pain and sorrow.

Finally, *live obediently*. I do not mean to offer a truism. Wisdom is to be applied and employed by godly men and women. It is skill for righteous living, a weapon for battlefield use and not a toy for vain display. We must walk by faith. We must live conditioned by the fear of God, directed by the Spirit of God, instructed by the Word of God, practicing the will of the Lord. The healthy Christian is the one who takes to heart and lives in accordance with the truth that God has given to save us and to keep us. When the Lord gives understanding, the true saint thinks and acts accordingly.

The world is a dangerous place for the child of God, and we have much work to do here, working out our own salvation with fear and trembling, for it is God who works in us both to will and to do for His good pleasure. We therefore ought to do all things without complaining and disputing, that we may become blameless and harmless, children of God without fault in the midst of a crooked and perverse generation, among whom we shine as lights in the world, holding fast the word of life, so that those who serve us for God's sake may rejoice in the day of Christ that they have not run in vain or labored in vain (Phil. 2:12–16). Our calling is to serve Him who "gave Himself for our sins, that He might deliver us from this present evil age, according to the will of our God and Father, to whom be glory forever and ever" (Gal. 1:4–5). So get wisdom from God:

> Give me understanding, and I shall keep Your law;
> Indeed, I shall observe it with my whole heart.
> Make me walk in the path of Your commandments,
> For I delight in it. (Ps. 119:34–35)

4

KNOW THE ENEMY

Sun Tzu is generally acknowledged to be the author of a book of military maxims titled *The Art of War*. One of the principles he urges upon his students runs something like this: If you know the enemy and know yourself, you need not fear the result of a hundred battles. If you know yourself but not the enemy, for every victory gained you will also suffer a defeat. If you know neither the enemy nor yourself, you will succumb in every battle.

Despite the absolute nature of the statement, there is much that is sound about this maxim and much that Christians would do well to grasp. It is all well and good to get a grip on our own identity and activity, but if we are to make our way in the world so as to bring glory to God, we also need to know our enemy's identity and activity. Perhaps in some circles today our problem is not so much that we do not know our enemy as that we have dismissed him substantially, ignored him greatly, or denied him completely. In the words of D. Martyn Lloyd-Jones, "I am certain that one of the main causes of the ill state of the church today is the fact that the devil is being forgotten."[1]

There is a reason our enemy is called the father of lies. This character manifests itself in various ways, but I wonder if, in our day and age in the modern West at least, he has pulled off perhaps his greatest coup: the lie that he is not even there. What more effective way for an enemy to strike at those whom he opposes than to convince them first of all that he does not even exist? When we are obstructed,

---

1. As quoted in Iain Murray, *Lloyd-Jones: Messenger of Grace* (Edinburgh: Banner of Truth, 2008), 215.

attacked, and wounded and do not realize that there is a spiteful intelligence and an adverse power setting out to bring us low, we will be at a great disadvantage.

And yet many pilgrims set out on the heavenly way through a hostile environment ignorant of and blind to the malicious foe who daily assails us. Such ignorance and shortsightedness only adds to the confusion and bewilderment as we are troubled by difficulties we did not anticipate and battered by attacks that constantly surprise us. Those who use the Book of Common Prayer are taught to ask, "From the crafts and assaults of the devil;…and from all the deceits of the world, the flesh, and the devil, Good Lord, deliver us." Here is an echo of the petitions in the outline of prayer that our Lord gave to His disciples:

> "And do not lead us into temptation,
> But deliver us from the evil one.
> For Yours is the kingdom and the power and the
>   glory forever. Amen." (Matt. 6:13)

So, as a pilgrim people, we need to know that we have an enemy, how he operates, and how we ought to respond to him. Only in this way can we go as we should to the coming kingdom.

Know the Enemy: Scriptural Framework

The scriptural framework stretches across the whole of our Bibles, and it provides a determinative understanding of our experience in the world as a people locked in combat with a fierce foe until the very end. It begins for us in Genesis 3:15, where the Lord God drops a diamond of promise into the mound of filth that is the serpent's curse:

> "And I will put enmity
> Between you and the woman,
> And between your seed and her Seed;
> He shall bruise your head,
> And you shall bruise His heel." (Gen. 3:15)

That sets the tone for the entire Bible. From there on in we find the seed of the serpent contending with and seeking to snuff out the Seed of the woman. We trace it through the experience of the patriarchs.

We find it in the lives of Joseph and Moses. We notice it in the line of David. We observe it, of course, from the moment of Christ's birth. We see it written large in His death, and we continue to see it in the experience of Christ's people.

So at the end of our Bibles, we find the following testimony to the intensification and the culmination of this antagonism:

> Now when the dragon saw that he had been cast to the earth, he persecuted the woman who gave birth to the male Child. But the woman was given two wings of a great eagle, that she might fly into the wilderness to her place, where she is nourished for a time and times and half a time, from the presence of the serpent. So the serpent spewed water out of his mouth like a flood after the woman, that he might cause her to be carried away by the flood. But the earth helped the woman, and the earth opened its mouth and swallowed up the flood which the dragon had spewed out of his mouth. And the dragon was enraged with the woman, and he went to make war with the rest of her offspring, who keep the commandments of God and have the testimony of Jesus Christ. (Rev. 12:13–17)

> Now when the thousand years have expired, Satan will be released from his prison and will go out to deceive the nations which are in the four corners of the earth, Gog and Magog, to gather them together to battle, whose number is as the sand of the sea. They went up on the breadth of the earth and surrounded the camp of the saints and the beloved city. And fire came down from God out of heaven and devoured them. The devil, who deceived them, was cast into the lake of fire and brimstone where the beast and the false prophet are. And they will be tormented day and night forever and ever. (Rev. 20:7–10)

Leaving aside any discussion of the particular details, I trust that it will be evident that the church of Christ—those "who keep the commandments of God and have the testimony of Jesus Christ"—remains the particular object of satanic malevolence to the very end. God's people will be actively hated by the adversary until he is finally cast down and brought utterly low. As Christians survey the ground, then, how does our enemy appear?

The Ruler of This World

> Be sober, be vigilant; because your adversary the devil walks about
> like a roaring lion, seeking whom he may devour. (1 Peter 5:8)

You have an adversary. The language echoes the experience of
Joshua the high priest in the days of Zechariah, who had "Satan
standing at his right hand to oppose him" (Zech. 3:1). He is the devil,
the slanderer—Revelation 12:10 describes him as "the accuser of our
brethren." He hates the saints and is in principle constantly set against
us in all things. All his desire is to strike and stab at the people of
God. He is full of intelligent malice and cunning deceit: Paul talks of
the wiles or scheme of the devil (Eph. 6:11) and tells the Corinthians
that we are not ignorant or unaware of his devices (2 Cor. 2:11), his
evil purposes and enterprises. In 1 Peter 5:8, the apostle describes
his activity, walking about, an unwearied and diligent foe, restless
in his desire to express his antagonism toward his would-be victims.
We also see his character, one like "a roaring lion," hungry, fierce,
strong, and cruel, expressing his violent rage, proclaiming his fierce
intent, seeking his intended prey. We are warned of his desire, for he
is actively seeking his victims, tracking them down and searching
them out deliberately and mercilessly. We are shown his aim, for his
whole business and appetite is to devour the saints. Satan prowls
and strikes not merely to scratch his enemies, but—if he could—to
swallow them, to destroy souls entirely. Here we have a portrait of
one whose whole being, in every fiber, is bent upon damaging and
destroying the kingdom of Christ, assaulting the saints by all means
possible to do all harm possible. Here is the grand persecutor of the
church, the great orchestrator of all her opponents, the archenemy of
our souls. Lest we are in any doubt regarding the primacy, power,
and sphere of the operations of our foe, we find him described as
"the ruler of this world" (John 14:30) and "the god of this age" (2 Cor.
4:4). The world in which we live, considered as fallen and corrupted,
is, in measure, under him.

Principalities and Powers

> Put on the whole armor of God, that you may be able to stand
> against the wiles of the devil. For we do not wrestle against flesh
> and blood, but against principalities, against powers, against

the rulers of the darkness of this age, against spiritual hosts of wickedness in the heavenly places.... Above all, [take] the shield of faith with which you will be able to quench all the fiery darts of the wicked one. (Eph. 6:11–12, 16)

But we have other enemies. Ranged alongside and fighting for the crown prince of hell are a host of others. Paul exhorts believers to use their armor because they are involved in combat with these armies of darkness. When we fight, it is not first and foremost with flesh and blood, the seen things of this world, but with principalities and powers, the unseen hordes of the spiritual realm. He hints at their power, present in their very name as "principalities," or rulers; "powers," or spiritual potentates of some sort; "the rulers of the darkness of this age," the foul lords of the fallen cosmos. If we consider the capacities of the angels described in the Scriptures and understand these to be fallen angels enjoying even a measure of their original strength, then we see something of the horror of these enemies. He makes plain their number, those relentless plurals suggesting the word "hosts" or "forces" in some translations, indicating a multitude of foes. He points to their nature as "the spirituals of wickedness"—the spiritual embodiments of all that sets itself against God, belonging entirely to moral darkness, characterized entirely by evil. He indicates their realm, and it answers to their nature, operating in the realm of the substantially unseen, the "heavenly places"—literally, simply "the heavenlies"—where they have their being and conduct their doing.

To read such a description isolated from the rest of our Bibles, or even the rest of the letter to the Ephesians, might make us throw up our hands in despair. What, we might feel, is the point of any armor against such a host of mighty foes? Battle with such hordes is a frankly terrifying prospect to any man.

In response to this we must remember certain spiritual realities. In Colossians 1:13, Paul writes that God "has delivered us from the power of darkness and conveyed us into the kingdom of the Son of His love." This is a definitive statement. It speaks with finality to the realm to which a Christian—every Christian—belongs. We are no longer under the tyrannical power of spiritual darkness. God, in His merciful might, has lifted us up and carried us from that state into the kingdom of the Son of His love. That is where we now belong, and that definitively informs our identity as citizens of the kingdom of light and love ruled by King Jesus. This reality runs through the book of Ephesians. Thus we are informed that "the God and Father of our Lord Jesus Christ" "has blessed us with every spiritual blessing in the heavenly places in Christ" (Eph. 1:3). Here is precisely the same language as in Ephesians 6:12. The very realm in which these spiritual hosts of wickedness operate is the realm in which God has blessed us. Again, Paul says that God has made His people to "sit together in the heavenly places in Christ Jesus" (2:6). Here is the same language once more, this time making entirely clear that our identity and security in that sphere of "the heavenlies" is found in our being made alive together with Christ and raised up together with Him (Eph. 2:6–7), and so being seated together with Him on account of that unshakeable union established between the Lord Christ and all His saints. Furthermore, though "you were once darkness," "now you are light in the Lord"; therefore, we should "walk as children of light," having "no fellowship with the unfruitful works of darkness," but rather exposing them (Eph. 5:8–11). Our fundamental nature and allegiance have shifted. We no longer belong to darkness, and that darkness no longer has any grip upon us. That is why the spiritual hosts of darkness hate us and why we contend against them. This shift explains the malice that is directed against us. It is what makes sense of our spiritual experience.

So we see that around us and against us are vigorous, numerous, unseen foes. Behind the opposition that we see is the opposition that is unseen, for wherever there is spiritual darkness we are right to trace satanic influence, as these enemies work through various agencies and employ various means to express their malevolence toward Christ and His church. In the language of Peter O'Brien, "The apostles' [sic] clarion call, then, in Ephesians 6 to believers is to recognize the nature and dimension of the spiritual conflict in which we are engaged, and to appropriate God's armour in order to resist vigorously the onslaught of the evil one (cf. Jas. 4:7)."[2]

Friendship with the World

> Do not love the world or the things in the world. If anyone loves
> the world, the love of the Father is not in him. For all that is in

---

2. Peter O'Brien, *The Letter to the Ephesians* (Grand Rapids: Eerdmans, 1999), 470.

the world—the lust of the flesh, the lust of the eyes, and the pride of life—is not of the Father but is of the world. And the world is passing away, and the lust of it; but he who does the will of God abides forever. (1 John 2:15–17)

Here is a statement and warning from John that echoes the declaration of James, considered earlier, that "friendship with the world is enmity with God," and so "whoever therefore wants to be a friend of the world makes himself an enemy of God" (James 4:4). Loving the world—the world considered as apart from and against God—is inconsistent with loving God.[3] John goes on to explain that there are certain things that belong to the world and participate in its character rather than reflecting that which is godlike: the lust of the flesh, the lust of the eyes, and the pride of life.

The point we need to understand here is that this fallen world is Satan's home territory: the environment serves the devil better than it does the saint and provides him with his means of assault. To use a typical Puritan illustration, our hearts are tinderboxes, and the world is full of sparks. Our enemy has at his disposal much with which to work on us and in us. Is John, perhaps, deliberately evoking the temptations of Eden, in which Eve and Adam fell even though they did not then have the same sinful nature that we now possess? Compare what John says here with what Moses records in Genesis 3:6, as Eve, her heart influenced by the sugary words of the serpent, gazes at the tree of the knowledge of good and evil: "So when the woman saw that the tree was good for food, that it was pleasant to the eyes, and a tree desirable to make one wise, she took of its fruit and ate." The woman saw that the tree was good for food; in the same way, Satan uses the things of this world to stir up the lust of the flesh, our bodily appetites, carrying us beyond what is right for us. The woman saw that the tree was pleasant to the eyes; so Satan dangles before us the lust of the eyes, engendering covetous desires, longing for what has been put out of our reach. Finally, the woman saw that the tree was desirable to make one wise; this is the pride of

---

3. Note again John's report in John 3:16 that God loved the world emphasizes that we must be careful to take into account not only the particular sense that the writers assign to this word but also the various contexts in which it is found. God may love the fallen world with a love of compassion and goodwill, but saints are not to love the world with a love of committed affection.

life, that arrogant ambition that is quite ready to have self sit on the throne rather than God, the aim to be like God on our own terms (Gen. 3:5). In short, we find that Satan is once more using the same weapons on the same targets: we are not ignorant of his devices (2 Cor. 2:11). He operates upon our humanity as he ever did, now taking advantage of the fact that fallen men are wholly inclined to evil and that even the redeemed, while they are on the earth, will have these susceptibilities.

No Neutral Ground

> Do all things without complaining and disputing, that you may become blameless and harmless, children of God without fault in the midst of a crooked and perverse generation, among whom you shine as lights in the world, holding fast the word of life, so that I may rejoice in the day of Christ that I have not run in vain or labored in vain. (Phil. 2:14–16)

As we have been stating, the world, considered in its fallen condition and in its rebellious state, is—in large measure—the place where Satan operates and where his power lies. The spiritual hosts of wickedness in the heavenly places work out their plans and purposes among men in the world. We have seen Satan called "the ruler of this world" (John 14:30). It is worth noting that even with Christ's death and resurrection accomplished, Paul still called him "the god of this age" (2 Cor. 4:4). John himself makes plain that we know two things at this present time: "We know that we are of God, and the whole world lies under the sway of the wicked one" (1 John 5:19). Revelation identifies him as "the great dragon...that serpent of old, called the Devil and Satan, who deceives the whole world" (Rev. 12:9).

Again, we must not overestimate our enemy and afford him an honor to which he is not entitled or a power he does not possess. This is not a denial of God's ultimate government over all things nor of His ultimate divine authority over the evil one. The opening verses of Job 1 clearly express that the boundaries of Satan's working are set by God. It is not a denial of the power of Christ to save and to keep His saints: our Lord is the stronger man who has entered the strong man's house and plundered his goods by first binding him (Matt. 12:29). But Christ does not deny that it is Satan's house He is plundering, even as He declares Satan's binding. What we are doing is acknowledging the reality of our present circumstances.

Paul would have the Philippians—and, by extension, Christians today—to understand that the people around us who do not belong to Christ's kingdom are not mere neutrals, but are slaves of Satan. They are lost in darkness, doing his will. We are part of twisted and perverse societies among those—even with the operations of common grace—who are fundamentally crooked and dishonest, perverted, depraved, and distorted. Again, we do not exaggerate the doctrine of total depravity. This is not an underhanded way of suggesting that all people are as bad as they could possibly be, although we should remember that the awful reality of total and entire depravity—thoroughgoing and unrestrained wickedness in every part of his being—does describe the adversary. But we are fools and blind if we imagine that this world entertains friendship toward the saints of God. The pressure in the world is always away from God, away from that which is straight and true toward that which is crooked and perverse. It is against such pressures and in such company that the saints are called to shine, striving to show the spiritual beauty of holiness in the face of the spiritual ugliness of godlessness.

The Assault on the Church

"For I know this, that after my departure savage wolves will come in among you, not sparing the flock. Also from among yourselves men will rise up, speaking perverse things, to draw away the disciples after themselves. Therefore watch, and remember that for three years I did not cease to warn everyone night and day with tears." (Acts 20:29–31)

At this point, we might feel rather relieved that at least we belong to the church, and there we are safe. We might even begin to entertain a degree of smugness. Not so fast! It is true that the church of Christ is under the care of Christ and is the safest place for any Christian to be and the people with whom every Christian ought to identify him or herself. However, the idea that it is a place of present and permanent peace is largely misguided. In the church also we must constantly be on our guard, for her very character as the body of Christ makes her the particular object of satanic malice. So Paul warns the elders of the church of savage wolves coming in from without and perverse speakers rising up from within to assault and deceive the disciples. The warnings are borne out by others. Peter warns his readers that

> there were also false prophets among the people, even as there will be false teachers among you, who will secretly bring in destructive heresies, even denying the Lord who bought them, and bring on themselves swift destruction. And many will follow their destructive ways, because of whom the way of truth will be blasphemed. By covetousness they will exploit you with deceptive words; for a long time their judgment has not been idle, and their destruction does not slumber. (2 Peter 2:1–3)

See how they have learned from their leader: destruction, blasphemy, covetousness, and deception—the very hallmarks of satanic work! Later in the same letter, Peter warns that Paul's teaching contains "some things hard to understand, which untaught and unstable people twist to their own destruction, as they do also the rest of the Scriptures" (2 Peter 3:16). Here again are those who take the substance of revelation and so corrupt the clear water as to make it a poison indeed.

Paul himself warns Timothy of those who have rejected faith and a good conscience and, therefore, "concerning the faith have suffered shipwreck, of whom are Hymenaeus and Alexander, whom I delivered to Satan that they may learn not to blaspheme" (1 Tim. 1:19–20). Later there is a further warning for his protégé: "But shun profane and idle babblings, for they will increase to more ungodliness. And their message will spread like cancer. Hymenaeus and Philetus are of this sort, who have strayed concerning the truth, saying that the resurrection is already past; and they overthrow the faith of some. Nevertheless the solid foundation of God stands, having this seal: 'The Lord knows those who are His,' and, 'Let everyone who names the name of Christ depart from iniquity'" (2 Tim 2:16–19).

Let there be no doubt, then, that Satan attacks the church of Christ by force and fraud. John Owen puts it in his typically quaint but vigorous way:

> The gates of hell, as all agree, are the power and policy of it, or the actings of Satan, both as a lion and as a serpent, by rage and by subtlety. But whereas in these things he acts not visibly in his

own person, but by his agents, he hath always had two sorts of them employed in his service. By the one he executes his rage, and by the other his craft; he animates the one as a lion, the other as a serpent. In the one he acts as the dragon, in the other as the beast that had two horns like the lamb, but spake like the dragon. The first is the unbelieving world; the other, apostates and seducers of all sorts. Wherefore, this work in this kind is of a double nature;—the one, an effect of his power and rage, acted by the world in persecution—the other, of his policy and craft, acted by heretics in seduction. In both he designs to separate the church from its foundation.[4]

Trace the history of the church and you will find it, in large measure, consisting in a series of assaults by means of force and fraud, withstood by the grace of God in Christ. Precisely because of her character as a pilgrim people traveling to the heavenly Zion, the church is subjected to all kinds of hostility from all quarters under demonic influences. These aggressors and betrayers reveal their spiritual parentage by their wicked character, their false teaching, and their rotten fruit, earning as surely as anyone else ever did the charge, "You are of your father the devil, and the desires of your father you want to do. He was a murderer from the beginning, and does not stand in the truth, because there is no truth in him. When he speaks a lie, he speaks from his own resources, for he is a liar and the father of it" (John 8:44).

Know the Enemy: Summary Thoughts

There is a deliberate and organized opposition to the church of God. The Bible delineates and describes it in terms of its spiritual dimension, its concrete manifestation, and its personal aggression. You have an adversary called the devil. He has hosts of wickedness at his ready command, operating by various means and through various agencies, seen and unseen, in a world substantially marked by satanic influence and operations. We are passing through a dangerous environment, better suited to the assaults of the evil one than the defense of the righteous ones. The church is the primary target,

---

4. John Owen, *Christologia, or, the Person of Christ*, in *The Works of John Owen*, ed. W. H. Goold (Edinburgh: Banner of Truth, 1965), 1:35–36.

and the susceptibilities and inclinations of the saints—not to mention those who do not know Christ—are viciously identified and relentlessly battered in order to express hostility toward Christ Himself and all those who belong to Him. Temptations will issue their siren call as God's people live in the midst of a crooked and perverse generation. From without, savage wolves will come in; from within, perverse speakers will rise up. We must be on our guard because the rebellious world is against us, and it is all an expression of the malice and malevolence of the dragon, who seeks to devour. As Charles Spurgeon writes,

> I think a genuine Christian cannot live long without believing in a personal devil. Some have thought his existence a myth. If they stood foot to foot with him in dire conflict they would know better. We speak our heart's convictions, that he has met us in the Valley of Humiliation and cast his fiery darts at us. We have had to contend with him by the hour and the day, ay, and even by the month, at a time, only too glad to defeat him at the last, though wounded in head, and hands, and feet.[5]

But before we move on, there is a note to sound once more: our foe is both conquered and doomed. Paul reports of Christ that, "having disarmed principalities and powers, He made a public spectacle of them, triumphing over them in it"—that is, in the cross (Col. 2:15). The Lord assures us through His apostle that "the God of peace will crush Satan under your feet shortly" (Rom. 16:20). John also paints a picture of his end: "The devil, who deceived them, was cast into the lake of fire and brimstone where the beast and the false prophet are. And they will be tormented day and night forever and ever" (Rev. 20:10).

Furthermore, even in the very contexts in which we are most clearly warned, we are also called to arms. As Spurgeon suggests, we are directed and enabled to stand and to prevail against him: "Resist the devil and he will flee from you" (James 4:7). We will consider this in more detail, but let us not lose sight of our need to know our enemy accurately—not to underestimate him, certainly, but neither to overestimate him. Christ has conquered him, and to that we cling.

---

5. C. H. Spurgeon, "Sorrowful Upbraidings," in *C. H. Spurgeon's Sermons beyond Volume 63: An Authentic Supplement to the Metropolitan Tabernacle Pulpit,* comp. Terence Peter Crosby (Leominster, U.K.: DayOne Publications, 2009), 69–70.

So let us remember that our adversary remains for the present a real, personal, malevolent, intelligent, purposeful, and committed enemy. Having been defeated by our Champion at the very point at which he thought he had snatched victory, he has nothing left to lose and is therefore a most dangerous foe.

Know the Enemy: Specific Counsels

So what must we do if we are to respond rightly to these things? First, we must *grasp these realities*. Bluntly, we need to wake up. We need to get real, and what we do not see is more real than what we do (see 2 Cor. 4:18). This is not scaremongering, but scriptural sense. It is not intended to breed paranoia, but to produce a right perspective. I have deliberately avoided some of the thornier questions of the devil's precise nature and origin, not prying into some of the difficulties and debates that surround his ongoing labors to assault the body of Christ and dishonor her Head. There are helpful resources, older and newer, that deal with these questions.[6] If you explore what is available, please be careful: many, especially more recent volumes, tend to be fantastical, sensationalist, and unscriptural—some are even casual and flippant. I am not dismissing those sometimes significant issues that I have deliberately overlooked, but they are not the point here.

What we need to get a grip on, at the very least, is the spiritual dimension, concrete manifestation, and personal aggression of this warfare. It is nonetheless real for being unseen; it works out in the world in definite and tangible ways; it is intended to do us all possible harm. We have already said that the world is not a playground, but a

---

6. Among older works, you might consider *A Treatise of Satan's Temptations*, by Richard Gilpin, ed. Alexander Grosart (Morgan, Pa.: Soli Deo Gloria, 2000); *The Christian in Complete Armour*, by William Gurnall, ed. J. C. Ryle (Edinburgh: Banner of Truth, 2002); *The Christian Warfare: Against the Devil, World and Flesh*, by John Downame (Norwood, N.J.: W. J. Johnson, 1974); or Benjamin Keach, *War with the Devil* (Leeds: John Binns, 1795). More modern works include *Satan Cast Out: A Study in Biblical Demonology*, by Frederick Leahy (Edinburgh: Banner of Truth, 1975); *The Victory of the Lamb*, by Frederick Leahy (Edinburgh: Banner of Truth, 2001); *Striving against Satan: Knowing the Enemy—His Weakness, His Strategy, His Defeat*, by Joel R. Beeke (Bryntirion, Wales: Bryntirion Press, 2003); or *Spiritual Warfare: A Biblical and Balanced Perspective*, by Brian Borgman and Rob Ventura (Grand Rapids: Reformation Heritage Books, 2014).

battleground. In the same way, the devil is not our playmate, but our fierce opponent. There are vile hordes at his command and various means at his disposal to assault Christ's church as an expression of his hostility to Christ Himself. Because of our identity and activity we become his target, and we cannot afford to ignore or deny it. Peter O'Brien writes:

> The devil and his minions are able to rule the lives of men and women who belong to his "tyranny of darkness" (Col. 1:13)—they are called "children of disobedience" at Ephesians 2:2—and the powers exploit culture and social systems in their attempts to wreck the creative and saving work of God. The first-century readers of the letter, and we ourselves, need to understand the spiritual dimension of this struggle, the supernatural, evil nature of the opposition, and the necessity of putting on divine armour for the battle.[7]

Again, we must be extremely careful not to derive our doctrine or form our practice from human wisdom and imagination. On the one hand, our world often forces us into a thoroughly materialistic and skeptical stance, an empirical approach to life in which what we cannot see and touch we will not accept. Even in reading a chapter like this it is possible that you will hear the mocking whisper, "Surely this isn't true! Do you really believe this stuff?" This is the conditioning of the worldview of the twenty-first-century Western world. My friend, let the plain matter of God's revelation be your guide, and not the wisdom of fallen men. By the same token, do not derive your ideas and responses from that pagan spirituality or popular superstition that reflects Satan's agenda, in which Satan's influence is either blurred or cloaked. That may be more of a temptation for readers from other cultures. All of us must learn to view the world—seen and unseen—through biblical spectacles.

Next, *understand Satan's strategies*: "We are not ignorant of his devices" (2 Cor. 2:11). Sun Tzu was right: at this point, knowing ourselves and knowing our enemy will help us. Perhaps the clearest and most immediately helpful work on this topic is by the Puritan Thomas Brooks, entitled *Precious Remedies against Satan's Devices*. Its particular benefit is its clear organization, with Satan's

---

7. O'Brien, *Letter to the Ephesians*, 468.

strategies arranged under various headings and a range of remedies or responses provided for each one. This makes it a sort of spiritual medicine cabinet for the saint wrestling with particular temptations or assaults. Brooks assures us that "Christ, the Scripture, your own hearts, and Satan's devices, are the four prime things that should be first and most studied and searched,"[8] giving Sun Tzu a biblical reworking. Brooks exposes Satan's tactics and erects defenses for the wise and humble believer, providing an armory for the child of God.[9]

We must expect artful malice and cruel intelligence to play on every weak point. This will not be a fair fight. Satan will employ every dirty trick learned over a long career to bring you down, keep you down, and kick you while you are down. No quarter will be given, and so the saints need to learn what to expect and how to respond. We have already seen from the apostle John the kind of approaches that the adversary takes, prying away at our bodily appetites, our covetous desires, our arrogant ambitions. When we begin to know how our enemy thinks and acts and put that into the context of our own being and doing, we might be able to start winning some of these battles. If we know how the enemy approaches, what weapons he uses, and where he strikes, we can prepare for his assaults, erect appropriate defenses, and prepare for holy retaliation. But let there be no spiritual bravado. He will strike hard and mercilessly at every weak point in your humanity. The saints know this by bitter experience. Is it not the case, Christian, that you find yourself being tripped and troubled repeatedly at precisely the same points? Is it not the case, Christian, that many of us have been fighting precisely the same battles over precisely the same ground for almost every day of our lives as the people of God? Time and time again battle is joined over the same issues. This is because Satan has been observing, learning, and plotting. He knows where you and I are at our weakest, and he keeps going back and hitting us at that point. He is the master of deceit and a reservoir of venom.

---

8. Thomas Brooks, *Precious Remedies against Satan's Devices*, in *The Works of Thomas Brooks*, ed. Alexander Grosart (Edinburgh: Banner of Truth, 1980), 1:3.

9. For a contemporary summary and discussion of Satan's devices relative to the invaluable, major Puritan books on this subject, see Beeke, *Striving against Satan*, 65–86.

We must learn the general approach that the enemy takes in assaulting the saints, the broad strokes of satanic strategy. We also must learn his specific tactics against particular churches and individuals, the particular ways and means that we come under assault. Why do I always fight this battle? How is it that Satan draws me into this web again? What are the particular baits that he dangles before my eyes to stir up the lusts of my flesh? What does he introduce that stokes the fires of my covetous desires, the wish to have or to be certain things? How does he foster again that pride of life that makes me begin to imagine that—in this or that matter—I should be in charge of my life, that this man rather than the Lord should call the shots? Satan will strike you where he knows you are most susceptible.

This should teach us to *look to Christ Jesus*. No fallen creature has ever lived entirely out of the devil's clutches in the absolute sense, but the Lord Jesus has delivered countless thousands from Satan's foul grip. No one has ever stood against him and triumphed in his own strength, but—out of weakness—many have been made strong by Christ to resist the devil. It is when we start to reckon with the fierce malice and cruel strength of this foe that we are, first of all, sent fleeing to Christ to be made free. We are slaves of Satan, captive in darkness, until God by His mighty power transfers us into the kingdom of the Son of His love. We cannot save ourselves! Our enemy is too strong for us. That is why Christ is described as the strong man who spoils His enemy: "When a strong man, fully armed, guards his own palace, his goods are in peace. But when a stronger than he comes upon him and overcomes him, he takes from him all his armor in which he trusted, and divides his spoils" (Luke 11:21–22).

It should keep the saints clinging to Christ, not just to be made free but to be kept free, that we may stand in the evil day. We have One who has conquered; He is still saving men and women from darkness and bringing them into His kingdom, a Deliverer on a white horse, one called Faithful and True, who in righteousness judges and makes war (Rev. 19:11). Because of the enemy, we need a great Champion, and the only one we have is our great God and Savior, Jesus Christ, as Isaac Watts reminds us:

> Should all the hosts of death,
> And powers of hell unknown,
> Put their most dreadful forms

Of rage and malice on,
I shall be safe, for Christ displays
Superior power, and guardian grace.[10]

Let these realities drive you to Jesus Christ. My strength fails, but Christ stands. Robert Hawker writes, "All our preparations, humblings, watchings, and the like, unless found in Christ, and Christ undertakes for us, will stand as nothing against the wiles of Satan."[11]

I urge you also to *count the cost*. We are called to Christ not for comforts, but for combats. The journey is first, then we arrive at home. The battle must be fought, and then the triumph is enjoyed. First the bloody fight, then the victory wreath. There is a careful calculation to be made when a man follows Christ (see Luke 14:25–35). Part of that calculation is that we are called into battle as the armies of the Lamb against a foe of prodigious strength and vicious cunning. But we should recognize that this is a good fight—a fight indeed, but a fight worth fighting. But let us not pretend that it is an easy fight. How they lie who tell sinners that following Jesus brings you immediate ease and comfort, as if the saints are carried into heaven on a bed of roses! The child of God enters on to a road of thorns: through many tribulations we enter the kingdom of heaven, and the kingdom of heaven makes all the tribulations worthwhile. It is the painful testimony of many of God's faithful people that we never had to fight until we were free. We never knew the malice of our captor until we were released from his bonds. Once enlisted in the army of God, then we knew what pain and sorrow were, contending as our Lord did for the glory of God and the health of His church. If you would follow Jesus, if you do follow Jesus, then count the cost: your allegiance to the King of kings will make you a prime target of His enemies. The King will sustain you and even use the battle to train you, but battle there must be.

Again, *be on your guard*. Do not let scientism or superstition blind you or dull your senses. Heed these warnings for yourself and for the church to which you belong. This life is not a game, but a constant warring. The stakes are higher than we often calculate. We cannot

---

10. Isaac Watts, "Join all the Glorious Names."
11. Robert Hawker, *The Poor Man's New Testament Commentary* (Birmingham, Ala.: Solid Ground Christian Books, n.d.), 3:387.

afford to take lightly what God speaks weightily. Divine revelation provides the children of God with all manner of instruction specifically intended to equip us to know our enemy and so to keep us from falling. The apostle Paul reminded the Corinthians of the idolatry of the Israelites after their escape from Egypt, their immorality, how they tempted God, how they complained, and how the Lord punished all these:

> Now all these things happened to them as examples, and they were written for our admonition, upon whom the ends of the ages have come. Therefore let him who thinks he stands take heed lest he fall. No temptation has overtaken you except such as is common to man; but God is faithful, who will not allow you to be tempted beyond what you are able, but with the temptation will also make the way of escape, that you may be able to bear it.
> Therefore, my beloved, flee from idolatry. I speak as to wise men; judge for yourselves what I say. (1 Cor. 10:11–15)

Let us then be wise, neither heedless nor careless. We will be taken by the roaring lion unless we listen to the warnings and guard our souls.

Then we must *get on our knees*. This is not the Christian's posture of surrender, but rather his most effective fighting stance. Remember how Christian fought Apollyon:

> In this combat no man can imagine, unless he had seen and heard as I did, what yelling and hideous roaring Apollyon made all the time of the fight—he spake like a dragon; and, on the other side, what sighs and groans burst from Christian's heart. I never saw him all the while give so much as one pleasant look, till he perceived he had wounded Apollyon with his two-edged sword; then, indeed, he did smile, and look upward! But it was the dreadfullest sight that ever I saw.[12]

But even then, his fighting was not over, for as he passed into the valley of the Shadow of Death he faced further strife. In the midst of the valley, he perceived the mouth of hell, with flames, smoke, sparks, and hideous noises coming out of it. His sword was ineffective against these things, so he used the weapon called "All-prayer; so he cried…O Lord, I beseech thee, deliver my soul." Still attacked

---

12. Bunyan, *Pilgrim's Progress*, 3:113.

by flames and troubled by sad voices and strange sounds, Christian believed he would be torn in pieces or trampled. Approached by what he thought was a "company of fiends," Christian contemplated going back, but remembered all the dangers he had passed through and decided that it would probably be far more dangerous to go back than to proceed. "So he resolved to go on; yet the fiends seemed to come nearer and nearer. But when they were come even almost at him, he cried out with a most vehement voice, I will walk in the strength of the Lord God. So they gave back, and came no farther."[13]

When all else fails, prayer lays hold upon the Lord Almighty and obtains help from Him. Our Savior has equipped us with specific frames for our prayers:

"And do not lead us into temptation,
But deliver us from the evil one.
For Yours is the kingdom and the power and the glory forever.
   Amen." (Matt. 6:13)

In prayer the frail and fainting child of God lays hold upon the One to whom belong the kingdom and the power and the glory, and by Him we are hedged about in our hour of need. Let us never forget the weapon of All-Prayer. This is why

Restraining prayer we cease to fight;
Prayer makes the Christian's armour bright;
And Satan trembles, when he sees
The weakest saint upon his knees.[14]

Satan has no fear of prayerless religion; prayerless study, prayerless preaching, and prayerless work are nothing to him, for there is no power in them. But prayer fetches fire from heaven, and that is why the adversary hates to see saints pray and why we must make prayer a matter of principled practice.

Finally, we must *learn to fight*. The Captain of our salvation does not send us into battle unprepared and underequipped. We are warned, trained, strengthened, nourished, prepared, and provided for in every stage of our journey and for every element of our

13. Bunyan, *Pilgrim's Progress*, 3:115.
14. William Cowper, "What Various Hindrances We Meet."

combat. The believer who finds himself unarmed and underarmored does so not because of any failing on Christ's part but because of his own laziness or carelessness. The child of God who is walking with Christ depends utterly upon his Redeemer and contends faithfully for Him, confident that Christ's triumph sets the stage for ours: "Be wise in what is good, and simple concerning evil. And the God of peace will crush Satan under your feet shortly" (Rom. 16:19–20). We will consider this more specifically, but let us rest our confidence in this, that in all our battles and tribulations "we are more than conquerors through Him who loved us. For I am persuaded that neither death nor life, nor angels nor principalities nor powers, nor things present nor things to come, nor height nor depth, nor any other created thing, shall be able to separate us from the love of God which is in Christ Jesus our Lord" (Rom. 8:37–39).

5

FIGHT THE BATTLES

When the children of Israel had been decisively delivered from Egypt, they had a long journey through the wilderness on the way to the good and spacious Promised Land. This journey was not a gentle stroll, but an arduous campaign. A hostile environment and aggressive enemies meant that they faced years of trials, assaults, and temptations. We need only read the opening chapters of Deuteronomy, in which Moses summarizes the experience of Israel, to get a sense of this: it is a catalog of troubles as they followed the fire by night and the cloud by day. In Numbers 1 and 2 the focus is on Israel as a fighting force, a people equipped for war as they move through the land. Judah is the vanguard of this highly organized throng, this army with banners, and God is in the midst of them as they camp around the points of the compass, centered on the presence of God with them. Although Psalms 78, 105, 106, and 136 have a slightly different function, showing Israel's repeated follies and failings and God's free and faithful mercies, still they give some sense of the constant tensions and tribulations of the life of God's people.

Life in the wilderness was and is a running battle. It is a picture of God's people still: delivered from the bondage of Satan, we pass through the wilderness, fighting as we go, until at last we cross the river into the Promised Land. Once we understand the environment and know the enemy, we will begin to see why the fight is inevitable. In such a place as this world and with such an enemy as the devil, the identity of the saints means not only that assaults are unavoidable but also that engagement is required if we are to be faithful to our heavenly calling, if we are to walk and to please God.

We must, however, note in all that follows that the exhortation to fight the battles is a command given to believers, to those who are in Christ Jesus. Only in union with the Lord Jesus is a sinner able to stand. Until united to Christ by the irresistible call of God, that sinner is a slave-soldier of Satan. Only as one delivered from Satan's clutches and transferred into the kingdom of Christ and under His command is a sinner able to obey God's orders. You cannot fight for Christ until you belong to Christ. We must first run to Christ before we can resist the devil; we cannot do the latter without having done the former, and any attempts we make to fight these battles in our own strength should convince us of our utter weakness and persuade us to come to Christ without delay. Apart from Christ, in this as in all things, you and I can do nothing. If we are to stand, it must be in the Lord and in the power of His might. Let us consider, then, the commands, exhortations, and realities pressed in on the souls of the saints as we fight the battles.

Fight the Battles: Scriptural Framework

Endure Hardship

> You therefore must endure hardship as a good soldier of Jesus Christ. No one engaged in warfare entangles himself with the affairs of this life, that he may please him who enlisted him as a soldier. (2 Tim. 2:3–4)

This command is given to Timothy specifically and primarily in his calling as a minister of the gospel. However, most commentators admit that it contains a principle more broadly applicable. Gospel ministers in particular, and all Christians in general, must endure hardships. When Barnabas and Paul made a circuit of various churches, they were "strengthening the souls of the disciples, exhorting them to continue in the faith, and saying, 'We must through many tribulations enter the kingdom of God'" (Acts 14:22). Paul uses the illustration of the soldier to press home the demands upon those whom God calls to serve Him. This calling invariably involves suffering, the experience of hardship.

Like a soldier under command, this issue is not whether he will suffer, whether he will live or die, but whether he will do his duty, committed to his cause and his Captain. The consequences of our

duty are less important than our fidelity in our duty. Alfred, Lord
Tennyson, wrote a poem titled *The Charge of the Light Brigade* about a
tragic military blunder during the Crimean War in which a brigade
of lightly armed cavalry charged entrenched Russian artillery. Tennyson's poem emphasizes the valor of the men on horseback as they
charged down the valley toward the guns. Remove the confusion
in command (which could never apply to Christ) and give us in its
place an all-wise and all-good Commander of the army of the Lord,
and Tennyson provides a fine example of the best spirit in a subordinate soldier:

> Theirs not to make reply,
> Theirs not to reason why,
> Theirs but to do and die:
> Into the valley of Death
> Rode the six hundred.
>
> Cannon to right of them,
> Cannon to left of them,
> Cannon in front of them
> Volley'd and thunder'd;
> Storm'd at with shot and shell,
> Boldly they rode and well,
> Into the jaws of Death,
> Into the mouth of Hell
> Rode the six hundred.

This is what a good soldier of Christ does if it should be required of
him. The issue is not the cost of our obedience, but our commitment
to Christ our Captain and His cause.

The Christian's existence is not a bed of ease, but often a path
of pain, a road of sacrifice. In 2 Timothy 2 Paul draws on military
imagery to paint soldiers in their best light: men of honor, courage,
resolution, obedience, and loyalty. Elsewhere he is happy to charge
Timothy "according to the prophecies previously made concerning
you, that by them you may wage the good warfare" (1 Tim. 1:18).
Archippus, perhaps one of the elders in Colosse, is "our fellow
soldier" (Philem. 1:2), and faithful Epaphroditus is likewise "my
brother, fellow worker, and fellow soldier" (Phil. 2:25). The apostle
is communicating and commending their willingness to serve and

to suffer, their pursuit of obedience with an eye to the Captain's commendation. For that is the Christian soldier's aim—to "please him who enlisted him as a soldier" (2 Tim. 2:4). Following the Captain and His orders and seeking to please Him and bring credit to Him, is the believer's goal. To do this, there must be single-minded devotion to the cause, that true zeal which makes a Christian a man of one thing: "Not that I have already attained, or am already perfected; but I press on, that I may lay hold of that for which Christ Jesus has also laid hold of me. Brethren, I do not count myself to have apprehended; but one thing I do, forgetting those things which are behind and reaching forward to those things which are ahead, I press toward the goal for the prize of the upward call of God in Christ Jesus" (Phil. 3:12–14).

Having been brought into service, Paul's great goal was to be and to do everything that Christ intended him to be and to do. Such a man cannot afford to be swamped by the accumulation of worldly attachments and commitments. To live like this the Christian minister more absolutely and every saint relatively must free himself from the entanglements of this life. Though he may be employed in the world, he cannot afford to be entangled in it, caught up in its cares and concerns, devoted to its demands and delights. Spurgeon urges the Christian to carry what is necessary to accomplish what is his priority, laying aside whatever hinders him in his warfare for the sake of his calling, cause, and Captain:

> Up, I pray you now. By him whose eyes are like a flame of fire, and yet were wet with tears, by him on whose head are many crowns, and who yet wore the crown of thorns, by him who is King of kings and Lord of lords, and yet bowed his head to death for you resolve that to life's latest breath you will spend and be spent for his praise. The Lord grant that there may be many such in this church—good soldiers of Jesus Christ.[1]

The Fight of Faith

Be sober, be vigilant; because your adversary the devil walks about like a roaring lion, seeking whom he may devour. Resist

---

1. Charles H. Spurgeon, "A Good Soldier of Jesus Christ," in *Metropolitan Tabernacle Pulpit* (Pasadena, Tex.: Pilgrim Publications, 1983), 16:370.

him, steadfast in the faith, knowing that the same sufferings are experienced by your brotherhood in the world. (1 Peter 5:8–9)

We have already seen from this text the character of our adversary, a cruel striker restlessly pursuing the children of God, intent on devouring his prey. What is our response to the destroyer? We must first be *sober*, temperate, self-controlled in our appetites, and not intoxicated by the dizzying, distracting, and destabilizing world around us: "You must moderate your affection to worldly things, or else Satan will soon overcome you."[2] If your heart and mind are taken up with the empty baubles and fading beauties of this world, if you are giddy with the sights and sounds of this life, you will not be ready for Satan's coming against you. We need a clear perspective.

Furthermore, we must be *vigilant*—the language calls us to wakefulness and watchfulness, to the alertness of a soldier called to stand guard deep in enemy territory crawling with hostile assault teams. No one accuses such a warrior of paranoia if he shouts, "Who goes there?" and rouses his comrades at the faintest rustle of the leaves on an otherwise still night. This is the stance of the believer.

This attitude prepares the saints for action when the enemy springs upon them like a lion; then they *resist* him, steadfast in the faith. Cowering under assault leads only to defeat. The only way to beat Satan is to stand against him toe to toe in the Spirit's strength. It is a terrifying prospect, but it is the only route to victory. The saints must stand, planting their feet and setting themselves against the foe, not giving place to the devil (Eph. 4:27)—giving him no foothold and relinquishing not one inch of ground willingly and without a monumental struggle.

In this battle, faith is the Christian's strength, for faith lays hold on God, engages Him on our behalf, and lays hold of His might and grace. Without faith, we have no resources on which to draw and no means of obtaining them. Faith is the primary armor of the saint: "Above all, taking the shield of faith with which you will be able to quench all the fiery darts of the wicked one" (Eph. 6:16). Faith, then, is the sphere in which victory is obtained, for it brings us into contact with eternal realities and draws on divine strength. Christ is our captain in this combat and our example of how to fight. Consider the

---

2. Unattributed, quoted in Henry, *Commentary*, 6:834.

testimony of Psalm 22, as the Messiah wrestles to keep hold on God
as His God in the midst of His trial, expressing His torment in the
"but Me" statements and declaring His faith in the "but You" testimonies of the psalm. Finally, he triumphs: "You have answered me"
(v. 21). Furthermore, this is a battle in which every child of God the
world over is involved: you know "that the same sufferings are experienced by your brotherhood in the world" (1 Peter 5:9). This combat
is the common experience of saints as we make our way through
the world, and therefore none of us is exempt from the call for sobriety, vigilance, and resistance. Indeed, the more we are assaulted, the
more they are demanded.

Submit to God

> Submit to God. Resist the devil and he will flee from you. Draw
> near to God and He will draw near to you. (James 4:7–8)

Again, the context places us firmly in the environment of a corrupted
world: "Adulterers and adulteresses! Do you not know that friendship with the world is enmity with God? Whoever therefore wants
to be a friend of the world makes himself an enemy of God" (James
4:4). In this context, God offers us through James *a gracious precept*:
"submit to God" and "resist the devil." We must resist Satan as those
who are in submission to God. Again, faith sees what is really taking place and embraces and obeys God in His divine authority as
the Lord of all, necessarily recognizing Satan's claims of dominion
for the falsehoods they are and rejecting them as such: "Do you not
know that to whom you present yourselves slaves to obey, you are
that one's slaves whom you obey, whether of sin leading to death,
or of obedience leading to righteousness? But God be thanked that
though you were slaves of sin, yet you obeyed from the heart that
form of doctrine to which you were delivered. And having been set
free from sin, you became slaves of righteousness" (Rom. 6:16–18).
We are to choose God's righteous and holy will and turn our backs
upon the claims of the liar on our affections and attentions. It was
said of Christ that Satan, as the ruler of this world, had nothing in
Him (John 14:30). Why was this? At least in part it was because our
Savior had submitted entirely to His heavenly Father. Christ was
committed to fulfilling His Father's will.

James reinforces what we learned from Peter: if we do not resist, we shall be taken captive, but if we resist, then there is hope. Satan treads carefully and fearfully when he meets with the grace of resistance in the soul of a saint: "Resolution shuts and bolts the door against temptation," Matthew Henry comments.[3] Again, we must join battle at the right point, for too often we invite Satan in and then ask him to leave when he starts getting pushy. The time to resist him is when he knocks at the door and demands entry. In resisting Satan in this way, we fight sin. The battle is not carried out by means of superstitions and charms. Prayer wheels, rehearsed rote petitions, pawing the crucifix, calling on pagan gods, rubbing the rabbit's foot, carrying our white heather, checking for promises in the stars, and all the collected nonsenses of the darkened mind will avail us nothing in this battle. Again, it is the faith that submits to God that wins the day. We must remind ourselves, "God is real, God has delivered me, and God has called me to do what he has said." Satan only beats us if we give in, for if we resist there is *a gracious promise* here too. Satan's power and advantage lie in our weakness and frailty. If we resist, the lion will turn tail, a cowardly lion indeed. If the saint does not consent to Satan, then he cannot be conquered by Satan, and he is no longer obliged to do Satan's will. The adversary is not omnipotent, though he would like you to believe that he is at least equal with God. Satan cannot make a Christian sin. He may bend all his malice and intelligence upon us, striking sparks around the gunpowder of our hearts, but while faith keeps the powder dampened, there will be no explosions. If we resist, he will be overcome. Will he return? Yes, until the end comes he will be back again and again, but if he is repeatedly resisted, he will repeatedly flee.

You may read this and be tempted to say, "That does not work!" Does it not? Is God a liar? I wonder if the reason why we find it so easy to doubt this is that we so rarely do it. We dress up our feeble efforts in the clothes of resistance, playacting about keeping Satan at the door but capitulating all too quickly because we actually want to traffic in the guilty pleasures that Satan has on offer. But faith draws near to God and so finds God drawing near to the believer, supplying grace and strength for the fight that the believer simply

---

3. Henry, *Commentary*, 6:797.

does not possess in himself. Faith judges these things rightly and wants no part of sin, but rather looks to and comes to God in Christ, and so resists.

The Armor of God

> For we do not wrestle against flesh and blood, but against prin-
> cipalities, against powers, against the rulers of the darkness of
> this age, against spiritual hosts of wickedness in the heavenly
> places. Therefore take up the whole armor of God, that you may
> be able to withstand in the evil day, and having done all, to
> stand. (Eph. 6:12–13)

This passage shows us not only the nature of the opposition but also the nature of our response. By definition, the Christian is one who wrestles, who fights the good fight: the aim is to get your opponent down and hold him there. We are fighting in a holy war in which we are called to set up and keep up our opposition to those who come against us. The apostle calls us to prepare to stand, to take a stand, and to make a stand. Again, we must not give way, must not back down. We are exhorted to equip ourselves in the light of this battle, taking up the whole armor of God.

We must take it to heart that the Lord does not send us out isolated and poorly equipped. Our modern age often glamorizes the notion of the solitary hero, and we can end up reading the Bible in individu-alistic terms. A recent and short-lived U.S. Army recruitment slogan invited recruits to become an "army of one." The problem with an army of one is that in real life it usually gets killed very quickly by an army of three or four, let alone several thousands. How do we picture ourselves? What Paul has in mind is not one little soldier with his armor marching alone into a pointless battle where he will be massacred, but the massed ranks of the church fully equipped for spiritual combat, striving together for the supremacy. This battle is not fought in isolation, and we must not transport our modern narcissism into the spiritual arena and try to go it alone. The Lord intended that this battle should be fought not only individually but also corporately. The church of Jesus Christ is the place in which and the people alongside whom this battle is fought—loving, protect-ing, helping, encouraging, exhorting, and admonishing one another.

We are not isolated, and we cannot afford to isolate ourselves in this combat. Every saint must grasp this, because one soldier falling out and turning tail leaves a gap where others are put at grave risk.

God prepares and bestows all that is needed for all His people, defensively and offensively. Too often we show no sign of the confidence of faith and holy aggression that ought to characterize the people of God. Sometimes we think and act as if we are a beaten people; we seem to have concluded that we have been, are being, or will be defeated. We approach the battle as if it is already lost, as if the field is taken, as if the enemy has won. But that is not so, and it is dishonoring to God to live as if it were. The whole point is that this battle is ongoing. You and I are called to fight and to win. The high days of the church are not entirely behind us. The times of blessing are not fixed forever in the haloed past. The battle is *now*, and God has promised to equip us to do His bidding in this present evil age.

With His provision, the regiments of God must tool up and turn out in an atmosphere of general hostility in which there will be specific occasions on which the raging and scheming of the wicked one break out, that "evil day" when "the wiles of the devil" (Eph. 6:13, 11, respectively) seem to be or are particularly fierce and cruel, the day when he sends the worst that he has against the saints. Even then, in the heat of the fiercest battles, we may stand. The whole church of Christ is provided with heavenly equipment by divine power for specific purposes on definite occasions.

Spiritual Weaponry

> For the weapons of our warfare are not carnal but mighty in God for pulling down strongholds, casting down arguments and every high thing that exalts itself against the knowledge of God, bringing every thought into captivity to the obedience of Christ, and being ready to punish all disobedience when your obedience is fulfilled. (2 Cor. 10:4–6)

Here Paul reminds us that both the means and the ends of our warfare are spiritual. Christ's kingdom is not of this world (John 18:36), so His people do not conquer by the means upon which men rely to extend their empires. We are equipped with God's weaponry for God's warfare, employing spiritual artillery for spiritual purposes in spiritual battles against spiritual enemies hiding in spiritual strong-holds. Our weapons are not carnal—they do not belong to this world and are not forged in its workshops. They are of God's design and construction, crafted of heavenly material. For this reason they have power, being "mighty in God," sufficient for everything for which they were intended. Paul tells us that purpose: these heavenly weap-ons are for the destruction and dereliction of "strongholds," those fortresses of proud human reason built on the lofty peaks of human self-sufficiency in which men take refuge, defending and protecting themselves in their sinful courses. They have potent effects, casting down the ignorance, prejudice, and entrenched desires of human wisdom, for this battle takes place in the realm of the intellect and the will, and these weapons are directed against the arrogant spirit of fallen men in rebellion against God, defiantly erecting their own thrones and seating themselves at the center of all things. In the face of all that can be known about the Lord from His world, men have rebelled against Him. The apostle Paul explains:

> Professing to be wise, they became fools, and changed the glory of the incorruptible God into an image made like corruptible man—and birds and four-footed animals and creeping things. Therefore God also gave them up to uncleanness, in the lusts of their hearts, to dishonor their bodies among themselves, who exchanged the truth of God for the lie, and worshiped and served the creature rather than the Creator, who is blessed for-ever. Amen. (Rom. 1:22–25)

Furthermore, by these weapons thoughts are captured—rebellion is quelled, truth prevails, and the Lord is acknowledged as sovereign and received with humility as men yield to the divine authority of the truth as it is in Jesus, becoming submissive to God's voice ringing out in the Scriptures.

So vital is this conviction and action that Paul—while confident that there are true believers among the Corinthians whose obedience will be plain—warns unequivocally that he is ready to bring a spiri-tual and ecclesiastical court-martial against anyone who abandons the God-ordained weapons of spiritual warfare and replaces them with the cheap and malfunctioning popguns of carnal wisdom. Such men and women have no place in the church of Jesus Christ because it does not and must not fight God's battles with worldly weapons.

Heeding God's Word

> How can a young man cleanse his way?
> By taking heed according to Your word.
> With my whole heart I have sought You;
> Oh, let me not wander from Your commandments!
> Your word I have hidden in my heart,
> That I might not sin against You. (Ps. 119:9–11)

What is the point of all this preparing and striving? It is godliness! Here in Psalm 119 is a young man eager to serve the Lord, but perhaps immature. He may be willful; he certainly needs wisdom. How will he reform and govern his life? William Plumer writes, "Taking heed to God's word is the means of leading a holy life."[4] Here is diligent obedience to divine truth, sincere prayers from an honest heart in pursuit of divine knowledge. This is a spirit willing not merely to read and hear the word and have it wash over and around him, but seeking to receive it in love, assimilate it in faith, meditate on it in humility, and store it in the soul with the intention of purity, stocking the armory of the heart with all that is needful to be kept from sin and to pursue holiness. With the heart so equipped, we are ready faithfully to bring forth our revelatory reserves in time of battle and, like our Savior, contend with the devil by those means which defeat him utterly: "It is written…" (see Matt. 4:1–11). Plumer explains, "He who accepts, believes, ponders and practises God's word hides it in his heart. Thus received, it warns, reproves and deters from all sin."[5]

Fight the Battles: Summary Thoughts

The Christian is not a neutral observer or a civilian bystander. The Christian is not a helpless victim, but an enlisted soldier in the armies of the Lamb of God. The Christian is a pilgrim warrior, at war and called to engage in battle, individually and corporately, within and without, contending in the spiritual realm for the glory

---

4. Plumer, *Psalms*, 1026.
5. Plumer, *Psalms*, 1026.

of God and the good of his brothers. Matthew Henry comments, "We have enemies to fight against, a captain to fight for, a banner to fight under, and certain rules of war by which we are to govern ourselves."[6] As such, we are constantly exhorted to take up arms, to stand, to fight, to resist evil, to pursue holiness, to engage in Christ's war at Christ's command by Christ's means for Christ's ends.

Our weapons from heaven are effective. We do this not as some kind of parodic cyber warrior, living on the cutting edge and adopting every latest gadget and gizmo in an attempt to keep up with the rest of the world. Neither do we do it as some kind of religious battle reenactment society, steadfastly and determinedly marching into the fight with the weapons and uniforms of a bygone age, as if antiquity were its own sufficient defense. Our weapons are neither ancient nor modern, but timeless. Our warfare is not bound by the stuff of this life and is not conducted by the world's rules, but we take up the weapons appointed by God for employment by His battalions to accomplish the purposes for which they have been given in the sphere in which they are intended to operate.

We fight, then, with weapons of truth by the strength of faith, aiming to please our Lord and Captain as we make our way through the world. Christian life in the wilderness is not a bed of roses, but a path of thorns. It is a running battle until the running is done and the battle is won, and it is necessary for us to identify the battle lines drawn in the place and the time where God has put us and to hold fast against the foe. In short, we are called to live as enlisted soldiers on a war footing.

Fight the Battles: Specific Counsels

In order to fight these battles, we must *remember the enemy*. We have briefly studied his character and operations, and we cannot afford to forget those against whom we fight. We must always consider the spiritual dimension, concrete manifestation, and personal aggression of the battle. We must take into account the fact that we have an enemy, the devil, with those "spiritual hosts of wickedness in the heavenly places" (Eph. 6:12) and countless willing slaves doing his cruel bidding in the world. We must not forget, neglect, or deny

---

6. Henry, *Commentary*, 6:579.

these realities. We should neither overestimate nor underestimate his strength and his malice, but rather take account of a real foe with whom we are locked in a real fight.

A further counsel is to *grasp the calling*. If you do not know who you are or are not willing to embrace this aspect of your identity and activity, you expose yourself and others to fearful danger. Neutrals expect and hope to avoid the horrors of war; they think to stand aside while the bloodletting rolls past. Civilians tend to be obliterated, their deaths dismissed under the chilling phrase "collateral damage." It is soldiers who stand and fight. If you name the name of Christ, this battle will not pass you by, and if you try to avoid it you will be taken down by shot and shell, overwhelmed by the tide of battle.

We are commanded to flee from sin, to avoid it at all costs (1 Cor. 6:18; 10:14; 1 Tim. 6:11; 2 Tim. 2:22), but we are commanded to resist the devil who tempts us to sin, and not to run from him. As various authors have pointed out over the centuries, the Christian's armor all presumes that he is facing rather than fleeing his foe.

We are called to exalt the Lord, fight the devil, oppose the rebels, and rescue the captives. If you have been converted, then you have been enlisted as a warrior in the spiritual realm, posted to a company of blood-bought brothers. That is part of a Christian's calling and character, and our attitudes and actions ought to reflect this reality.

Again, we must *follow the Captain*. Our great goal should be to please Him who has freed us, called us, enlisted and equipped us, in whose livery we fight and for whose cause we contend. Having been delivered through His faithfulness to God, we are to submit to God as He did and in His strength, resisting the devil, obeying the truth, defying the enemy, and pursuing righteousness. Our Christ is a warrior, and it is not very becoming when His people give the impression that they are cowards following a weakling rather than holy fighters in the train of their victorious King.

When did Christ back down? When did Christ fail to hold the line? When did Christ turn tail and run? His life was a constant resisting of the devil, a constant testimony of submission to God, a constant choosing of God's will over every enticement set before Him to depart from the path of righteousness. We will not face greater foes than Christ has already faced and conquered on our behalf, nor will we ever find ourselves alone in the fight, for He Himself has said, "I will never leave you nor forsake you" (Heb. 13:5). Following, obeying, and depending on Him bring us into the best and the safest of places, even if it carries us into the midst of the fiercest battles, for there we find Christ closest to us. The best place to be is standing where Christ has told us to stand and fighting where Christ has told us to fight. The sweetest place to be will be with Him, near Him, striving in His strength, as hymn writer Isaac Watts points out: "I shall be safe, for Christ displays / Superior power, and guardian grace."[7]

In addition, we must correctly *choose the weapons*. How tempting it is to meet the challenges of the world with the weapons of the world, to meet the seeming triumphs of carnal policy with carnal repulses and counterattacks. Have you felt the pressure to stand toe to toe with the world on the world's terms and with the world's tools? It is a recipe for disaster! Too readily the church operates within the paradigms established by the enemy, relying on human wisdom, performance, eloquence, organization, entertainment, and institutions. If we can only be bigger, stronger, richer, grander, flashier, prettier, and cleverer than they are, all will be well! Such a strategy has been disproved time and time again through the history of God's people, but it seems a sad truth that every generation must prove or see proved the emptiness of this approach. What a tragedy when the church thinks and acts in this way! If the church secularizes (even with the perfume of religiosity to adorn it) in order to meet secular challenges, if she becomes like the world to compete or contend with the world, then she has already lost the battle. By fighting in this fashion, she has surrendered the very means by which God intended for her to claim the victory.

The saints, individually and together, must deliberately and self-consciously turn their backs upon those things upon which the world relies and by which the devil does his work and take to hand those things which God has designed, provided, and appointed. Philip E. Hughes describes the Christian's arsenal:

> They are the weapons, scorned by the world and yet most feared
> by the powers of darkness, of truth, righteousness, evangelism,

---

7. Isaac Watts, "Join All the Glorious Names."

faith, salvation, the Word of God, and prayer, enumerated by Paul in Eph. 6:14ff. They are the very weapons which he wielded in the unremitting warfare that he was called upon to wage as Christ's apostle, which enabled him at last to testify that he had fought the good fight, and which won for him the victor's crown of righteousness (II Tim. 4:7ff.).[8]

We must not let the world set our agenda and appoint our equipment. We hear its sneers, we look at the weapons with which God provides us, and we are tempted to turn up our noses. They seem such weak things, as if I were to send my sons into combat with the foam and plastic blades to which they, as mere boys, are so ardently attached. But, again, faith sees things as they are and not as the eye of flesh imagines them to be. What the blinded and befuddled world accounts a pathetic toy is by God's intention and hell's estimation a fearsome weapon, a true Jerusalem blade in the spiritual realm. Wielded with faith, we will discover that God's weapons are never out of date, never malfunctioning, and never superseded, but effective in all the ways and means in and for which God has appointed them.

However, we must not forget to *establish the defenses*. Faith is at the heart of the battle, offensively and defensively. It is how we resist the devil in his assaults against us; it is the strength in which we contend for the cause of Christ, as Robert Hawker explains:

> When a poor buffeted child of God, against all Satan's accusations, and all the alarms of conscience, which the enemy takes care to bring before him, pleads guilty to all, but takes confidence, at the same time, in the Person, blood and righteousness of Jesus Christ; the devil can fight no longer. And this is what the Apostle meant when he said: *Resist the devil, and he will flee from you. Draw nigh to God, and he will draw nigh to you.* James iv. 7, 8. But how shall a self-condemned sinner resist the devil but in Christ's strength; or draw nigh to God, but in Christ's Person, blood and righteousness? Christ is the alone *way, and truth, and life; for none can come to the Father, but by him.* John xiv. 6.[9]

---

8. Philip E. Hughes, *Paul's Second Epistle to the Corinthians* (London: Marshall, Morgan & Scott, 1962), 351.

9. Hawker, *Poor Man's New Testament Commentary*, 2:682.

Faith is the starting point for all liberties and triumphs in the heavenlies, the abiding foundation of all our spiritual progress: "For whatever is born of God overcomes the world. And this is the victory that has overcome the world—our faith" (1 John 5:4). If we wish to win these battles, we must begin at the cross of Christ. This must be where we send those who are slaves to sin and who have no strength to stand. Every other remedy is hopeless. Looking to Christ, we are transferred from the reign of darkness and brought into the kingdom of light, uniformed and equipped for the new life in Him, operating on a new basis, with new appetites and expectations, pursuing a new and glorious destiny. This faith goes on looking to Christ. We stand insofar as we stand in Christ; we stand insofar as we are steadfast in the faith. If we wish to resist the devil and win these battles, we must get to Christ, hold to Christ, and stand in and with Christ Jesus, for we will otherwise fall.

Faith lays hold of things that are unseen, relies on what is unshakably real, assumes what is divinely true, and expects that all the promises of God will prove in Christ to be Yes and Amen, "to the glory of God through us" (2 Cor. 1:20). Faith takes up the heavenly weapons that the world despises and fights in the way that God commands us to fight. Faith obeys God and therefore triumphs in Christ Jesus. It stands by believing every word that proceeds from the mouth of God and rests on the whole counsel of God. It hides God's Word in the innermost depths of the believer's being and seeks to have its heat and light radiate through the whole of redeemed humanity. Faith proves divine truth to be a sure defense against wickedness, finding—as has always been so—that the revelation of God is a lamp to the feet and a light to the path of every saint who swears and confirms that he will keep God's righteous judgments (Ps. 119:105–6).

We must pray for an increase of faith, seek to cultivate our faith by dwelling upon and meditating upon and resting upon and praying over the Word of the living God, desiring the Spirit's gracious illumination of every phrase. We must know our God, and only then shall we do exploits (Dan. 11:32). When Moses was sent back to Egypt by God, he reeled off a number of excuses, and God's answer was, in part, to make Himself known as the great I AM. This is not about you or me! This is not about what we can do or what glory we can obtain, and we must slay once and for all the twisted pride that attempts nothing for the honor of God because of our own feeble strength. We know that our great God has called us and has determined to accomplish His great purposes by employing frail creatures, and so to magnify His great name.

Faith considers divine reality and eternity and determines before the battle begins that Christ must be obeyed and Satan defied. A friend of mine who has seen the horrors of physical combat affirms that a crisis does not form a man's character, but simply reveals it. In the same way, spiritual battles do not form us, but expose us, for better or worse. This is not the time to work out or to decide whose side we are on, to discover that our armor is loosely strapped about us, or that we have taken the wrong weapons for our warfare. Faith prepares to engage, and faith engages when the battle begins.

And therefore we must actually *fight the battles*. This may seem a little on the obvious side, a mere truism, but the reason why so many Christians are so swiftly defeated is that they fail to do just this. We may know all the theory, but when Satan comes roaring in, we fail faithfully to put these truths into practice. By God's grace we can conquer in Christ if we take a stand.

It may be that you will face a battle before you have finished reading this paragraph, page, or chapter. I would be greatly surprised if you do not do so before you have finished the book. It may happen when you are driving to work or back home, when you are sitting in church or in front of a computer, playing sport or checking your phone messages, lying in bed or taking a walk, reading your Bible or watching television, chatting with your wife or husband or talking with a colleague or neighbor, witnessing to a stranger or relaxing with a friend. The one thing you can be sure of is that it will happen. We cannot avoid this: "In the world you will have tribulation" (John 16:33). Our victory does not consist in avoiding these tribulations:

> The true victory is not found in escaping or evading trials, but in rightly meeting and enduring them. The questions should not be, "How can I get out of these worries? How can I get into a place where there shall be no irritations, nothing to try my temper or put my patience to the test? How can I avoid the distractions that continually harass me?" There is nothing noble in

such living. The soldier who flies to the rear when he smells the battle is no hero; he is a coward.

The questions should rather be, "How can I pass through these trying experiences and not fail as a Christian? How can I endure these struggles and not suffer defeat? How can I live amid these provocations, these reproaches and testings of my temper, and yet live sweetly, not speaking unadvisedly, bearing injuries meekly, returning gentle answers to insulting words?" This is the true problem of Christian living.[10]

So when the predator attacks, will you prove to be food or a fighter? Will you cower or will you conquer? As temptations rush in, when the fiery darts of the wicked one rain down upon you, will you then take a stand, deploy your defenses, take up your weapons, and resist? Will you hold fast against sinful fears and appetites? Will you battle Satan as he assaults you with temptations to unbelief, selfishness, greed, covetousness, anger, cruelty, laziness, and lust? When called upon to stand up for the honor of God and His Christ, will you do so with fortitude, relying on the weapons that God has appointed and determined in faith to hold fast and by grace to press on, though "storm'd at with shot and shell"?

We must be so careful here. There are parts of the modern church that seem to revel in a sort of martial machismo when it comes to life in the world. We hear all manner of religious militaristic bombast, in which all or some Christians are commandos, special forces operatives, and so on. And while all the chest-beating and roaring is going on, there are battles being lost by these very men and churches that have, in some instances, failed to discern the battle lines and recognize the enemy. All the military jargon and paraphernalia is so much empty bravado if we do not fight for a holy God against the devil and his temptations, standing apart from the world. It simply does not sound very special when it comes from men weighed down with the gaudy stuff of this life, like a soldier going into the field towing a wagon full of the comforts of home or fighting with the flimsy, insubstantial, childish, and ineffective weapons of the world.

---

10. J. R. Miller, *Week-day Religion* (Philadelphia: Presbyterian Board of Publication and Sabbath-School Work, 1880), http://gracegems.org/Miller/weekday _religion.htm.

Here, too, it is worth remembering that it has often proved among soldiers in training that those who are noisiest and most boastful—full of proud claims about what they will do once they get on the battlefield—are often found cowering once the bullets start to fly while the quiet men with little to say for themselves get on with the job efficiently and effectively. We hear too many grand prayers not backed up by the pursuit of godliness and contention for the truth. Here we might say, after a fashion, "Let not the one who puts on his armor boast like the one who takes it off" (1 Kings 20:11). Fewer armchair soldiers and bombastic chest-beaters and a few more understated but valiant foot soldiers would do the army of God a great deal of good.

Finally, let us fix our eyes on and *pursue the reward*. The battles will soon end, peace will follow, commendations will be given, and prizes bestowed. The fight will be hard and seem long, but it will be over soon. The peace and blessings that follow will put all the pains and struggles of the warfare into the shade, "for I consider that the sufferings of this present time are not worthy to be compared with the glory which shall be revealed in us" (Rom. 8:18).

Will you be able to say with Paul, "I have fought the good fight, I have finished the race, I have kept the faith" (2 Tim. 4:7)? If so, then you can also look forward with Paul to that crown of righteousness that the Lord, the righteous Judge, will give not only to Paul on the day of His glorious return but also to all who have loved Christ's appearing (2 Tim. 4:8). That is the day on which staunch pilgrim-warriors will hear their Lord and Master speak in tones of sincere love and rich approval, "Well done, good and faithful servant; you were faithful over a few things, I will make you ruler over many things. Enter into the joy of your lord" (Matt. 25:21).

James assures us, "Blessed is the man who endures temptation; for when he has been approved, he will receive the crown of life which the Lord has promised to those who love Him" (1:12). The truly and lastingly happy man is the one who is matured through the testing of these battles against sin and who comes finally to receive that crown of life promised to those who fight for the Lord they love.

John, too, holds out rich and precious promises in his own distinctive, Christ-modeled language:

He who has an ear, let him hear what the Spirit says to the churches. To him who overcomes I will give to eat from the tree of life, which is in the midst of the Paradise of God. (Rev. 2:7)

Do not fear any of those things which you are about to suffer. Indeed, the devil is about to throw some of you into prison, that you may be tested, and you will have tribulation ten days. Be faithful until death, and I will give you the crown of life. He who has an ear, let him hear what the Spirit says to the churches. He who overcomes shall not be hurt by the second death. (Rev. 2:10–11)

He who overcomes shall inherit all things, and I will be his God and he shall be My son. (Rev. 21:7)

What more glorious prospect can there be for the Christian soldier? A day is coming when the sword will be beaten into the ploughshare, when the saint will at last take off his armor and lay aside his weaponry. Then he will enter into a life of eternal peace and enduring rest, in the company of Christ and of the redeemed hosts who overcame their adversary by the blood of the Lamb and by the word of their testimony, and who did not love their lives to the death (Rev. 12:11). This calling and character echo through George Duffield's well-known verses:

Stand up, stand up for Jesus, ye soldiers of the cross;
Lift high His royal banner, it must not suffer loss.
From victory unto victory His army shall He lead,
Till every foe is vanquished, and Christ is Lord indeed.

Stand up, stand up for Jesus, the trumpet call obey;
Forth to the mighty conflict, in this His glorious day.
Ye that are brave now serve Him against unnumbered foes;
Let courage rise with danger, and strength to strength oppose.

Stand up, stand up for Jesus, stand in His strength alone;
The arm of flesh will fail you, ye dare not trust your own.
Put on the Gospel armor, each piece put on with prayer;
Where duty calls or danger, be never wanting there.

Stand up, stand up for Jesus, the strife will not be long;
This day the noise of battle, the next the victor's song.

To him that overcometh a crown of life shall be;
They with the King of Glory shall reign eternally.

Faith fixes its eye on the crown beyond the cross. We must live and labor and fight and strive with this destiny in view. Faith fights every step of the way until the battle is over and the victory is gained. If we will fight this good fight, before long we shall receive the conqueror's crown to cast at the feet of our Captain.

6

PURSUE THE MISSION

We take for granted that the spread of the gospel is the great object of your desire. Without this it will be hard to prove that you are Christian churches. An agreement in a few favourite opinions, or on one side of a disputed subject, or even a disagreement with others, will often induce men to form themselves into religious societies, and to expend much zeal and much property in accomplishing their objects. But this is not Christianity. We may be of what is called a sect, but we must not be of a sectarian spirit, seeking only the promotion of a party. The true churches of Jesus Christ travail in birth for the salvation of men. They are the armies of the Lamb, the grand object of whose existence is to extend the Redeemer's kingdom.[1]

This was the ardent contention of the Particular Baptist pastor and theologian Andrew Fuller, writing a letter in 1810 to various churches that pressed home the promise of God's Spirit as our grand encouragement in the promotion of the gospel. Fuller was profoundly concerned that the churches with which he was involved should recognize "that the time for the promulgation of the Gospel is come."[2] Have you and I, and the churches to which we belong, been gripped by that recognition and its implications?

Are you impressed by Fuller's declaration? Are you constrained by it? Are you ready to dismiss it, perhaps as an exaggeration? Are you even scared by it? Here we are, pilgrims passing through a hostile environment, facing numerous foes, and having to fight various

---

1. Andrew Fuller, *The Armies of the Lamb: The Spirituality of Andrew Fuller,* ed. Michael Haykin (Dundas, Ont.: Joshua Press, 2001), 223–24.

2. Fuller, *Armies of the Lamb,* 233.

battles. You might have thought we had enough on our plate just taking the next step—but apparently not! The central element of our combat, the great duty that we are called to embrace as we go, is the making of disciples. We must call others—in accordance with our Captain's Great Commission—through the narrow gate on to the narrow way that leads to life (Matt. 7:14) to walk that way with us, denying ourselves, taking up our cross, and following the Lord Jesus.

Pursue the Mission: Scriptural Framework

Here we face a true embarrassment of riches. We could trawl through the New Testament almost at will and pluck many choice gems of truth from the pages of the Old Testament to enforce and illustrate this element of the pilgrim life. We are obliged to restrict ourselves to a few that I trust—in the context of the study as a whole—will bring to our attention and highlight some appropriate particulars.

The Commission

> And Jesus came and spoke to them, saying, "All authority has been given to Me in heaven and on earth. Go therefore and make disciples of all the nations, baptizing them in the name of the Father and of the Son and of the Holy Spirit, teaching them to observe all things that I have commanded you; and lo, I am with you always, even to the end of the age." Amen. (Matt. 28:18–20)

We find something similar at the end of Mark's gospel, and the same command in essence at the beginning of the Acts of the Apostles: "But you shall receive power when the Holy Spirit has come upon you; and you shall be witnesses to Me in Jerusalem, and in all Judea and Samaria, and to the end of the earth" (Acts 1:8).

Christ's words at the end of Matthew bring us face-to-face with the implications of His atoning death and triumphant resurrection. We are dealing with Christ as the risen Redeemer in His glorified majesty, looking at all the things that Jesus continued to do and teach (see Acts 1:1) after His resurrection. Indeed, there are some readings of Matthew's gospel which suggest that—in terms of its overarching structure—we are provided with a deliberately open-ended and somewhat inconclusive conclusion. Here at the end of the history is a narrative passage shorn of its subsequent activity, as if Matthew is deliberately leaving a tantalizing open space for the movement that must inevitably follow upon such a command as the one Christ gives here.

We are confronted with *Christ's authority*: "All authority has been given to Me in heaven and on earth." It is entire and universal. Although we might contend that it is His by right as the eternal Son of God, here He declares it His by grant, the rightful possession of the risen Messiah, the incarnate Son triumphant now over sin and death and hell and God's appointed Mediator between God and man. He stands before His church with the right to save, to sanctify, to strengthen, and to send in order that His Father may be glorified: "Glorify Your Son, that Your Son also may glorify You, as You have given Him authority over all flesh, that He should give eternal life to as many as You have given Him" (John 17:1–2). We are in the presence of the Lord of hosts, the supreme King over all creation.

But we should also note *Christ's assumption*, which comes to us forcefully, with some of the pressure of a command: "Go therefore." We might translate this, "going," or "as you go." Christ assumes that we will be making our way through this world as His followers, and as we do so, we are to have our wits about us and our eyes wide open and our hearts and hands primed for the carrying out of the duty committed to us by our heavenly King. There is something for us to do as we are going. Because all authority has been given to the King, the citizens of His kingdom have work to do as we make our way in the world.

And that brings us to *Christ's command*: "Make disciples of all the nations, baptizing them in the name of the Father and of the Son and of the Holy Spirit, teaching them to observe all things that I have commanded you." At the core of the mission is the call to "make disciples," with its inevitable corollaries of baptism and instruction. This mission takes the church to "all the nations." Under Christ's authority we can go to any place to carry out our appointed task. As Matthew Henry says,

> Christ the Mediator is setting up a kingdom in the world, bring the nations to be his subjects; setting up a school, bring the nations to be his scholars; raising an army for the carrying on of the war against the powers of darkness, enlist the nations of the earth under his banner. The work which the apostles had to

do, was, to set up the Christian religion in all places, and it was honourable work; the achievements of the mighty heroes of the world were nothing to it. They conquered the nations for themselves, and made them miserable; the apostles conquered them for Christ, and made them happy.[3]

Such a commission with such a joyful prospect should put a smile on a servant's face. The disciples are to call men out of the world to become followers of Christ, bring them into the church by baptism in the triune name as a sign of their whole-souled identification with Christ and with His people, and then train them up so that they might increasingly demonstrate a full-orbed obedience to the commands of the Lord Jesus to His church, individually and corporately.

We should recognize here that conversion is the starting point for the commission, not the finishing line. The church should expect to have among it spiritual infants, those who are recently made disciples. At the same time, it should not be a body composed solely of spiritual infants. Its task, under God, is to train men and women to spiritual maturity within the congregation of the righteous, instructing and equipping them through the Word of God and under the influence of the Spirit of God to "walk worthy of God who calls you into His own kingdom and glory" (1 Thess. 2:12). In the language of the apostle Paul concerning his ministry of Christ, "Him we preach, warning every man and teaching every man in all wisdom, that we may present every man perfect in Christ Jesus" (Col. 1:28). The task to which we are called is grand and demanding. Although all depends on the power of the Spirit, from the human perspective I should imagine that many undershepherds consider the training element more wearying, demanding, and sometimes maddening and saddening than the making disciples of men in the first place. In this regard it would be well for all believers to remember that if they are true disciples, then they ought to be baptized and identify themselves openly with Christ and with His people. This assumes a full participation in the life of a local church and the awareness that they have been put there not to coast along to glory but in order that they might "grow in the grace and knowledge of our Lord and Savior Jesus Christ" (2 Peter 3:18). It is in this environment that they come

---

3. Henry, *Commentary*, 5:362.

under the influence and discipline of the church and her appointed leaders in order that sin might be increasingly rooted out and holiness increasingly planted and cultivated. So we learn to serve Christ as part of His church in our own turn: He has given gifts to the church "for the equipping of the saints for the work of ministry, for the edifying of the body of Christ, till we all come to the unity of the faith and of the knowledge of the Son of God, to a perfect man, to the measure of the stature of the fullness of Christ." The purpose of this ministry is our maturity as godly believers:

> that we should no longer be children, tossed to and fro and carried about with every wind of doctrine, by the trickery of men, in the cunning craftiness of deceitful plotting, but, speaking the truth in love, may grow up in all things into Him who is the head—Christ—from whom the whole body, joined and knit together by what every joint supplies, according to the effective working by which every part does its share, causes growth of the body for the edifying of itself in love. (Eph. 4:11–16)

We ought also to note that the commission our Lord gives us embraces and anticipates the planting of churches, where those who are called together to Christ out of the world are gathered into communities of true faith for the working out of their life in Him together.

In the pursuit of this task, we go under cover of *Christ's promise*: "Lo, I am with you always, even to the end of the age." Christ seems to draw particular attention to this element of the commission: "Look! Behold this!" It is a little like His assertions during His humiliation that He must suffer many things and be killed and rise again on the third day. The disciples seem most likely to overlook that last element, so the Lord points to it very plainly, that we should not overlook it or forget it. He tells us that in all times and places until the end comes, He Himself, as the sovereign King of the universe, will be present with His saints as we carry out His commands. He will equip, enable, protect, preserve, and bless us in our obedience to all His commands, and in particular obedience to this command. J. C. Ryle comments on this passage:

> It is impossible to conceive words more comforting, strengthening, cheering, and sanctifying than these. Though left alone, like orphan children in a cold, unkind world, the disciples were

not to think they were deserted. Their Master would be ever "with them." Though commissioned to do a work as hard as that of Moses when sent to Pharaoh, they were not to be discouraged: their Master would certainly be "with them." No words could be more suited to the position of those to whom they were first spoken. No words could be imagined more consolatory to believers in every age of the world.[4]

The whole of this commission, then, resonates with absolute completeness and complete absoluteness: Christ has *all* authority to send us to *all* the nations to teach *all* His commands as He goes with us *all* the days. And this continues to be the mission of the church of Jesus Christ. Ryle pulls no punches when he presses this home: "Let us never forget that this solemn injunction is still in full force. It is still the bounden duty of every disciple of Christ to do all he can in person, and by prayer, to make others acquainted with Jesus. Where is our faith, if we neglect this duty? Where is our charity? It may well be questioned whether a man knows the value of the gospel himself, if he does not desire to make it known to all the world."[5]

In similar fashion, the great pastor-evangelist of the Victorian Baptists, Charles Spurgeon, closes his devotional commentary on Matthew, aptly originally entitled *The Gospel of the Kingdom*, with this stirring charge:

> This is our commission as well as theirs. From it we learn that our first business is to make disciples of all nations, and we can only do that by teaching them the truth as it is revealed in the Scriptures, and seeking the power of the Holy Spirit to make our teaching effective in those we try to instruct in divine things. Next, those who by faith in Christ become his disciples are to be baptized into the name of the triune Jehovah; and after baptism they are still to be taught all that Christ commanded. We are not to invent anything new; nor to change anything to suit the current of the age; but to teach the baptized believers to observe "all things whatsoever" our Divine King has commanded.
>
> This is the perpetual commission of the Church of Christ; and the great seal of the Kingdom attached to it, giving the

---

4. J. C. Ryle, *Expository Thoughts on Matthew* (Edinburgh: Banner of Truth, 2012), 330.

5. Ryle, *Matthew*, 328.

power to execute it, and guaranteeing its success, is the King's assurance of his continual presence with his faithful followers: *"Lo, I am with you alway, even unto the end of the world. Amen."* May all of us realize his presence with us until he calls us to be with him, "for ever with the Lord"! Amen.[6]

Serpents and Doves

"Behold, I send you out as sheep in the midst of wolves. Therefore be wise as serpents and harmless as doves." (Matt. 10:16)

We find a similar statement in Luke 10:3: "Go your way; behold, I send you out as lambs among wolves." Again, while recognizing that this command was given to the Twelve at a particular point in redemptive history, its principles and its lessons are abiding. Here is our *obligation*. Christ is sending us out. He defines the task. For the apostles, the specifics of their work are immediately given with appropriate warnings and counsels about the challenges they must face, the difficulties they must overcome, the responsibilities they must sustain. Surely the essence of these things resonates down to us! Given what follows, one would contend that the mission would be utter madness—and, indeed, is often considered such by the world— if it were not for the fact that Christ Himself sends us to carry it out. However, it is precisely this fact that gives us the assurance that we need as we go forth in His name.

Christ further identifies our *nature*: He sends us out as sheep. Luke reports it as "lambs," which rather seems to rub it in a little, for the immediate sense we have is of our innate helplessness and defenselessness. Sheep are not renowned for their personal qualities in defense or attack, but rather for their susceptibility to danger. No one ever envisions Flossie the Wonder Sheep, hurtling vigorously across the sward fully equipped for countless deeds of derring-do. That is simply not our image of a sheep, still less of a lamb. And yet if we stop there, we have missed part of the point, for it is not only our character in ourselves that we must see but also that this identity is found in reference to the Shepherd. Where we are weak, He is strong. Where we are foolish, He is wise. It is He who speaks: our character is formed in

---

6. C. H. Spurgeon, *Commentary on Matthew: The Gospel of the Kingdom* (Edinburgh: Banner of Truth, 2010), 442.

relation to His, and we receive His leadership as those in need of His wise and loving care. He does not act rashly or negligently. If we are sheep, if we are lambs, then this command presupposes and implies the consequent care that the Shepherd will extend.

And we need such assurance because Christ speaks of our *enemies*: We are sheep "in the midst of wolves," surrounded by destroyers and devourers who take after the character and intent of their father the devil. Again, this is a dangerous but not an unforeseen environment; these are cruel but not surprising foes.

Furthermore, our Lord directs us as to our necessary *character* in surviving and thriving in such an environment. We are to be "wise as serpents" and "harmless as doves." Wisdom is required for legitimate self-preservation, for "we do not overestimate the kindness of wolves."[7] We must show a measure of holy guile and craft, manifesting prudence and discretion in pursuit of a proper and reasonable defense of our lives. The call to deny yourself, take up your cross, and follow Christ (Matt. 16:24) is not a call to a suicidal mind-set. We do not need to thrust ourselves into the greatest possible danger, either as an act of spiritual bravado or out of the mistaken notion that there is some necessary virtue in our suffering. We must be ready to die, but we do not need actively to seek death.

The famed historian of the early church, Eusebius, tells the story of the misguided zeal of the church father Origen. During his younger years, persecution was sweeping through the church, and his father was seized and imprisoned. The teenaged Origen wrote his father a letter of exhortation urging him to hold fast in the face of death. Possessed with what seems to have been an unhealthy sense that martyrdom was inherently virtuous, when his father was then executed, Origen was apparently determined to go out and join him. His mother, grieved at the prospect of losing husband and son simultaneously, found the only way she could of preventing her son's effective self-destruction. She hid his clothes in the confident expectation that Origen would be too embarrassed to pursue his martyrdom naked. There is nothing in the Scriptures that speaks of martyrdom as something actively to be desired and pursued, nothing that endorses the

---

7. Daniel M. Doriani, *Matthew* (Phillipsburg, N.J.: P&R, 2008), 1:428.

kind of spiritual sadomasochism that would drive one to an unnecessary death. This is not the wisdom of the serpent.

But at the same time we are to display the harmlessness of the dove. Just as the serpent is renowned for its self-preserving instinct, so the dove is celebrated for its peaceful nature. Apparently the dove is the last bird to flee when danger approaches; in the same way, though there is a legitimate wisdom to be employed in preserving the life of the saints, there ought to be a holy and gentle fearlessness that should characterize believers. We are not to be quickly alarmed, fleeing whenever there is a hint of danger, panicky and frantic under pressure, plotting to preserve and quick to defend ourselves. Spurgeon remarks, "The Christian missionary will need to be wary, to avoid receiving harm; but he must be of a guileless mind, that he do no harm. We are called to be martyrs, not maniacs; we are to be simple-hearted, but we are not to be simpletons."[8]

There is a fine line to tread between cowardice and compromise on the one hand and brashness and brutishness on the other. The Christian might wait confidently while danger approaches or simply walk away from it; he is not invariably required to rush into it or to race from it in fear or to wait in ambush for it. Ryle's religion is, as so often, eminently practical, as he observes that few of our Lord's instructions are as difficult as this one:

> There is a line marked out for us between two extremes, but a line that it requires great judgment to define. To avoid persecution, by holding our tongues and keeping our religion entirely to ourselves, is one extreme; we are not to err in that direction. To court persecution, and thrust our religion upon every one we meet, without regard to place, time, or circumstances, is another extreme: in this direction also we are warned not to err any more than in the other.[9]

And that, too, is where Spurgeon leaves us with this prayer: "Lord, in my work for thee, so teach me that I may display the wonderful blend of serpent and dove, which thou dost here commend to

---

8. Spurgeon, *Matthew*, 119.
9. Ryle, *Matthew*, 80–81.

thy ministers. Never allow me to become to others like a wolf, but
may I conquer by the meekness of a lamb!"[10]

God's Fellow Workers

> "And now the LORD says,
> Who formed Me from the womb to be His Servant,
> To bring Jacob back to Him,
> So that Israel is gathered to Him
> (For I shall be glorious in the eyes of the LORD,
>   And My God shall be My strength),
> Indeed He says,
> 'It is too small a thing that You should be My Servant
> To raise up the tribes of Jacob,
> And to restore the preserved ones of Israel;
> I will also give You as a light to the Gentiles,
> That You should be My salvation to the ends of the earth.'"
>   (Isa. 49:5–6)

In this passage we hear the voice of Messiah, the Servant of the Most
High, speaking with believing confidence of God's goodwill and
purpose for Him and of the Father's determination to accomplish
great things by His Christ, and calling and forming Him accordingly. The Servant is to be God's appointed and anointed means of
raising and restoring a remnant from Israel. He will bring from the
people those set apart to God. But this is not all. There is something
more, something greater and more glorious even than this. He will
be the only saving illumination of the pagan nations of the earth.
"I am the light of the world. He who follows Me shall not walk in
darkness, but have the light of life" (John 8:12). Here is the world
considered as lying in the darkness of sin and ignorance, and here
is the light flooding in as an end to darkness. Thus God's elect from
the nations will also be brought into the kingdom, to the divine joy:

> Thus says the LORD,
> The Redeemer of Israel, their Holy One,
> To Him whom man despises,
> To Him whom the nation abhors,
> To the Servant of rulers:

---

10. Spurgeon, *Matthew*, 119.

"Kings shall see and arise,
Princes also shall worship,
Because of the LORD who is faithful,
The Holy One of Israel;
And He has chosen You." (Isa. 49:7)

But, we might ask, what does this have to do with you and me? The answer to this question is found in the book of Acts, where Paul and Barnabas are in Pisidian Antioch, preaching in the synagogue. As the gospel is proclaimed and the word spreads, the Jews take it upon themselves to oppose the preachers, and Paul and Barnabas answer them boldly: "It was necessary that the word of God should be spoken to you first; but since you reject it, and judge yourselves unworthy of everlasting life, behold, we turn to the Gentiles. For so the Lord has commanded us: 'I have set you as a light to the Gentiles, that you should be for salvation to the ends of the earth'" (Acts 13:46–47). E. J. Young says, "These men of God have no hesitation in taking the words spoken by and about Messiah to themselves. Paul's use of this verse (Acts 13:47) supports the identification of the servant as the Messiah and His people. When His people labor in His Name as Paul and Barnabas were doing, He works through them."[11]

Messiah's people actively participate in Messiah's mission; we can unashamedly employ the same language of the church as Christ employed of Himself. To be sure, we are not the light in the same way that Christ is the light, but we bring *His* light to those who are in darkness. This was the reason why Paul and Barnabas pressed on from the Jews to the Gentiles. It still provides a measure of constraint, a sort of holy impetus, a divinely ordained momentum that impels the saints onward from those who reject to those who have not yet heard. In the parable of the great supper, the master sends out the servant, but he is rejected for all kinds of relatively petty reasons. He reports back to his master, who sends him out again:

"'Go out quickly into the streets and lanes of the city, and bring in here the poor and the maimed and the lame and the blind.' And the servant said, 'Master, it is done as you commanded, and still there is room.' Then the master said to the servant, 'Go

---

11. Edward J. Young, *The Book of Isaiah* (1972; repr., Grand Rapids: Eerdmans, 2000), 3:276.

out into the highways and hedges, and compel them to come in, that my house may be filled. For I say to you that none of those men who were invited shall taste my supper.'" (Luke 14:21–24)

The church continues to carry out Messiah's commission to the glory of His name and the joy of the Father, doing so under Christ's direction and protection as the members of the body of which He is the sovereign and saving Head. In this we are called to be God's fellow workers (1 Cor. 3:9). Let us make no mistake: Christ is not obliged to rely upon us. He chooses to employ us, and it is our privilege to participate. That ought to astound and delight us, that we should have the opportunity to stand alongside Christ in His determination to make the good news of His death and resurrection known to every corner of the globe.

Spreading the Light

> The people who walked in darkness
> Have seen a great light;
> Those who dwelt in the land of the shadow of death,
> Upon them a light has shined. (Isa. 9:2)

This centrality of and relationship to Christ is borne out in measure by this glorious promise in Isaiah 9, where the prophet—in the context of a gracious promise to Israel—draws attention to the work of Messiah in salvation. Isaiah emphasizes the *horror of darkness,* the profound spiritual gloom in which the unconverted dwell, the deathly shadow of the ignorance, idolatry, and insurrection of the soul. This is the condition of every human being who does not know Christ, exposed to the judgment against sin. At the same time, there is a contrast with the *blessing of light.* Messiah is at work! Isaiah depicts the subjective experience of this on the one hand—"the people...have seen a great light"—and its objective substance on the other—"a light has shined." This is spoken of the Christ, and this is the blessing of every sinner who is saved. Messiah is the light in the darkness, the help of the helpless, the hope of the hopeless, the bright dawn after the oppressive night. "The darkness of sin can only be dispelled by something that is its very opposite, namely, light," says Young. "Light is a gift of God; it cannot be produced from a human heart which itself is in darkness. The whole work of Christ and all the blessings which He brings may be characterized by the one word 'light.'"[12] It is this light that the church spreads. Christ is the light; Him we proclaim, bringing the healing and wholesome illumination of the gospel to bear upon those who have lived in the dismal darkness of alienation from God.

Proclaiming God's Praise

> But you are a chosen generation, a royal priesthood, a holy nation, His own special people, that you may proclaim the praises of Him who called you out of darkness into His marvelous light; who once were not a people but are now the people of God, who had not obtained mercy but now have obtained mercy. (1 Peter 2:9–10)

In this portion of Scripture, Peter draws attention first to the *gospel character* of the church. He reaches into the Old Testament and takes these sweet descriptions and designations that he invests with the riches of New Testament fullness in Christ. The church is "a chosen generation," called by the God of grace to be His; "a royal priesthood," privileged servants of the Most High who serve His person and abide in His presence; "a holy nation," set apart by God, to God, for God, distinctive among all others; "His own special people," the personal, prized, and purchased possession of the Lord God by virtue of the blood of the Lamb. Once we were not a people, but now we are the people of God—made not just a people generically, but His own people specifically. Once we had not obtained mercy, laboring under the condemnation of sin. Now we have obtained mercy full and free and have been brought into all the privileges of the sons of God. It is a picture of all the ripeness of gospel blessing that the saints enjoy. But Peter ties in that gospel character with our *gospel calling*, just as Isaiah did before him: "This people I have formed for Myself; they shall declare My praise" (Isa. 43:21). Peter tells us that the reason why we have been blessed in this way is in order "that you may proclaim the praises of Him who called you out of darkness into His marvelous light."

This is one of the reasons we have been focusing on the light of the gospel, the salvific shining of Christ—because this is the light

---

12. Young, *Isaiah*, 1:325.

into which we have been called. We can say with all the assurance of experience, "Oh, taste and see that the LORD is good; blessed is the man who trusts in Him!" (Ps. 34:8). As those who have received these blessings ourselves, we are to number out and make widely known all that is praiseworthy in the Lord our God. When the world hears us and sees us, it should be left in no doubt that there is a great, gracious, and glorious God in heaven who lives and saves and rules. The church is designed by God and formed by grace to be a pedestal for the display of the divine beauties of holiness. Saints are to be a living advertisement constantly broadcasting the eminent qualities and noble acts of God the Creator and Deliverer. At the heart of the church's mission is this testimony of praise from a grateful soul: "Christians are to 'publish abroad' the mighty works of God, which include both his activity in creation and his miracle of redemption in the life, death, resurrection, and revelation of Jesus Christ.... This heraldic praise is their reason for existing."[13]

In his magnificent commentary on 1 Peter, John Brown tells us that "Christians, as the called of God, are intended to show forth the excellencies of God, both passively and actively. Those wonderful dispensations of power, and righteousness, and benignity, the incarnation and sacrifice of the divine Son, and the regenerating and sanctifying influences of the divine Spirit, are the most remarkable displays which probably ever have been, or ever will be, made to the intelligent universe of the virtues, the powers, the excellencies, of the divine character." Everything else is, by comparison, a hiding rather than a revealing of the excellence of Jehovah. Brown continues, "If a man wishes to know the true character of God, let him study it as embodied in these dispensations; let him look at God in Christ; 'the glory of God in the face of Christ Jesus.'"[14]

This ought to fill our hearts with abounding joy at the privilege that belongs to us, not only in the possession of these things but in the declaration of them. Consider how Brown weaves together both these elements, showing how Scripture repeatedly links together what God has made us and why He has made us those things.

---

13. Peter H. Davids, *The First Epistle of Peter* (Grand Rapids: Eerdmans, 1990), 93.
14. John Brown, *1 Peter* (Edinburgh: Banner of Truth, 1975), 1:288.

Believers are not passive instruments, but active workers in making known God's praises:

> The manifestation of God made to them in their calling, and the privileges into which it conducts them, produce in their minds just views of the Divine character, and a corresponding mode of thinking and feeling, and speaking, and acting, so that they cannot but show forth the praises of Him who has called them. This is the great design of God in giving them the privilege. If they are "predestinated to the adoption of children by Jesus Christ to himself, according to the good pleasure of his will," it is "that they might be to the praise of the glory of his grace." If they are planted by Him as "trees of righteousness," it is "that he might be glorified." If they are "bought with a price," it is that they may "glorify Him with their souls, and with their bodies, which are his." If they are "filled with the fruits of righteousness," it is "to the praise and glory of God." If they "obtain the inheritance," it is "to the praise of His glory." If "the purchased possession" at last is redeemed completely and forever from all evil, still it is "to the praise of His glory."[15]

Whatever privileges we enjoy, whatever blessings we receive, whatever mercies have been bestowed upon us, they are fuel to the fire of praise, that God in His glory as the Deliverer may be exalted by us and through us in the world. Our experience and existence declare that there is a God who saves. Praising Him is no chore, no burden, to the Christian who has grasped what he has been made by God in Christ. Brown says, "To be made capable of, disposed to, and actually to be employed in, showing forth the praises of Jehovah, is the highest dignity and happiness which can be conferred on created intelligent beings."[16] Do we believe that? Is that our heart's conviction?

Our lives ought to manifest this praise as the spontaneous outflow of delight of a saved man in his Savior and His so-great salvation. This is why Peter lavishes upon us this rich description of what we have received in Christ—so that we should stop asking, "Why should I?" and begin to confess, "How can I do otherwise?"

---

15. Brown, *1 Peter*, 1:290.
16. Brown, *1 Peter*, 1:291.

Pursue the Mission: Summary Thoughts

Our Lord and Master sends us out into this environment against this enemy, fighting these battles, in order that He might build His kingdom, against which the gates of Hades cannot prevail (Matt. 16:18). We, His church, are His privileged instrument in the work, witnesses to the Savior and His salvation by our experience of grace and our testimony to grace, our declaration of His saving might and mercy.

Christ Himself is the saving light. That light reflects from the soul of the saints and refracts through the prism of the church so that it is manifest in all its purity and intensity, all its component shades made splendidly and gloriously plain. We are so closely bound to Christ in our identity and our work that He can use of His church the same language that He uses of Himself: "You are the light of the world. A city that is set on a hill cannot be hidden. Nor do they light a lamp and put it under a basket, but on a lampstand, and it gives light to all who are in the house. Let your light so shine before men, that they may see your good works and glorify your Father in heaven" (Matt. 5:14–16). We have been ordained of God that Christ may be seen in us and made known by us. In Christ's hands and by the Spirit's might, we are the means of manifesting and declaring the unsearchable riches of Christ to the nations, of bringing the incalculable blessings of Christ in salvation to those who are lost in darkness.

How far would you go to give bread to a starving man? What would you pay for a dying man to obtain life-giving medicine? How hard do we labor to relieve the temporal sufferings of the body? How far, how costly, how painful are our efforts to bring light to lost souls?

And this is not to be merely incidental, but intentional. Our gospeling must be active and deliberate. We ought consciously and conscientiously to pursue that high and holy calling of declaring God's saving works in Christ in accordance with our own experience, identity, and character, rooted and grounded in Christ Jesus.

This is no short-term or shallow work. It is not a matter of moments to do a few surface repairs. It is a work of deep-rooted renovation and ongoing reformation. We are to reach the lost and teach the reached, calling men to be true disciples, followers of our Lord and Savior Jesus Christ. Our stated aim is to bring them in through

God's grace, to see Christ formed in them in the context of the local church, exalting Jesus as Savior and Lord to the ends of the earth and the end of days. The church of Jesus Christ is the only missionary organization that Christ ever established, and we must embrace our joyful duty and high privilege of making Christ Jesus known as we make our way through the world. Though you might not have expected him to sound a little like a church-growth guru, and though he must be understood in his Genevan context, note the comments of John Calvin. Preaching on Acts 6:7, where Luke records that "the word of God spread, and the number of the disciples multiplied greatly in Jerusalem, and a great many of the priests were obedient to the faith," Calvin says:

> Therefore, in keeping with the teaching Luke gives here, let us learn that we constitute a true church of God when we try our best to increase the number of believers. And then each one of us, where we are, will apply all our effort to instructing our neighbours and leading them to the knowledge of God, as much by our words as by our showing them good examples and good behaviour.

Calvin goes on to insist on the way in which the Bible molds our thinking with regard to those cut off from God's church and our duty to them. The people of God must encourage all to come and truly join with them in worshiping the one true and living God. Without this, says the preacher,

> we give a clear indication that we have scarcely learned anything in the school of our Saviour Jesus Christ. Each of us must extend our hand to our neighbour and encourage one another to grow more and more in the knowledge of God's truth, which he has been pleased to reveal to us.... Now, as I have already said, we must make every possible effort to lead those who have not been instructed in the knowledge of God so that they and we may serve and honour Jesus Christ, and in so doing increase the numbers of believers. But is that all? We are far from doing all we should. Surprisingly, we have, it seems,

conspired against God by obscuring the truth of his gospel by no longer talking about it.[17]

Pursue the Mission: Specific Counsels

Considering these things, let every believer and every church labor to *understand the mission*. On this subject much confusion abounds. Many today would have us be culture warriors or social renovators or reformers. To be sure, there is a legitimate call to do good and a real measure of value in so doing, but the primary calling of the church is to be witnesses to Jesus Christ.[18] The church is created and commissioned to be a body of disciple-making disciples. We are to bring in and bring on those who—seeing in us and hearing from us the enduring truths of life in Christ—turn to Him as Savior and bow the knee to Him as Lord. So doing, new disciples enter His bright kingdom and learn increasingly to do the bidding of the heavenly King. In this way, as the Word of God dwells richly in the saints in all wisdom, so others will hear and see and will come to trust in Him, existing churches will grow in the grace and knowledge of our Lord and Savior Jesus Christ, and new churches will be established. So the gospel will progress intensively, taking ever deeper root and producing ever sweeter fruit in the lives of the saints, and, extensively, breaking through barriers of race and geography and culture and spiritual opposition and bringing sinners to a crucified Christ in repentant faith.

Heraldic praise is our reason for existing.[19] The grand object of our existence is to extend the Redeemer's kingdom.[20] We are to pray for it and—lest we prove gilded hypocrites—to set out actively to do it, for His glory's sake:

"Our Father in heaven,
Hallowed be Your name.

17. John Calvin, "Learning, Teaching, and Living the Gospel Message" (sermon on Acts 6:7–9), in *Sermons on the Acts of the Apostles (Chapters 1–7)* (Edinburgh: Banner of Truth, 2008), 335–36.

18. An excellent book-length study of this matter is *What Is the Mission of the Church? Making Sense of Social Justice, Shalom, and the Great Commission*, by Kevin DeYoung and Greg Gilbert (Wheaton, Ill.: Crossway, 2011).

19. Davids, *First Epistle of Peter*, 93.

20. Fuller, *Armies of the Lamb*, 224.

Your kingdom come.
Your will be done
On earth as it is in heaven....
For Yours is the kingdom and the power and the glory forever.
    Amen." (Matt. 6:9–10, 13)

In this, our simple calling is to *obey the Master*. How often in the Gospels does our Lord strictly instruct those who have received a blessing to keep silent about His person and His work, and how often do those so blessed go away and immediately begin to make it known? Here is a typical sequence:

And [Christ] strictly warned him and sent him away at once, and said to him, "See that you say nothing to anyone; but go your way, show yourself to the priest, and offer for your cleansing those things which Moses commanded, as a testimony to them."
    However, he went out and began to proclaim it freely, and to spread the matter, so that Jesus could no longer openly enter the city, but was outside in deserted places; and they came to Him from every direction. (Mark 1:43–45)

Leave aside for a moment the reason for these warnings in that time and place. We might imagine ourselves justified in rolling our eyes, shaking our heads, and perhaps even indulging in a little sanctified tut-tutting at the inability of these men and women to obey such a clear and simple command. To be sure, we can perhaps understand a little of their joy at their blessing, the pressure to go and speak of the mercies received, but did they not hear Christ explicitly telling them to keep silent?

What of us? Are we better than they? For them, the constraint was in a sense unnatural, the requirement to say nothing to anyone they had known of the greatest mercy they had known. Christ calls us to do what ought to come naturally to the blessed man. We have something great to speak of and orders to go and tell. Yet we justify our sinful silence for reasons of policy, perhaps telling ourselves that we are waiting for the right moment. Fortunately for our fearing hearts, we feel that it never quite arrives, or we excuse ourselves on grounds of politeness. The earliest generations of believers needed persecutions and visions to get them moving. Shall we criticize them when we have all that they have and still do not speak? The wisdom of serpents was never intended to muzzle us, and the harmlessness of doves was not designed to make milksops of us. Christ our Lord expects us to be going wisely and harmlessly, and—as we go—to proclaim God's praises and call men to Christ, to taste and see that the Lord is good. As a church and as individuals we ought to be counting the cost of that and then doing Christ's bidding.

Let us then *seize the opportunities*. Some are there to be found, others will need to be made. Every child of God is party to the gospel character of the church of Christ, and all therefore participate in the privilege of our gospel calling to proclaim the praises of Him who called us out of darkness into His marvelous light:

> So let our lips and lives express
> The holy gospel we profess;
> So let our works and virtues shine,
> To prove the doctrine all divine.
>
> Thus shall we best proclaim abroad
> The honours of our Saviour God,
> When His salvation reigns within,
> And grace subdues the power of sin.[21]

The saints individually and the church as a whole ought to plan, to organize, and to invest so as to seek, find, and take our opportunities. We all have them, whether in seeking the lost or teaching the found. Our witness ought to be spontaneous and opportunistic on one level, but that does not exclude any possibility of plans and schemes: "The fruit of the righteous is a tree of life, and he who wins souls is wise" (Prov. 11:30). Too often we sit and linger, excusing ourselves into a kind of practical hyper-Calvinism by simply waiting for opportunities to present themselves to us or telling ourselves with a false modesty that others are better equipped and we have nothing to offer. As Isaiah says, "A generous man devises generous things, and by generosity he shall stand" (Isa. 32:8). There is no plan more generous, more noble, than to take the good news to those who sit in darkness. As individuals and as churches we must make disciples as we go. There is no reason why we should not plan and purpose to go by the way that makes fruitful obedience intentional. It is a noble thing to see a church full of saints at

---

21. Isaac Watts, "So Let Our Lips and Lives Express."

different stages of their pilgrimage encouraging, exhorting, teaching, and training one another along the road.

Of course, we must consider our individual callings, characters, and circumstances. You are not a preacher? Fine—bring a friend to hear one! You are a busy mother of children? There is your mission field! You have unconverted family members and neighbors? Go home and tell them what great things the Lord has done for you and how He has had compassion on you! You are too weak or sick of body to go? Then show your strength of spirit and pray! Are there no moments on the Lord's Days when you could go week by week to a younger saint to inquire after his soul and gently urge him on? Are there no communications that you could write, no calls you could make, no relationships you could cultivate with the aim of seeing Christ more evidently formed in a soul? A little holy ingenuity and wise investment would soon enough make some space for the gospel to go forth and for godliness to be encouraged. We must discern our role and then go about our gospel business. Too much is at stake with regard to the glory of God and the eternal destiny of men's souls and the enduring health of the church for us to hold our tongues. We ought to speak more readily, more willingly, more cheerfully, and more tellingly than we do.

The same is true corporately. It is too easy to equate smallness with purity and ineffectiveness with faithfulness. We piously profess our confidence in God's sovereign purposes but practically fail to yoke it with confident employment of the means God has given. John Berridge put the following prayerful poetry in the mouth of ministers, but there is a principle that applies to all:

> The means of grace are in my hand,
> The blessing is at God's command,
> Who must the work fulfil;
> And though I read, and watch and pray,
> Yet here the Lord directs my way,
> And he works all things still.

Here is no lack of confidence, but a proper awareness of the relationship between the means and the blessing. In the course of his hymn, Berridge expresses further his entire reliance on God. That drives him ultimately not to the suspension or abandonment of the appointed means, but to an active yet dependent embrace of them:

Prepare my tongue to pray and praise,
To speak of providential ways,
And heavenly truth unfold;
To strengthen well a feeble soul,
Correct the careless, rouse the dull,
And silence sinners bold.[22]

So the church, her ministers, and all her other members ought to be considering how most faithfully and effectively they can bring the good news to their communities and regions. We must be praying over and planning for and participating in both the regular life of the church and those particular expressions of her urgent desire to see sinners saved. All too often, that which weakens our hands and closes our mouths is faithless fear.

That is why we must learn to *face the dangers*—not in our own strength, for that would be madness. We go in the name of Christ our King as sheep among wolves. Our Savior knows what He is doing and with whom He is doing it when He sends us out. He has not promised us an easy task, but a worthy one. He has never suggested that this is an easy road, but He assures us that it leads to a glorious place. He has never offered a coward's peace, but called us to a good fight.

These things are hard, for the eye of flesh sees all the dangers, and only the eye of faith can see that the mountain is full of horses and chariots of fire (2 Kings 6:17), that the Lord of hosts is with us always. Why are we so easily scared? Why are we so quickly discouraged? Why do we so swiftly retreat? Why do we trim our words and fudge our testimonies to the beauties of divine grace and goodness? Have we forgotten the King and His promises? He has warned us of the dangers. He has sent us to the task, and that ought to put some steel in our spines. He has equipped us for the fight, and that ought to put some confidence in our hearts. He has declared his intention to accomplish all His saving purposes through His saved people—weak, frail, stumbling people like you and me. One of the reasons He works this way is so that He will obtain the glory, and not us. The issue is not our strength and competence but God's. Often we seek to make Christ known and walk away feeling ourselves abject

---

22. John Berridge, "The Means of Grace Are in My Hand."

failures. What happens if those to whom we spoke are converted? Do we reassess our contribution and conclude that perhaps we did not do so badly after all? No, we were probably just as shabby in ourselves as we imagined, and perhaps more so, "but God has chosen the foolish things of the world to put to shame the wise, and God has chosen the weak things of the world to put to shame the things which are mighty; and the base things of the world and the things which are despised God has chosen, and the things which are not, to bring to nothing the things that are, that no flesh should glory in His presence" (1 Cor. 1:27–29). God has not said that it would be easy, and it is not pleasant. It is war, but Christ is triumphant, and He is with us as we go.

So we should stir up our hearts as we *ponder the privileges*, the blessings of being who we are and doing what we do and speaking what we speak and offering what we offer in the name of our God and our Redeemer. You and I are the worm that threshes the mountains and beats them small (Isa. 41:14–15). We are the people who once were no people, but now have been made the people of the living God. We are the rebels granted mercy and brought into the family of God. We are the blasphemers who have become witnesses of the very Lord whom once we hated. We are the redeemed of God who hold out redemption to those who sit enchained in death's dark shadow. We are of Christ, in Christ, for Christ, and will one day be with Christ. Who can sing His praises the way we can? Let us meditate on this so-great Savior and His so-great salvation until our hearts burn within us. Let us gaze on all His loveliness and dwell upon the unsearchable riches of the Lord of glory until we have something to say and a reason to say it. Let us take account of the privileges we possess and the prospect we are granted of living so as to hear the Master say, "Well done, good and faithful servant. Enter into the joy of your Lord."

If we are to do that, we must *preach the person*: our great God and Savior Jesus Christ—*Him* we proclaim. Christ crucified is the Master we serve and our motive to go and the message we carry. We are to employ His means to accomplish His ends. Our fidelity, our purity, and our testimony ought to be compelling, demanding a hearing and offering something to hear. To be sure, some of our battles are necessarily defensive, but these are righteously offensive strikes as we go to win souls for our Lord. We have in our hand and our heart the sword of the Spirit, which is the Word of God. So equipped, we go out at Christ's command to compel men to enter His kingdom. We speak the truth in love, presenting the King in His beauty and majesty, in His humiliation and exaltation, in His atoning death and justifying resurrection, in His past cross and His present crown, in His coming once to put away sin by the sacrifice of Himself and His coming again a second time, apart from sin, for salvation. We are to speak, in dependence on the Holy Ghost for spiritual power, making known the only name given among men by which sinners like us are saved, so that men will be saved and will learn to serve and will themselves be sent, that Christ may be glorified in salvation. "And I," said our Lord, "if I am lifted up from the earth, will draw all peoples to Myself" (John 12:32). He was lifted up on the cross to make atonement for sin, and He must be lifted up as crucified by His people before the gaze of the world. We must placard Him before the nations as the dying but risen Lord, the light of the world, the hope of the hopeless and the help of the helpless, to the conversion of the lost, the edifying of the saints, and the glory of His eternal name.

7
RESPECT THE AUTHORITIES

As I have pointed out, there are many common misconceptions about the role and priorities of the Lord Jesus Christ's church. Many of those misconceptions arise from a failure to reckon with the identity of the church, not least in its relation to the world. Some people seem to labor under the misapprehension that the church is, or ought to be, a political force, a social force, or an economic force. Listen to some, and you might even imagine that she is a deliberately subversive, if not outrightly a rebel, force. I would go so far as to contend that if we see the church simply or merely as a moral force, we are again falling short of our calling.

All this is to put the church in entirely the wrong sphere, to assess her on entirely the wrong plane. To look for such priorities in the life of the church of Christ is to seek for oranges on an apple tree. The church, by divine design and intention, is a spiritual force, a gospel organism. Her involvement in and impact upon the world socially, politically, and economically may not be insignificant, but it will be substantially incidental. The church does not exist to have a political life or role.

By this I mean that when the church pursues her mission and fights her battles in this world, the specific intention is that sinners will be saved, in the fullest sense of the word: brought into the kingdom of God and trained up in the kingdom of God. What is the effect when that happens? Well, for example, the drunkard ceases to empty his glass. The thieves stop lifting their goods. The fanatics stop idolizing the people and things of the world, as it loses its sparkle in their eyes. The philanderers leave their bits on the side. The pornography consumers clean up their acts. The addicts begin to break their addictions. The lazy begin to work. The distant spouses begin to speak and to love one another. The liars begin to tell the truth. The parent begins to care for the child. The student begins to heed the teacher. The cheat begins to live with integrity.

Nothing is more practical in its impact than salvation! Such things as these are happening all the time on a small numerical scale in the lives of repenting, believing, saved sinners in countless countries on every continent. Suppose that were to happen on a larger scale. What would be its effect?

To take one example, consider the consequences of a revival of religion that took place in Ireland in the nineteenth century through God's blessing on the preaching of W. P. Nicholson. As he declared the gospel in the dockyards of Belfast, men's hearts were touched by the truth, and many were convicted on account of their sin, repenting of their transgressions and trusting in the Lord Jesus. As the work of the Spirit developed, the owners of the Harland and Wolff Shipyard had to open a warehouse to store all the tools returned by the repentant thieves of the dockyard, men who had once thought nothing of walking away with what did not belong to them—one of the unwritten "perks" of the job, as it were.

Similar stories can be told of pubs and brothels bereft of customers, of whole streets characterized by family religion and peace where strife had once reigned, of entire regions transformed by the power of the gospel. It happened in Ephesus when Paul preached the gospel there. The silversmiths of the city—the makers of the idol figurines of Diana—felt robbed of their customers as the appetites of fallen hearts were radically and practically redirected by the power of the Spirit of Christ.

And what would happen in your community? What pubs, bars, and liquor stores would close? What stores would cease trading, and which services would stop being offered? What download patterns would change? What antagonism might ensue? What transformations in schools, workplaces, homes, and streets there would be! But these would be the consequences of the church pursuing her priorities, not a reflection of their shift.

Again, I am not suggesting that individual Christians should be careless or dismissive of their place and opportunities in particular cultures and societies. We are not required by our Christianity to abandon, retire from, neglect, or despair of opportunities in the civic sphere. Indeed, this is one of those areas where Christian salt and light are desperately needed.

In the Old Testament, for example, we have Daniel advising Nebuchadnezzar to "break off your sins by being righteous, and your iniquities by showing mercy to the poor. Perhaps there may be a lengthening of your prosperity" (Dan. 4:27). Esther, like Daniel a relatively isolated figure under a pagan government, has to face a challenge: "If you remain completely silent at this time, relief and deliverance will arise for the Jews from another place, but you and your father's house will perish. Yet who knows whether you have come to the kingdom for such a time as this?" (Est. 4:14). Stirred to action, Esther uses the position in which God has placed her and the influence He has given her to contend for righteousness. Doing so, she delivers both herself and her people.

In similar fashion, when John the Baptist was calling men to repent, he was asked by tax collectors and soldiers how they ought to live as citizens of God's kingdom: "Then tax collectors also came to be baptized, and said to him, 'Teacher, what shall we do?' And he said to them, 'Collect no more than what is appointed for you.' Likewise the soldiers asked him, saying, 'And what shall we do?' So he said to them, 'Do not intimidate anyone or accuse falsely, and be content with your wages'" (Luke 3:12–14).

Notice that John did not tell the tax collectors to stop collecting tax nor the soldiers to give up their commissions and lay down their weapons. Politicians, officials, businessmen, entrepreneurs, soldiers, and civil servants—nothing prevents them from being Christians and nothing prevents Christians from excelling in those roles, with God's blessing. When William Wilberforce was converted, some well-meaning counselors advised him to retire from politics as a sphere unfit for a child of God. It was John Newton who advised him to stay where God had put him and do all the good that he could. To be sure, someone already converted might find it hard to climb the slippery poles of the political or business realms simply because of the principles (or lack of them) that may be in operation in particular times and places. These things must all be taken into account, as we shall see below.

Nevertheless, we need to recognize that the blessings outlined above are the consequence of the church embracing her priorities, not the result of her altering them. It is not the business of the church as such, or of Christians individually, to get into influential positions with the aim of securing the progress of some political agenda. We do not set out to transform the world apart from the preaching of the gospel. That is potentially to conflate and confuse the priorities of two different kingdoms and quickly leads to the church losing her distinctiveness and effectiveness. Christ's kingdom is not of this world (John 18:36), and this transforms the perspective of God's people on the world in which they live, their expectations, aims, and approaches. For precisely this reason the Scriptures give such clear light as to how the church of God is to relate to "the powers that be." To be sure, there is much that could be said about the calling and responsibility of those powers, but our focus in the pages that follow will be on the calling and responsibility of the church in relation to those powers.

Respect the Authorities: Scriptural Framework

A Proper Subjection

> Let every soul be subject to the governing authorities. For there is no authority except from God, and the authorities that exist are appointed by God. Therefore whoever resists the authority resists the ordinance of God, and those who resist will bring judgment on themselves. For rulers are not a terror to good works, but to evil. Do you want to be unafraid of the authority? Do what is good, and you will have praise from the same. For he is God's minister to you for good. But if you do evil, be afraid; for he does not bear the sword in vain; for he is God's minister, an avenger to execute wrath on him who practices evil. Therefore you must be subject, not only because of wrath but also for conscience' sake. For because of this you also pay taxes, for they are God's ministers attending continually to this very thing. Render therefore to all their due: taxes to whom taxes are due, customs to whom customs, fear to whom fear, honor to whom honor. (Rom. 13:1–7)

This is part of the apostle's treatment of practical Christian living in the real world, and here Paul traces a tight, logical sequence. What he says may be considered an outworking of the full spiritual force of the fifth commandment, "Honor your father and your mother, that your days may be long upon the land which the LORD your God is giving you" (Ex. 20:12). The implications of this commandment concern our relationship to God-appointed authority, and its demands reach far deeper and wider than parental authority. The Shorter Catechism helpfully expands the essence, reminding us that the fifth commandment requires us to preserve the honor of and perform the duties belonging to all people in their various places and relations, whether as superiors, inferiors, or equals. By way of negative contrast, it forbids the neglecting of or doing anything against the honor and duty that belong to all people in their various places and relations.

Here Paul takes that principle and applies it to the relationship of believers to the civil magistrate. It is a rule for all people: each one must be subject to the governing authorities, "the powers that be," in the evocative phrasing of the King James Version. It is a call not merely to grudging quietism or passive acceptance but to an active and comprehensive embrace of submission in all lawful duties and services. It is not a mere matter of obligatory constraint or restraint, but a positive pursuit of a disposition and deeds that show one's awareness that the Lord has appointed authorities.

There is a recognition inherent in this submission that the power exercised by these authorities is by divine appointment (Prov. 8:15). God has devised, designated, and delegated the exercise of all earthly powers subordinate to His own. The highest and lowest civil authorities have been ordained in principle and in person by the Lord of heaven and earth. There is a clear sequence of corollaries: to resist these authorities is to resist what God has ordained, which is to resist God, which is to invite wrath or judgment. Although the context suggests that the primary reference is to the judgment meted out by civil magistrates in accordance with God's appointment, there may be a hint of eternality in the language as well.

All this is bounded in the intended benefits of government. Rulers are appointed to be a terror to evil—to spook the bad guys, keeping evil at bay—so that the citizen who acts uprightly should have nothing to fear. We must recognize that God has appointed earthly authority to be a blessing to men. Civil magistrates have been granted the sword to defend good and to punish evil. Even usurped or abused authority—which we might and should as Christians and citizens speak against—ought to and often does provide a measure of control and order in a nation against the outbreak of open sin, a protection against those times when every man does what is right in his own eyes (Judg. 21:25).

Two reasons are provided for this principled submission. The first is "wrath," the fear of temporal judgments against evildoing, but this is not the only reason and would in itself be a fairly shallow one. The saints also obey "for conscience' sake," recognizing their obligations to the God who has appointed those authorities and having their consciences bound ultimately to Him.

The implications are clear and practical. Christians are to offer to the government whatever belongs to the government by right—appropriate maintenance and appropriate reverence: "Render therefore to all their due: taxes to whom taxes are due, customs to whom customs, fear to whom fear, honor to whom honor" (Rom. 13:7). Whether in the material or the moral spheres, governments ought to receive from us what God has called us to give.

Before we begin to buck at this and start offering exceptions to the rule, we would do well to recognize that this commandment was not issued to a church basking in the hazy afterglow of the largely tragic Constantinian settlement. It did not float down to saints enjoying the benefits of a post-Enlightenment liberal democracy, but to believers who were living in the Roman Empire under the tyranny of such beasts as Claudius and Nero Caesar. These men were no friends to humanity, let alone to Christianity, but despots who ruled with the proverbial fist of iron as those who considered themselves gods. The issue is not first and foremost the character of the magistrate or his abuses of the power put in his hands, but the position to which he has been appointed by God as an agent of temporal justice in some measure. We must acknowledge that this does not suspend the believer's ultimate obligation to God. The apostles themselves were perfectly clear that they ought to obey God rather than men whenever the civil or religious authorities commanded something that God forbade or forbade something that God commanded. Peter challenged the Sanhedrin, "Whether it is right in the sight of God to listen to you more than to God, you judge" (Acts 4:19). Not long after, he and the other apostles were even plainer: "We ought to obey God rather than men" (Acts 5:29).

While we will consider this tension in more detail as we move on, we should note that this understanding dictates the occasions on which and the tone in which some form of resistance or disobedience is legitimized. Perhaps the finest examples are found in the book of Daniel. In the first instance, Daniel's three friends refuse to bow to the image of gold erected by Nebuchadnezzar. Threatened with death in the fiery furnace if they will not obey, their reply is a model of gracious refusal. Their language is polite and eminently respectful. Their recognition of the king's authority is sincere and humble. Their refusal to obey is absolute. Their faithfulness to God is complete: "O Nebu hadnezzar, we have no need to answer you in this matter. If that is the case, our God whom we serve is able to deliver us from the burning fiery furnace, and He will deliver us from your hand, O king. But if not, let it be known to you, O king, that we do not serve your gods, nor will we worship the gold image which you have set up" (Dan. 3:16–18). How infuriating it must have been to Nebuchadnezzar to have men who humbly and reverently accepted his right to throw them into a fiery furnace and politely refused to obey him anyway!

Daniel is no less noble and gracious when forbidden to pray to anyone but Darius. He will not lay aside God's law in the matter and is willing to be thrown into the lions' den as a consequence. And how does he respond to the concerned emperor who hurries down to the den the morning after? With words like these: "O king, live forever! My God sent His angel and shut the lions' mouths, so that they have not hurt me, because I was found innocent before Him; and also, O king, I have done no wrong before you" (Dan. 6:21–22). Daniel honors his sovereign, testifies to God, and defends his actions, all at once. Recognizing the authorities as appointed by God conditions our attitudes and actions toward them, even when as disciples of Christ we are legitimately obliged to refuse particular demands.

The Prayers of the Saints

I exhort first of all that supplications, prayers, intercessions, and giving of thanks be made for all men, for kings and all who are in authority, that we may lead a quiet and peaceable life in all godliness and reverence. (1 Tim. 2:1–2)

Paul calls Timothy to fulfill his appointed role with fidelity. Part of that requires Timothy to be truly and righteously publicly minded. We may be separate from the world, but we do not cut ourselves off from those around us, from the world in which we live. One of the ways in which we show our engagement with the world is by prayer.

Here is a *command* that all kinds of prayers be offered for all kinds of men, including and especially kings and all who are in authority. Paul speaks of various approaches made to the Lord God: seeking to obtain needful things, making requests, having close dealings with God on behalf of ourselves and others, also giving thanks to God for His goodness bestowed on others and on ourselves. Why does Timothy need to pray in this way? The desired *consequences* are not to obtain wealth, power, influence, or prominence in society or among its rulers, but simply to be able to get on with the job of being the saints of God without interference or oppression. God's people wish simply to conduct themselves in godliness and reverence, discharging the duties we have toward God and men. The commentator Patrick Fairbairn says that these are prayers that we "may be allowed freely to enjoy our privileges, and maintain the pious and orderly course which becomes us as Christians, without the molestation, the troubles, and the unseemly shifts which are the natural consequence of inequitable government and abused power."[1] Up to a point, we wish merely to be left alone to get on with the life that God has called us to lead.

Here is a new covenant echo of the prayer that the exiles of Jeremiah's day had commended to them: "Seek the peace of the city where I have caused you to be carried away captive, and pray to the LORD for it; for in its peace you will have peace" (Jer. 29:7). We do not wish to suffer from rapid shifts of power, from abuses of authority, or from threats to civil order. Pray, then, that the Lord would guide those in authority so that you may have peace to pursue righteousness. Paul goes on to say to Timothy that such a disposition to pray and such a righteous expectation is pleasing to the Lord God.

---

1. Patrick Fairbairn, *1 & 2 Timothy and Titus* (Edinburgh: Banner of Truth, 2002), 112.

A Godly Life

> Beloved, I beg you as sojourners and pilgrims, abstain from fleshly lusts which war against the soul, having your conduct honorable among the Gentiles, that when they speak against you as evildoers, they may, by your good works which they observe, glorify God in the day of visitation. (1 Peter 2:11–12)

At the core of Peter's exhortation is the principle that a godly life—honorable conduct—provides a measure of defense to strangers and pilgrims in this hostile environment. The saints are given instructions that have to do more with the inward life: "abstain from fleshly lusts which war against the soul." There follows the evidence of those working principles in the outward life: "having your conduct honorable among the Gentiles." The saints, conscious of the eye of the world upon them, ought to cultivate attractive and blameless lives. Our interactions with those around us ought to be truly righteous. This is so that when our religious convictions bring a measure of reproach or persecution, those who speak evil of the children of God will be obliged to acknowledge the practical and generally beneficial godliness of the saints.

As they see your righteous living they will be caught between their rejection of the Christ whom you follow and the undeniable difference that your following of Christ makes in your treatment of those around you. They must acknowledge that your life is exemplary; that your Christian convictions raise you above the aggressive and bestial living that increasingly characterizes our societies; that our fundamental neighborliness is on open but unostentatious display (Luke 10:36). Such good works of the church will ultimately lead these critics to "glorify God in the day of visitation." This is a difficult phrase that some suggest refers to a personal and searching encounter with the Lord, perhaps prompted by or certainly driven home by the testimony of the believers in the world. There may come a day when God deals with the souls of our friends, neighbors, and colleagues who may presently pour scorn on our convictions, dismiss our religion, or deride us as mere do-gooders. In that day the honorable conduct of the saints may be one of the means that the Lord uses to press home the realities of His salvation in Jesus Christ. The following verses spell out what this looks like with regard to the state:

Therefore submit yourselves to every ordinance of man for the Lord's sake, whether to the king as supreme, or to governors, as to those who are sent by him for the punishment of evildoers and for the praise of those who do good. For this is the will of God, that by doing good you may put to silence the ignorance of foolish men—as free, yet not using liberty as a cloak for vice, but as bondservants of God. Honor all people. Love the brotherhood. Fear God. Honor the king. (1 Peter 2:13–17)

You will notice that Peter establishes absolutes that are similar to those which Paul makes clear in Romans 13. Peter explains that if the ' saints are to suffer, at least it ought to be for the right reasons and not because of their rebellion against God's appointed authorities. What is particularly interesting is the way in which Peter connects lawlessness and rebellion in relation both to God and to men. As with Paul, rebellion against the authority that the Lord has appointed is *de facto* rebellion against the Lord who appointed it. Rebellion against one authority often reflects an ill disposition to authority in general, including divine authority. It is no surprise that a generation in which sinners very willingly and eagerly enthrone themselves as the only authority worth heeding tend to disregard both the laws of men and the laws of God. Verse 17 provides a potent summary of what Peter has been addressing: "Honor all people. Love the brotherhood. Fear God. Honor the king" (1 Peter 2:17).

Respond Prayerfully

So when they heard that, they raised their voice to God with one accord and said: "Lord, You are God, who made heaven and earth and the sea, and all that is in them, who by the mouth of Your servant David have said:
'Why did the nations rage,
And the people plot vain things?
The kings of the earth took their stand,
And the rulers were gathered together
Against the LORD and against His Christ.'
For truly against Your holy Servant Jesus, whom You anointed, both Herod and Pontius Pilate, with the Gentiles and the people of Israel, were gathered together to do whatever Your hand and Your purpose determined before to be done. Now, Lord, look on their threats, and grant to Your servants that with all boldness

they may speak Your word, by stretching out Your hand to heal, and that signs and wonders may be done through the name of Your holy Servant Jesus." And when they had prayed, the place where they were assembled together was shaken; and they were all filled with the Holy Spirit, and they spoke the word of God with boldness. (Acts 4:24–31)

Here Luke depicts the response of the righteous when the God-appointed authorities set out to play God. The context is one that goes well beyond background antagonism—it is one of outright opposition and persecution. The Sanhedrin "called them and commanded them not to speak at all nor teach in the name of Jesus. But Peter and John answered and said to them, 'Whether it is right in the sight of God to listen to you more than to God, you judge. For we cannot but speak the things which we have seen and heard'" (Acts 4:18–20). Again, as in Acts 5:29, God's authority is ultimate, man's authority is subordinate, and the church is now facing a human civil and religious authority that is requiring her to disobey God.

In the verses that follow we see the response of the church as a church, the people of God gathered together in a particular place. It may be that some of them in this place were converted priests, perhaps Roman soldiers or officials, members of Herod's or Caesar's households, or women with extensive circles of contacts or the wives of men with particular influence. There may have been some or many who might have had personal opportunities to do good in the circumstances. Doubtless such sincere believers, given the chance in the days following, might have used whatever legitimate influence they had or whatever means lay lawfully at their disposal to protect the apostles or to divert the march of persecution. But notice what the saints do as a church: They do not begin to organize and orchestrate a plan of civic resistance. They do not plan marches and establish alliances and coalitions and institutes to carry their voices to the upper echelons of society. They do not reach out to other oppressed and concerned parties to establish campaigns of belligerency. They do not make contact with lobbyists nor print leaflets and redesign their websites, working up a more effective advertising campaign. They do not draw up petitions, design banners with catchy titles, print T-shirts with telling slogans, and work up posters with vivid images. They do not conclude that they need to engage the world on the world's terms. They do not seek to obtain a voice on the political and cultural stage. They do not pursue larger numbers, greater prominence, cutting-edge websites, pithier sound bites, all the while whipping up publicity campaigns to sweep the floor with the opposition. None of that is remotely what you find in Jerusalem (allowing for a little modernization).

Rather, they get on their faces before God Most High and pour out their hearts to the One who governs, appoints, ordains, and judges—the Lord to whom all in heaven and earth are ultimately accountable. They raise their voices not to men but to God. This is most assuredly not mere mindless quiescence or fawning, groveling submission to human authorities. If you read their prayer, you will see that they first *recognized* the divine authority and government, ascribing honor to God as the King enthroned over all, the Creator of all things, the Governor of all things, and the Revealer of Himself to men. They also *reckoned with* the human opposition as it really was, fierce and united against the Christ and all those who named His name. Natural enemies found a common cause in opposing Christ and His kingdom. Like Hezekiah reading Sennacherib's letter (Isa. 37:14–20), they spread the whole matter out before the Lord. Therefore, faced with such a challenge, they *requested* divine equipment from God's hands. But note the specific requests. They do not pray against the government, but rather for the gospel. They do not ask to be made able to avoid the threat, but rather to be given grace to meet it as true and steadfast believers: "In the face of opposition, make us yet more distinctive as those who live for and proclaim Jesus the Christ. Take away our fear, and give us courage to declare the truth." And so they *received* specific answers to their prayers, being filled with the Holy Spirit and speaking the word of God with boldness.

The church's response to the assaults made on her is not a rallying cry to civic resistance or even civic engagement, but to get on her knees before the living Lord and to seek His face, crying for heavenly power to declare divine truth faithfully and fruitfully even in the face of opposition and persecution.

Remember Our Heavenly Hope

For our citizenship is in heaven, from which we also eagerly wait for the Savior, the Lord Jesus Christ, who will transform our lowly body that it may be conformed to His glorious body, according to the working by which He is able even to subdue all things to Himself. Therefore, my beloved and longed-for brethren, my joy and crown, so stand fast in the Lord, beloved. (Phil. 3:20–4:1)

The governing power of the saints is a heavenly one. The church takes her identity, her sense of privilege and priority, her direction for behavior, and her enduring hope from her heavenly King and the realities of citizenship in His kingdom. This conditions all our relationships with the authorities here. The men of the world set their minds on earthly things, but the citizens of Zion set their minds on heavenly things. The saints operate here as belonging there. Our character, conduct, and convictions are conditioned by the world to come rather than by the world that is passing away. Paul is probably quite deliberately employing the language that would be used of Caesar to ascribe to him semidivine functions in order to emphasize that the saints have a Savior and a Lord who is most certainly not Caesar. Caesar is a lord and a deliverer by the Lord and Deliverer's appointment. Commentator G. Walter Hansen explains: "Their hope for the future is not fixed on Caesar, the savior and Lord of the Roman Empire, but on Jesus Christ, the heavenly Lord and Savior.... The power of earthly tyrants to humiliate the followers of Christ will be overcome by Christ when he subjects all things to himself and transforms our bodies of humiliation to be like his glorious body."[2]

Not only will the saints themselves be transformed at the coming of Christ but all things will be subdued under Him—*all things*, including all those who stand over and against the church, which is His body. Our home is heaven, and we are here only for a little while. All too often our problem is that we are reaching into the future and trying to bring our hopes and expectations into this world rather than anticipating them in the next. We try to build our empires here. We see things in terms of time, and we lose sight of eternity. But we are Christ's heavenly kingdom, and our citizenship is in heaven. Our King is in heaven.

2. G. Walter Hansen, *The Letter to the Philippians* (Grand Rapids: Eerdmans, 2009), 270, 275.

This ought to be a transforming realization. If my hope is heavenly, then I know who and what I am in relation to the things of this passing world. I show proper honor to my earthly rulers but am not bound to this world as if it were the only thing that matters. With this confidence, the church is able to stand fast in the Lord. Her convictions, character, and conduct are conditioned by her relationship with her heavenly King establishing a heavenly citizenship and providing a heavenly hope.

Respect the Authorities: Summary Thoughts

In relation to the civil magistrates whom God has appointed, the Lord's pilgrim people live in the space between our Christ's declaration that His kingdom is not of this world (John 18:36) and His command that we are to give to Caesar the things that are Caesar's and to God the things that are God's (Matt. 22:21). There is a divinely appointed and righteous tension at this point. We are of the kingdom of Christ, and that situates us finally and ultimately in and of Christ in the heavenlies. While we are here, that allegiance must be reflected in our giving to God's appointed authorities what is their rightful due as well as rendering to the Lord that which belongs to Him alone.

It is precisely because Jesus Christ's kingdom is not of this world that we obtain perspective on the world and its authorities. It is because we serve the eternal King, being citizens of heaven, that we are the best citizens on earth, measured by divine standards. I remember the story of a pastor called before a communist dictator in Eastern Europe before the collapse of the Iron Curtain. The autocrat upbraided the man of God for being subversive and rebellious. "Not at all," answered the pastor humbly. "We Christians respect our leaders. We are faithful citizens, and we pray for you every day." What if we were brought before men like Claudius Caesar or Nero Caesar, men like Stalin, Hitler, Mao Zedong, Pol Pot, Ceausescu, and others who may yet be raised up in our nations, perhaps superintending and even directing what we are persuaded is a moral decline and advancing wickedness? Would we be able to say with a clear conscience, "Sir, I am one of your best citizens. I hear what you say even when I cannot heed it, and I pray to my God for you every day"?

As citizens of heaven we recognize that we are sojourners here and that our convictions, character, and conduct should reflect our true homeland and bring honor to our true King. Part of our duty as we make our way through the world is to regard and respect rulers and authorities as God's appointed temporal vicegerents in the civil sphere to promote righteousness and to prevent wickedness. At their best, they provide a peaceful environment in which the church can go about its gospel business in peace, simply being what God has called us to be. At their worst, the civil authorities make themselves the agitators and architects of all that is most vicious and violent about opposition to the church, employing all the machinery of government in an attempt to crush the people of God.

If the influence of the authorities is benign, we should be genuinely thankful and express that thanks to God, but we should not make the mistake of yoking our hopes for Christ's heavenly kingdom to the vehicles of political, social, or economic power or renewal. Our confidence does not lie in the politics and parties and pressure groups of any culture. If the rulers over us are malign, we should not orchestrate campaigns of civil resistance or rebellion nor despair of the kingdom of God because that does not rise or fall depending on the state of any nation or nations. In one sense, the progress of God's kingdom has nothing to do with the civil authorities. Christ is our king, and His kingdom is not of this world.

Even if we face explicit opposition, even if a government should forbid what God commands or command what God forbids, even if we reach the point of confessing that "we ought to obey God rather than men" (Acts 5:29), the Christian's noncompliance should reflect his supreme commitment to the God who governs all and who will one day subdue all. As such, his demeanor, behavior, and speech should all communicate an acknowledgment of the subordinate authority, even as he obeys the higher one.

The Christian's spirit is to be one of cheerful, willing, comprehensive submission as required of him by God. We are to offer legitimate support and reverence wherever we are able to the rulers appointed over us by our sovereign Lord, and to pray for them and for ourselves, that the gospel may readily advance as the church pursues the mission entrusted to her by her Redeemer.

Respect the Authorities: Specific Counsels

Almost nothing agitates Christians as much as discussion of the relationship of the church to the state. Some seem to imagine that theological and political allegiances are inextricably bound together. Others set out to avoid any kind of commitments. Some practice an extreme separatism, as if no Christian should care about or be involved in any political, social, or economic discussions or processes. Others fling themselves into this realm with what can appear to be thoughtless abandon. I trust that the discussion of this issue so far has at least provided a measure of clarity. Without the deliberate intention of slaying any particular sacred cows, let me offer what I hope are some clear and coherent principles based on what we have seen from the Word of God.

First, we must *remember the distinction*. Do not mix or confuse the kingdoms of the world and the kingdom of God. Perhaps one of the most helpful volumes in assessing our attitude and developing our responses to this issue is a very old one—*The City of God* by the theologian Augustine. Written at a time when the Roman Empire was collapsing, when many believers feared that the kingdom of God would collapse with it under the ravages of the barbarians, when many were confused about God's intentions and perhaps feared that the unshakeable was being shaken, Augustine's weighty work provides a corrective to such shortsightedness and a counterbalance to such fearfulness.

Augustine looks at the world from the perspective of the last day, recognizing that there are really only two peoples on the earth, citizens of two kingdoms or cities. One of those kingdoms is marked by supreme love to the Creator, and one by supreme love to the creation. These cities exist in stark antithesis to one another. Each has its own distinctive identity, activity, and destiny, although at present they coexist in one environment—those who worship and serve the creature rather than the Creator (Rom. 1:25) and those who worship and serve the Creator rather than the creature are side by side in this present age. Every person on the planet belongs to one city or the other. Each person bows to only one sovereign. You are either God's in Christ or of this present world, building your hopes and dreams here. The church cannot confuse her identity. We are the Creator's, and we do not wed ourselves to this present creation. The church is the city of God, and it is separate from the cities of men.

Here is the key point: though the citizens of the two kingdoms necessarily mingle as they make their way through this world, God's people cannot be finally identified with any nation, party, society, or institution in the earth. There is no such thing as a Christian nation, though there may be nations in which we find many Christians. There are no Christian governments, though there may be governments well seasoned with Christians. As we saw before, "this City has no home here in this world, but is on its way to its true home in the world to come."[3]

All this taken into account, it is vital that every one of us consider the issue of our allegiance. Where do you belong? To whom do you bow? Are you wedded to the creation, or waiting for the Creator? Where is your treasure, your home, your hope, your heart? Are you a resident here, with all your anchors dropped in this present world, or are you a pilgrim here, with your eyes fixed on the heavenly city? It is only when the Christian understands himself to be unequivocally and distinctively a citizen of heaven that he knows how to relate to the kingdoms of the earth.

In the church I serve there have been people from many different nationalities who have been in my country temporarily. If you ask them where they live, they know that they are in England. If you ask them where they belong, they know it is somewhere else. They know what it is to be resident aliens. Christians too recognize where they are and where they belong, and they do not blur the lines.

Once he knows who and whose he is and where he belongs, the Christian can then *recognize the appointment* of the earthly authorities by the God of heaven. He can both see it as true and respond to it in righteousness. God has appointed subordinate authorities in various spheres. He has appointed His regents in the home, the church, and the state. If we rebel there, we are rebelling not just against men but against the God who has put those men over us. Children would do well to remember this as they arrogantly react to their parents. Church members would do well to remember this as they contend or buck against the shepherds appointed for them. Citizens would

---

3. Haykin, "'Most Glorious City of God,'" 51.

do well to remember this as they carelessly and carnally complain about, ignore, or despise the civil authorities in their nations. This is not the same as saying that parents, pastors, and governments are infallible. Nevertheless, our underlying attitude toward them reveals something about our attitude to authority in general and—by virtue of the particular relation that underpins them—our attitude to God's authority in particular. Raise the fist against whom or what God sends, and you are raising the fist against God Himself.

With specific regard to governments and rulers, it is because our allegiance is ultimately to God and to His Christ that we submit to the authorities He has called into being and into whose hands He has put a measure of responsibility. This recognition conditions even the manner in which we express our ultimate allegiance when there is a conflict between our obedience to God and our submission to God's appointed authorities. Who can submit even while he disobeys without wisdom and grace from God? The examples of Daniel and his friends and later of the apostles and the early church demonstrate what this can and should look and sound like.

The fact that God has put these authorities in place governs how we should think about, speak of and to, and act toward civil magistrates. Often it will show itself in smaller things: in our driving habits, in our tax returns, in our patience with what seems like so much nonsensical bureaucracy. The fifth commandment has penetrating implications that must be embraced. We are to uphold and respect God's authorities.

Then we should *appreciate the protection*. Paul was not ashamed to appeal to Caesar when threatened with unjust judgments and unlawful imprisonment. He relied upon the protections afforded by the rule of law under Nero (Acts 25:11), the man who was becoming the great enemy of the Christian church. Even oppressive and persecuting governments may provide a measure of control against open sin, a measure of legitimate protection against lawlessness. I traveled some time ago to a country that had for many years lain behind the Iron Curtain. It was interesting to hear even younger people, including Christians, reminisce about the perceived benefits of the days of communism when their parents had work and homes, when they had little to eat but were thankful when it came, when they could play outside in safety until all hours of the night. They recognized the privations and oppressions that communism involved. They valued their newfound liberty, and in some cases had labored long and hard to obtain it. Many had waited years for such freedoms and suffered much in seeking them. But they also suggested that they could now buy everything and afford nothing, and that a materialistic spirit was increasingly evident in society. They found that the church too had lost something of its edge, its sense of community and its expressions of loving sacrifice in the face of difficulty and opposition. Neither were they nor am I offering some kind of apologetic for any form of totalitarianism with all its typical abuses and cruelties. Nevertheless, there was a tacit recognition that even this oppressive form of government, with all its evils, afforded them something valuable and appreciated. Despite the iniquities of totalitarianism, life under that system still offered a measure of protection in society at large, but also put an edge upon their sense of belonging to another kingdom. In a more developed liberal democracy, we ought to be properly thankful for the rule of law as it provides us with a measure of peace and stability and freedom, even if we might bemoan the spiritual flabbiness of the church under the circumstances.

There is an exegetical tradition that interprets the restraint of the man of sin—the man of lawlessness—in 2 Thessalonians 2:7 as the rule of law. The suggestion is that the man of sin himself will thrive in and arise out of an environment of undiluted and aggressive self-determination, unrestrained by strong and just government. Whether or not one accepts this interpretation, it at least underlines that we ought to be more thankful than perhaps we are for what we presently have. How many freedoms do we enjoy of which countless thousands past and present have been and are deprived? Many Christians ought to be slower to complain and quicker to express gratitude for the rulers and authorities over us.

This being so, we ought to *use the freedoms* we are presently afforded, wherever we might be. While we have the opportunity to live undisturbed and pursue our mission as the people of God, we ought to get on with the job. Many readers of this book still live in an environment of almost unprecedented civil liberty, and we ought to seize the day, pursuing open, frank, and full obedience to our Sovereign, carrying out our happy duty as the church of Christ in relative peace and safety. One of the tragedies is that we often use our freedoms not to labor but to relax and take our ease. We have scope to live righteously, to worship faithfully, and to preach truthfully. We should readily walk, worship, and witness as unashamed Christians while God provides us a safe environment in which to do so. We should pray that these blessings may long abide and labor as private citizens of our particular nations to preserve them.

We should remember that it is a relatively rare thing, historically and geographically, for believers to enjoy such freedoms as these. The kind of honor that has been afforded to Christian truth in much of the Western world in recent centuries is not the norm, and we might have come to assume too much. We are probably returning to the real historical norm of persecution, and we should be the more thankful for our relative freedoms while we have them, remembering those who do not as if we suffered with them (Heb. 13:3).

We must not forget to *pay the dues*. We must offer the civil authorities what is theirs by right of divine appointment, whether inwardly or outwardly. We do it because the civil magistrate bears the sword and because God has put it in his hands. This is not a call to pander to every whim of careless and thoughtless governments. It is not encouraging mindless quiescence of the most abject sort. It is not the suggestion that there is virtue in constituting yourself some craven holy doormat. It is the simple fact that—not just because of wrath but also because of conscience—we are to render to Caesar whatever belongs to Caesar. Whether it is a financial obligation (such as in the matter of taxes), a matter of legal recognition (obeying the laws of the land), or simply the expression of our outlook in speech and behavior, it ought to be clear from our attitudes and actions that we offer the civil authorities the support and the reverence to which they are entitled as those whom God has appointed.

We are also free to *address the government*. We must realize that it is not the task of the church to dictate policy nor to dabble in politics. That, again, is to confuse the spheres in which we operate: "Christ's kingdom is not of this world." The church is to declare the gospel to all, but she is also to make clear the duty of all to God, both as a prompt to true repentance and as a help to true obedience.

Gospel ministers have duties in several respects. First, God's servants are—as occasion provides—to preach to authorities concerning their duties as men and ministers of temporal justice, accountable to the God who has put them in their place. It is, of course, perfectly appropriate for a Christian pastor to make clear the responsibilities of governing authorities, but that is not the same as preaching to the authorities. There may be legitimate opportunities to do this. Some legislatures or executives invite the preaching of the word of God in some measure. Perhaps there are those in authority in a congregation, and to them the word of God must be addressed as part of the regular ministry, publicly and privately, in accordance with their calling in the world. It may be that a preacher, in his capacity as a private citizen as well as a preacher, might address his local or national representatives, if he has them. Perhaps if a Christian is dragged before authorities, he might take the opportunity to declare the truth of God. But all this is very different from railing at rulers from the pulpit or in the street when they are not present. For example, you might hear hotheaded pulpiteers or throaty street preachers attacking some local or national policy that they consider unchristian, tearing into the legislators or executive powers even though they are not present to hear. To whom are they preaching? Certainly not to the people in front of them. They are on their soapbox, aiming high and wide of the souls before them who—though they might applaud or deplore what they are hearing—are hardly involved in the matter. If there were representatives of the authority present, perhaps even then it is not mere official failure (in which the individual may or may not have a personal stake), but real, personal sin that ought to be the core concern.

Further, God's servants ought to instruct the church and her members—both as saints and as private citizens, as a matter of Christian witness and testimony—in their relations to the state in her specific roles. Preachers might also, publicly or privately, offer counsel and guidance in particular matters in which the saints as private and concerned citizens might speak. So, for example, there are issues with which the church as a church is not politically concerned. However, as a spiritual force for truth and righteousness, she might act for the good of those involved, and the members of the church might need particular instruction as to how they should engage. Think, to take one example, of the matter of abortion. Preachers might and should proclaim the sanctity of life and the crime of murder as it is appropriate. They might encourage and equip individual Christians to represent these truths. It would not be wrong for the church to draw attention to legitimate ways and means by which the feelings of believers might be communicated. A church might seek a particular opportunity to minister in various ways to women who face pressures to abort (perhaps because of social or economic demands) or who are wracked with guilt on account of their sin. A church might encourage Christians to consider adoption as a means of caring for unwanted children. But should the church be spearheading and organizing political campaigns, with pastors lobbying politicians and influencers on behalf of their congregations? I fear that this might distract from the work that the Lord has primarily given them to do.

We have already noted that in Acts 4 there may have been present Christian men and women who might have had some, even significant, opportunities to serve Christ in the world at large. As a church, though, they prayed. I am not suggesting that they returned to their homes and their employments, suspended their Christian convictions, and watched blithely or participated readily as the church was put under the hammer of persecution or as natural law was flouted and tramped upon. But there is a difference between how they acted as a church and how they might have acted as private individuals. We can and should discharge our responsibilities as Christians who have been placed in a particular time and place, living in certain nation-states by God's appointment. We can write and speak and visit and engage with those who are in authority, but this is not the business of the church as a church. We must, then, both recognize the boundaries and discern the overlaps—those points at which our Christianity has a necessary impact on the way we relate to governments and authorities on particular issues.

I do not offer these counsels lightly. Every child of God, every church, must sincerely seek to discern—in the light of God's written truth—where such boundaries lie. We need to work out where responsibilities as the citizens of heaven's kingdom and members of earth's societies touch and overlap.

With all this in mind, we must *manage the expectations*. Those who rule on the earth do not have the answers; they are not our saviors. There seems to be a constant temptation for the people of God to believe that if only we can marshal enough rich and important people, if only we can obtain enough celebrity endorsements, if only we can generate a big enough wave of public opinion, then we can help the church out of its troubles. But such men and women, however well meaning, cannot sustain or prosper the church in the world. Again, it is to look for apples on an orange tree.

Earthly authorities and celebrities are not the answer to the needs and pursuits of the church, any more than the world is its home and destiny. There are certain things that we can and should expect of civil governments, and there may be certain times when the church, through appropriate spokespeople given appropriate opportunities, might remind government of its obligations to God. But human authority and power are not the solution to the church's problems. The kingdom of God is not yoked to any nation, party, policy, platform, coalition, or organization and will not rise or fall with any kingdom of the earth:

> Through the rise and fall of nations
> One sure faith yet standeth fast:
> God abides, His Word unchanging,
> God alone the first and last.[4]

Or, singing of the providence of God:

> The kingdoms of this world
> Lie in its hand;
> See how they rise or fall
> At its command!
> Through sorrow and distress,
> Tempestuous storms that rage,
> God's kingdom yet endures
> From age to age.[5]

As we wrestle with these things, we need to remember that God does know what He is doing. Even those things that men mean for evil He has intended for good. Kings and kingdoms rise and fall by His divine and all-wise appointment. Even the individual activities of rulers are not outside his control:

> The king's heart is in the hand of the LORD,
> Like the rivers of water;
> He turns it wherever He wishes. (Prov. 21:1)

---

4. George Wallis Briggs, "God Hath Spoken by His Prophets."
5. David Charles, "Great Providence of Heaven," trans. Edmund Tudor Owen.

We may look at some of those who have risen to prominence or power, who have abused that platform horribly, and wonder how this can be securing the glory of God or the good of men. Often the answer will simply be that we do not know, and we may never know. Perhaps heaven itself will not make plain the answers to all the questions we may now have.

But we must bow before God. Our hopes for the kingdom of Christ—whether the advance of the gospel or the health of the church itself—hang upon the divine King and not upon mortal men. Ultimately, we are waiting upon Him and waiting for Him.

That being the case, we should *approach the throne.* Prayer ought to be our first port of call as the church—whether institutionally or individually—in dealing with the civil magistrates. We should pray and give thanks for the rulers and authorities themselves, seeking "that we may lead a quiet and peaceable life in all godliness and reverence" (1 Tim. 2:2), able to live as saints without unnecessary difficulties or distractions. We should pray to God for His appointments, that His glory and our peace might be secured. We should pray concerning the Lord's kingdom, that all God's purposes would be accomplished for the ingathering of the elect and the building of His church. We should pray for the equipping of the church in all her circumstances, whether at peace or persecuted, not looking to worldly powers nor relying upon worldly means to accomplish kingdom ends. We should pray that the Lord would fill us with His Spirit and give us bold speech, enabling the saints to be witnesses for Christ in every circumstance that we face, not looking to or relying upon worldly means (Acts 4:8, 31). We do not trust in legislation, adjudication, or intimidation to obtain the things we desire for the glory of God and the good of men, but on the proclamation of the truth as it is in Jesus with power from on high. To that end we should remember who is on the throne and call upon Him. We pray,

> "Your kingdom come.
> Your will be done
> On earth as it is in heaven." (Matt. 6:10)

We remember that there is One who sits enthroned above the earth, and He is our God and our King.

8

RELIEVE THE SUFFERING

It may be that for many readers of this volume, the very idea of a social gospel is anathema, a well-known spiritual bogeyman. It may be synonymous with the idea of bodily concerns swamping spiritual ones and a concern for temporal well-being that gradually leads to the neglect of the eternal. It conjures up the specter of a concentration on the tent of the present body without regard for its undying inhabitant. But there is a danger of overreaction. The notion of a social gospel may trouble us so deeply that we have allowed ourselves to neglect some of our wider responsibilities as pilgrims in this world. Could it be—perhaps as a reaction to this perceived and even real deficiency—that this is one of the reasons why many evangelicals today, especially those who are younger, are focusing on social justice as one of the great and pressing concerns of the church in the modern world? *Social justice* is undoubtedly a slippery phrase. It is as hard to define as it is to argue against. It sounds so positive, so worthy, so…right! Who would wish to say that they are against social justice? And yet you seek for substantive forms and concrete classifications, and the thing so often remains nebulous. In their helpful book dealing with this topic at some length, Kevin DeYoung and Greg Gilbert point out that the popular conception of the term points to "something ambiguously connected with poverty and oppression."[1] They go on to make a plea for a more intelligent and nuanced employment of the phrase.

However, there is in some circles a persistent drive to put mercy ministries and care for the poor not just back on the agenda

---

1. Kevin DeYoung and Greg Gilbert, *What Is the Mission of the Church? Making Sense of Social Justice, Shalom, and the Great Commission* (Wheaton, Ill.: Crossway, 2011), 179.

of God's people, but even front and center. Many go too far in this opposite direction and make the mission of the church to consist of these things, speaking and acting as if Christ's kingdom can be established in the world by these means. This is not always the intention—far from it—but you might reach the conclusion that by means of a program of practical endeavor accomplishing social or political transformation, we might be able to achieve heaven on earth, or at least make some headway in a Christianized version of the campaign to make poverty—or any other number of social ills—history, as the catchy slogan has it.

There should, of course, be no denying that the Lord God delights in justice and mercy. We read our Bibles and see these attributes shining in the principles and practices of the saints of those days. There should be no doubt that Christians, seeking godliness in all things, ought to be champions of equity[2] and charity. Historically, true Christians have been at the forefront of genuinely philanthropic concern. True saints have often been renowned for—even mocked for—their selfless and countercultural care for the poor and needy. One can go back to the early church, in which believers would go out at night to find and rescue unwanted infants abandoned in the streets in order to remove the burden of care from parents who did not want them, a burden gladly and sacrificially assumed by the selfless saints. The church was distinguished in the world by deeds like this. Such a spirit can be traced easily through the ages. However, I would suggest that many in the modern church, perhaps in certain circles, have lost sight of this. Determined to keep the gospel of salvation as the main thing, we have perhaps allowed ourselves to lose sight of or lose hold of those things that ought invariably to accompany the gospel of Christ. Those who have made this mistake need to regain this element of the pilgrim life, putting it in its proper place and scriptural proportion.

Relieve the Suffering: Scriptural Framework

Let Your Light Shine

> "Let your light so shine before men, that they may see your good works and glorify your Father in heaven." (Matt. 5:16)

---

2. Please note that I use the word *equity*—justice and righteousness—rather than *equality*.

In the Sermon on the Mount, Christ is explaining and enforcing what it means to belong to the kingdom of God. Though the saints are persecuted for the sake of righteousness, they must not withdraw from the world, becoming isolated from it and ignorant of it. Rather, Christians must remain engaged with the world as God's chosen people, their lives and works a testimony to the reality of God's salvation. Even when despised by the world—perhaps especially when so treated—we cannot afford to muffle our testimony before men. We must not forget that the greatest good we can do to any person is to make Christ known to him as Savior, but that is not the only good we can do. With regard to a life that exudes the savor of Christ, neither a skewed sense of modesty nor a cowardly appetite for self-preservation should make us slink into retirement— hiding our light under a bushel. Rather, we are to live distinctively and unashamedly as followers of the risen Christ, and so to season and illuminate the world.

Christ calls His people to live so that the light shines. This light should be seen by men, the good works of the saints—their "practical acts of kindness and neighborly love,"[3] their Christlike labors of duty and charity and devotion to God—evident before all. In this way the light can be traced back to its ultimate source, men being obliged to acknowledge that the only foundation of such a life must be in a divine operation upon the soul. Our works of piety, equity, and charity declare to the world that the only possibility behind their exercise is that there is a saving God in heaven who has changed our hearts and altered our dispositions in such a way as to make us distinct from the world at this point. There is a literal sense to Christ's solemn assurance, "For I say to you, that unless your righteousness exceeds the righteousness of the scribes and Pharisees, you will by no means enter the kingdom of heaven" (Matt. 5:20). Where are our holiness, righteousness, and love?

We have already, in a slightly different context, seen Peter make essentially the same point: "Beloved, I beg you as sojourners and pilgrims, abstain from fleshly lusts which war against the soul, having your conduct honorable among the Gentiles, that when they speak against you as evildoers, they may, by your good works which they

---

3. Doriani, *Matthew*, 1:136.

observe, glorify God in the day of visitation" (1 Peter 2:11–12). If we are a God-honoring people, then our good works will oblige those who are not converted to acknowledge the existence and activity of the God who is saving us. What are these good works? Spurgeon answers:

> Upright actions, honest dealings, sincere behaviour. When a man is scrupulously true, and sternly faithful, all rightminded persons admit that his works are good works. Good works are works of love, unselfish works, works done for the benefit of others and the glory of God. Deeds of charity, kindness, and brotherly love are good works. As also careful attendance to duty, and all service honestly done, together with all courses which promote the moral and spiritual good of our fellow-men. Works of devotion in which you prove that you love God and his Christ, that you love the gospel, that you desire to spread the kingdom of Christ.[4]

This is clearly not the self-centered performance of Matthew 6:1–4, in which charitable deeds are done to be seen and rewarded by men: "When you do a charitable deed, do not sound a trumpet before you as the hypocrites do in the synagogues and in the streets, that they may have glory from men. Assuredly, I say to you, they have their reward." Rather, this is the selfless and God-centered life of a godly man with no desire to draw attention to himself and no time or energy to do so even if he wished it. Nevertheless, a genuinely and consistently gracious life inevitably makes light to shine into the surrounding darkness. It is unavoidably visible to those all about. Those who are truly doing good are not doing it to be applauded and do not have the time or energy to waste on seeking that applause. They are doing it because it needs to be done and they are there to do it. Such deeds will eventually shine out into the darkness to the praise of God's glory. Even those who do not know that such a Christian is doing good may still benefit from and enjoy the good being done. Believers are a community of "do-gooders" in the best and highest sense, and they are pursuing that character for the exaltation of their Lord.

---

4. Charles H. Spurgeon, "The Candle," in *Metropolitan Tabernacle Pulpit* (London: Passmore & Alabaster, 1881), 27:226.

Do Good

> "God anointed Jesus of Nazareth with the Holy Spirit and with power, [and He] went about doing good and healing all who were oppressed by the devil, for God was with Him." (Acts 10:38)

In the context, Peter is demonstrating the heavenly character and mission of Jesus as Messiah, providing us with a miniature portrait of His glory as God's Anointed One. His works demonstrate His holy character and His heavenly mission, proving His identity. Yet we must recognize in reading this rich description that we are not looking at someone grudgingly carrying out a task in his official capacity, divorced from his personal concern and investment. Being the Messiah is not a professional role, but a divine calling in which the personal qualities of the Christ shine out in His works. His power and His person, as well as His honor and His heart are evident in what He does. That is why in Isaiah 49:6, for example, we are reminded that the Servant is Himself God's salvation to the ends of the earth—He does not just accomplish it or bring it, He *is* it.

What we see here is the expression of a heart governed by heavenly mercy. How often do we read of our Lord Jesus being "moved with compassion," His heart wrung with pity and His stomach churning over the physical and spiritual plight of men and women and children subject to sin and burdened by its effects? The incarnate God is revealing His concern for those who are in need, showing us the kind of person He is. Our Lord lived among and labored among and loved people. As He "went about"—as He passed through the world and as He went among the people—He was marked by acts of mercy and demonstrations of goodness. Kindnesses shone out of Him. Peter highlights the work almost universally appreciated by others and acknowledged as representative of His engagement with those around Him. Christ did good. Matthew Henry writes:

> They knew what a benefactor he was to that nation, both to the souls and the bodies of men; how he made it his business to do good to all, and never did hurt to any. He was not idle, but still doing; not selfish, but doing good; did not confine himself to one place, nor wait till people came to him to seek his help, but went to them, went about from place to place, and wherever he came he was doing good. Hereby he showed *that he was sent of*

God, who is good and does good; and does good because he is good: and who hereby *left not himself without witness* to the world, *in that he did good*, ch. 14:17. And in this he hath set us an example of indefatigable industry in serving God and our generation; for we came into the world that we might do all the good we can in it; and therein, like Christ, we must always abide and abound.[5]

We are not Messiah, or even little messiahs, in any saving sense. Nevertheless, we are called to imitate those who imitate Christ, and how can imitating Christ—whose reputation was of being a do-gooder in the sweetest sense—not involve works of mercy? How far do we—how far do you—imitate Christ in this "indefatigable industry in serving God and our generation"?

Sowing and Reaping

And let us not grow weary while doing good, for in due season we shall reap if we do not lose heart. Therefore, as we have opportunity, let us do good to all, especially to those who are of the household of faith. (Gal. 6:9–10)

But as for you, brethren, do not grow weary in doing good. (2 Thess. 3:13)

Paul exhorts the members of the churches in Galatia and the church in Thessalonica not to become faint and weary in well-doing. He reminds us that these labors are a sowing carried out with an eye to the day of reaping. The prospect of a reward, with all the incentives that carries with it, is too often overlooked today. We are not saying that we are saved because of our good works. However, having been saved, we always ought to do good works. It is the outflow of our redemption, and there is a blessing for it, as John Brown explains:

The Christian shall be rewarded for his well-doing. Every act of Christian duty, every sacrifice made, every privation submitted to, every suffering endured, from a regard to Christ's authority, with a view to Christ's honour, shall assuredly be recompensed. This reward is often—usually—granted in part, even in the present state, and shall be most certainly conferred in the future. This reward shall grow out of, and correspond to,

---

5. Henry, *Commentary*, 6:108.

the dutiful exertions of the Christian. It shall be his harvest. The happiness of a Christian, both in this world and the next, is, in a great measure, the natural result of his conformity to the will of God. Every holy temper is a capacity of enjoyment, and a source of enjoyment at the same time.[6]

Here is an *opportunity noted*. Time is short! The harvest is coming! Get sowing! Paul exhorts his readers to use the time that they have to accomplish what work they can in light of the coming day. You might, under normal circumstances, have decades left to serve God and men, but who knows whether or not you might have only years, months, or even days to store up for eternity? Paul also points out the *labor pursued*. Saints are to be doing good in all its complex variety, both giving whatever is someone's rightful due and meeting whatever is someone's legitimate need, doing acts of justice and of mercy in their proper spheres,[7] operating in every realm: "Whatever its immediate form, whether kindness, or beneficence, or mercy, whether temporal or spiritual in character, it is still good in its nature, and is 'the good thing,' adapting itself to each case as it may turn up, in reference to all, generally or more specially."[8] Whatever is good in these instances is defined by the matter in hand in accordance with the divine character and law and ought to be apparent in every Christlike person. Philip Ryken suggests that it means "meeting people's needs by performing the six acts of charity: feeding the hungry, giving drink to the thirsty, showing hospitality to strangers, clothing the naked, caring for the sick, and visiting prisoners (Matt. 25:34–36)."[9]

Then we have the *sphere described*. We are to do good to all. A love of mankind in the broadest and most general sense ought to galvanize the saints. At the same time, there is a *focus prescribed* because the family of God, the fraternity of the righteous, has the first and highest claim on us: "If a *brother or sister* is naked and destitute of daily food, and one of you says to them, 'Depart in peace, be warmed and filled,' but you do not give them the things which are needed for

---

6. John Brown, *Galatians* (Edinburgh: Banner of Truth, 2001), 344.

7. Brown, *Galatians*, 349.

8. John Eadie, *A Commentary on the Greek Text of Paul's Letter to the Galatians* (Birmingham, Ala.: Solid Ground Christian Books, 2005), 452.

9. Philip Ryken, *Galatians* (Phillipsburg, N.J.: P&R, 2005), 266.

the body, what does it profit? Thus also faith by itself, if it does not have works, is dead" (James 2:15–17, emphasis added). Again, Brown drives home the point:

> Christians, therefore, are particularly bound to do good to one another. Every poor and distressed man has a claim on me for pity, and, if I can afford it, for active exertion and pecuniary relief. But a poor Christian has a far stronger claim on my feelings, my labours, and my property. He is my brother, equally interested with myself in the blood and love of the Redeemer. I expect to spend an eternity with him in heaven. He is the representative of my unseen Saviour, and he considers everything done to his poor afflicted brother as done to himself. For a Christian to be unkind to a Christian, is not only wrong, it is monstrous.[10]

Christians doing good to one another is righteousness. It is a practical demonstration of the ties of Christ's blood. Such acts are the proper and natural expression of the family bond among the people of God, who have the first and most legitimate claim on the love of other family members. Here we are working out the command given that we should love one another and in doing so prove to whose household we belong and the character of that household (John 13:34–35 and Rom. 12:10, not to mention the other "one another" commands). Charity does begin at home, though it should not end there.

Offering the Heart

> He has shown you, O man, what is good;
> And what does the LORD require of you
> But to do justly,
> To love mercy,
> And to walk humbly with your God? (Mic. 6.8)

In this passage, the Lord has been calling His people back to Himself. They have been responding defensively, even aggressively, complaining that God Almighty is being demanding and unreasonable. Their response is essentially a half-serious, half-sarcastic display of corruption. They think that they can buy God off, suggesting a series of increasingly extravagant sacrificial gestures:

---

10. Brown, *Galatians*, 348.

With what shall I come before the LORD,
And bow myself before the High God?
Shall I come before Him with burnt offerings,
With calves a year old?
Will the LORD be pleased with thousands of rams,
Ten thousand rivers of oil?
Shall I give my firstborn for my transgression,
The fruit of my body for the sin of my soul? (Mic. 6:6–7)

God's response—echoing other passages in which it is made clear that outward sacrifice is no substitute for inward obedience—is that these people are offering everything but themselves, everything but their hearts. God is not interested in our stuff for Him to be blessed but in our souls that we might receive a blessing. Those who truly turn to Him will then live life for Him, embracing a pattern of godliness that Dale Ralph Davis describes as clear, simple, social, and relevant.[11] It consists essentially in imitation of God and relation to God, reflecting the two tables of God's moral law. The people of God must *do justly*, a command that comes to us in the context of Micah as a whole. In those days, as in our own, people who turned their backs upon God began to despise and abuse those made in His image. A lack of regard for the Creator always becomes a disregard for the creation. So Micah records a litany of injustice, cruelty, and oppression. Wicked men "devise iniquity, and work out evil on their beds." Once they have concocted their cruel schemes, they rise in the morning to carry them out. Their covetousness leads to violent aggression and cruel oppression. There is no regard for the weak and the needy (Mic. 2:1–2, 8–9). The prophet goes on to emphasize in graphic language the injustice of the rulers:

"Hear now, O heads of Jacob,
And you rulers of the house of Israel:
Is it not for you to know justice?
You who hate good and love evil;
Who strip the skin from My people,
And the flesh from their bones;
Who also eat the flesh of My people,
Flay their skin from them,

---

11. Dale Ralph Davis, *Micah* (Darlington, U.K.: Evangelical Press, 2010), 127–28.

> Break their bones,
> And chop them in pieces
> Like meat for the pot,
> Like flesh in the caldron." (Mic. 3:1–3)

These are the men who "abhor justice and pervert all equity," whose empire is built on bloodshed and iniquity, who are motivated by greed in all their works. All the while they claim, if not quite divine sanction, then at least divine protection (Mic. 3:9–11). In such a context, the sons of light are those who live by God's righteous standards and eschew all oppression and deceit, in accordance with God's character:

> He is the Rock, His work is perfect;
> For all His ways are justice,
> A God of truth and without injustice;
> Righteous and upright is He. (Deut. 32:4)

Those who walk in God's ways provide for the needy, protect rather than oppress the vulnerable, and give to all their proper due rather than deceiving in order to store up for themselves.

Furthermore, God's true worshipers *love mercy*. They have a willing delight in grace and compassion, going beyond the strict requirements of justice alone and showing the heart attitude that lies behind the actions. Again, their model is the Lord Himself: "The LORD, the LORD God, merciful and gracious, longsuffering, and abounding in goodness and truth" (Ex. 34:6). Or, as Micah himself declares Him to be:

> Who is a God like You,
> Pardoning iniquity
> And passing over the transgression of the remnant
>   of His heritage?

> He does not retain His anger forever,
> Because He delights in mercy.
> He will again have compassion on us,
> And will subdue our iniquities.

> You will cast all our sins
> Into the depths of the sea. (Mic. 7:18–19)

Again, true worshipers *walk humbly*: "With the humble is wisdom" (Prov. 11:2). This is a way of life characterized by reverence toward and dependence on the Lord God. It means to treat this gracious Sovereign as an honored and sustaining companion rather than a kind of divine rescue squad whose appearance and attentions are demanded whenever the need is imagined or felt.

Micah is giving us the heart of the law: "'You shall love the LORD your God with all your heart, with all your soul, and with all your mind.' This is the first and great commandment. And the second is like it: 'You shall love your neighbor as yourself.' On these two commandments hang all the Law and the Prophets" (Matt. 22:37–40).

A Life of Holiness

> For the grace of God that brings salvation has appeared to all men, teaching us that, denying ungodliness and worldly lusts, we should live soberly, righteously, and godly in the present age, looking for the blessed hope and glorious appearing of our great God and Savior Jesus Christ, who gave Himself for us, that He might redeem us from every lawless deed and purify for Himself His own special people, zealous for good works. (Titus 2:11–14)

Where there has been a gracious saving, a holy living and an eager looking will always follow. Christ has redeemed His people from lawlessness springing out of a carnal heart to lawfulness rising up from a renewed heart. His design was to purify for Himself His own special people, and their identity will be revealed in part because they are invariably zealous for good works. What are these good works? They certainly include those mentioned earlier by Paul, the stark evidence in a godless world of men and women living for God:

> But as for you, speak the things which are proper for sound doctrine: that the older men be sober, reverent, temperate, sound in faith, in love, in patience; the older women likewise, that they be reverent in behavior, not slanderers, not given to much wine, teachers of good things—that they admonish the young women to love their husbands, to love their children, to be discreet, chaste, homemakers, good, obedient to their own husbands, that the word of God may not be blasphemed. Likewise, exhort the young men to be sober-minded, in all things showing yourself to

be a pattern of good works; in doctrine showing integrity, reverence, incorruptibility, sound speech that cannot be condemned, that one who is an opponent may be ashamed, having nothing evil to say of you. Exhort bondservants to be obedient to their own masters, to be well pleasing in all things, not answering back, not pilfering, but showing all good fidelity, that they may adorn the doctrine of God our Savior in all things. (Titus 2:1–10)

Moreover, Matthew Poole makes clear that the saints are to be "studious to do, and warmly pursuing, *all such* works as are acceptable to God, and profitable to ourselves and others":[12]

Each one's work will become clear; for the Day will declare it, because it will be revealed by fire; and the fire will test each one's work, of what sort it is. If anyone's work which he has built on it endures, he will receive a reward. (1 Cor. 3:13–14)

And God is able to make all grace abound toward you, that you, always having all sufficiency in all things, may have an abundance for every good work. (2 Cor. 9:8)

For we are His workmanship, created in Christ Jesus for good works, which God prepared beforehand that we should walk in them. (Eph. 2:10)

For this reason we also, since the day we heard it, do not cease to pray for you, and to ask that you may be filled with the knowledge of His will in all wisdom and spiritual understanding; that you may walk worthy of the Lord, fully pleasing Him, being fruitful in every good work and increasing in the knowledge of God. (Col. 1:9–10)

Now may our Lord Jesus Christ Himself, and our God and Father, who has loved us and given us everlasting consolation and good hope by grace, comfort your hearts and establish you in every good word and work. (2 Thess. 2:16–17)

Good works are a distinctive mark of true saints, who are eager to be a means of blessing to others. Matthew Henry offers a summary: "Let us see then that we do good, and have zeal in it; only looking

---

12. Matthew Poole, *A Commentary on the Holy Bible* (Edinburgh: Banner of Truth, 1963), 3:803 (emphasis added).

that zeal be guided by knowledge and spirited with love, directed to the glory of God, and always in some good thing. And thus of the motive to the duties directed, from the end of Christ's death."[13]

Proactive Kindness

> Do not withhold good from those to whom it is due,
> When it is in the power of your hand to do so.
> Do not say to your neighbor,
> "Go, and come back,
> And tomorrow I will give it,"
> When you have it with you. (Prov. 3:27–28)

James makes a similar point when he informs us that "to him who knows to do good and does not do it, to him it is sin" (James 4:17). Note those to whom this proverb is written. It is not offering the poor a right to demand relief, but it does impose upon the rich an obligation to offer it, and the giving is not restricted to the material. Charles Bridges writes, "Every one has a claim upon our love. Every opportunity of doing good is our call to do so.... Kindness is therefore a matter, not of option, but of obligation; an act of justice no less than of mercy."[14] This sounds and truly is sweet until it starts to bite upon our conscience and our time, energies, and wallets. Our kindnesses are not to be measured out in accordance with the deserving lives of those who receive, but ought to be a reflection of the loving hearts of those who give.

The principle enshrined here once more goes well beyond the mere avoiding of harm. It requires of us active justice and mercy and militates against complacency, carelessness, procrastination, and selfishness. It requires that we do as much good as we are able as quickly, kindly, and fully as we are able to those in need—all possible good of all possible sorts to all possible people in all possible circumstances at all possible times. William Arnot advises us to "keep as few good intentions hovering about as possible. They are like ghosts haunting a dwelling. The way to lay them is to find bodies for them. When they are embodied in substantial deeds they are

---

13. Henry, *Commentary*, 6:700.
14. Charles Bridges, *Proverbs* (Edinburgh: Banner of Truth, 1968), 38.

no longer dangerous."[15] We should speak words that do good and pursue deeds that secure good. Christ's people seek actively to be a blessing and—without the neglect of plain duties already assigned— take every legitimate opportunity to accomplish good.

Show Mercy

> Pure and undefiled religion before God and the Father is this: to visit orphans and widows in their trouble, and to keep oneself unspotted from the world. (James 1:27)

James is not telling us that this is all that pure and undefiled religion is, but he does make plain that this is one indispensable mark of such religion. He is opposing the hypocrites whose profession of faith reaches no further than their mouths. James tells us *what* the true believer does—he visits. This is shorthand for all the duties of Christian love. It involves considering the needs of certain ones, attending upon them, and seeking to relieve them. And *whom* does he visit? Orphans and widows, not exclusively but representatively of those who are particularly vulnerable or defenseless, poor and exposed, easily neglected and oppressed—those about whom the Lord is concerned and for whom He has a particular regard, those to whom the saints show mercy as those who have themselves received mercy:

> "You shall not afflict any widow or fatherless child." (Ex. 22:22)

> For the LORD your God is God of gods and Lord of lords, the great God, mighty and awesome, who shows no partiality nor takes a bribe. He administers justice for the fatherless and the widow, and loves the stranger, giving him food and clothing. Therefore love the stranger, for you were strangers in the land of Egypt. (Deut. 10:17–19)

> A father of the fatherless, a defender of widows, is God in His holy habitation. (Ps. 68:5)

> The LORD watches over the strangers;
> He relieves the fatherless and widow;

---

15. William Arnot, *Studies in Proverbs: Laws from Heaven for Life on Earth* (Grand Rapids: Kregel, 1978), 115.

But the way of the wicked He turns upside down. (Ps. 146:9)

"Put away the evil of your doings from before My eyes.
Cease to do evil,
Learn to do good;
Seek justice,
Rebuke the oppressor;
Defend the fatherless,
Plead for the widow." (Isa. 1:16–17)

Matthew Henry would have us understand that "visiting is here put for all manner of relief which we are capable of giving to others; and fatherless and widows are here particularly mentioned, because they are generally m st apt to be neglected or oppressed: but by them we are to understand all who are proper objects of charity, all who are in affliction."[16]

And *when* does the godly man visit? "In their trouble." In the time of their affliction, when they are in their greatest need. I am not denying that rich widows and richly endowed orphans need comfort and should not be neglected, but they are not exposed to dangers as others are. This is not a call to an easy courtesy but to a necessary charity, a genuine giving: "Do not forget to do good and to share, for with such sacrifices God is well pleased" (Heb. 13:16).

It may be worth noting in passing that James does not make kindness to displace holiness at this point. These are not contrasting options, but complementary graces. Mercy and righteousness are not offset. They belong together in any and every demonstration of true religion.

Relieve the Suffering: Summary Thoughts

A merely social gospel we do and must abominate. Any system that relegates or evacuates the declaration of redemptive truth in Christ to men and women dead in their sins from the core of the Christian calling is misguided and dangerous and ought to be resisted. If we elevate time over eternity, establish the body and disregard the soul, then we are being faithless to God and cruel to our fellow possessors of immortal souls. However, we should not let this conviction betray

---

16. Henry, *Commentary*, 6:786.

us into forgetting our duties of mercy and justice. The redeemed must recognize that lasting social change should and must occur—indeed, only will occur—if and when the gospel of Christ permeates a society. That begins with us.

A godly man loves his neighbor and shows mercy. Christ was not joking when He made the application of the parable of the good Samaritan: "Go and do likewise" (Luke 10:37). The godly man has compassion on the whole person of his neighbor, his soul above all, but not his soul alone. Our Father in heaven "makes His sun rise on the evil and on the good, and sends rain on the just and on the unjust" (Matt. 5:45)—there is in God an indiscriminate mercy. It cannot be put in the same category as His saving mercy, but the Lord does good in abundant measure to His creatures, giving to all life and breath and all things (Acts 17:25). God in the flesh went about doing good, and we should go and do likewise, pursuing what is both right and kind in accordance with our callings and capacities, with regard to the souls and bodies of all those around us, to the glory of our God and Savior. If we claim holy principles but they are never joined with loving practices, James tells us that we are lying to ourselves about our faith.

True religion embraces practical mercies as well as pure principles. If we are willing to perform the greatest of all goods by pointing suffering people to Christ as Savior, ought we not to be willing to perform all lesser goods besides? Relief of physical suffering and meeting of physical needs in this world is not the essence of the gospel, but it is an inevitable corollary of the gospel. Inequalities are unavoidable and ineradicable in this life, but they do give an opportunity for the saints to show their character: "The poor you have with you always" (John 12:8). If we wish to restrict our ideas of heaven simply to those of equity and charity, there is no heaven on this earth. (And who would deny that heaven is abundantly more than that, though it surely includes it?)

To our shame, the world and false religion sometimes seem to have not quite a monopoly, but at the very least a head start on works of mercy. Too readily Christians have allowed this to happen and even appreciated and depended on it. Philanthropic labors initiated and for a time sustained by the followers of Christ have been taken on by the secular state. Charitable organizations have sometimes lost sight of their Christian origins, and with them the Christian sense of charity. The church has been in many instances displaced. I am not denying, deriding, or wishing to dismiss the common-grace labors and investments of unconverted men and women, but it simply ought not to be that the world should outlove the church either in scope or degree. We must do good to all men, loving even our enemies. At the same time, we must never permit our love to allow us to become a sort of glorified subsidiary of social services. Whatever else we give—and we must give readily and cheerfully and graciously—we must give the gospel. We are God's people and must remain distinctively so, and both our lips and our lives must reflect our God and His Christ, thereby expressing the holy gospel we profess.

Relieve the Suffering: Specific Counsels

How, then, do we strike a biblical balance in all this? How do we define and pursue our duties in this respect?

First, we must *train the heart*. We can do this only by gazing much and intently upon God in Christ. Here we see justice and mercy, righteousness and truth. This is the only real and lasting antidote to carelessness, bitterness, and weariness in doing good to all. We must "consider Him who endured such hostility from sinners against Himself, lest you become weary and discouraged in your souls" (Heb. 12:3). Always we are pointed back to how God acts, to what Christ did and does.

Paul was never ashamed to go back to the example of God in Christ, the heart of the Most High revealed, and to press Him into the conscience of the saints, to make us feel the weight of His perfect example. Think, for example, of the sustained reasoning of 2 Corinthians 8 and 9, where the apostle reminds us that "you know the grace of our Lord Jesus Christ, that though He was rich, yet for your sakes He became poor, that you through His poverty might become rich" (2 Cor. 8:9). Pushing on, Paul concludes,

> So let each one give as he purposes in his heart, not grudgingly or of necessity; for God loves a cheerful giver. And God is able to make all grace abound toward you, that you, always having all sufficiency in all things, may have an abundance for every good work. As it is written:
> "He has dispersed abroad,

> He has given to the poor;
> His righteousness endures forever."
> Now may He who supplies seed to the sower, and bread for food,
> supply and multiply the seed you have sown and increase the
> fruits of your righteousness, while you are enriched in every-
> thing for all liberality, which causes thanksgiving through us to
> God. (2 Cor. 9:7–11)

He closes that section with a heart-lifting, heart-compelling cry:
"Thanks be to God for His indescribable gift!" (2 Cor. 9:15).

Those who have received most ought to be most generous toward
others. Our hearts need to be formed by God's dealings with us in
Christ. When we understand how God has dealt with us justly and
mercifully, then we will make much of justice and mercy in our dealings with others. Only a godlike heart and a Christlike spirit will see
the doing of good as a priority. It is in the holy light of mercy received
that we feel the holy demand for mercy bestowed. This cannot be a
matter of mere deserving, for that is not the way that the Lord has
dealt with us—equity must be joined with charity:

> But I say to you, love your enemies, bless those who curse you,
> do good to those who hate you, and pray for those who spite-
> fully use you and persecute you, that you may be sons of your
> Father in heaven; for He makes His sun rise on the evil and on
> the good, and sends rain on the just and on the unjust. For if you
> love those who love you, what reward have you? Do not even
> the tax collectors do the same? And if you greet your brethren
> only, what do you do more than others? Do not even the tax col-
> lectors do so? Therefore you shall be perfect, just as your Father
> in heaven is perfect. (Matt. 5:44–48)

Furthermore, we must *cultivate the empathy* required for this
work. Again, every Christian is in possession of something he has
received without his deserving the least part of it—indeed, all of us
deserve the very opposite of all the good we have received: "For who
makes you differ from another? And what do you have that you did
not receive?" (1 Cor. 4:7). All of us know need in some measure. Some
of us have tasted greater measures of deprivation and poverty than
others, both in the spiritual and other spheres. All of us who are
Christians have experienced profound poverty of soul. We ought to

know and remember its pains and pressures. This in itself should prevent so-called compassion fatigue, in which we grow weary of being presented with fresh needs. It ought also to prevent the kind of crass comparisons that we use to avoid and evade our responsibilities in this regard. It is, perhaps, relatively easy to look around our privileged society and make the judgment that no one is really poor and needy or that others can and should be helping them. Indeed, in an absolute and material sense, there may be an element of truth in that. At the same time, we need to take account of the relative poverty and need. Someone does not need to be absolutely poor to be considered genuinely poorer, to be entirely destitute before he is needy. Remember, "do not withhold good from those to whom it is due, when it is in the power of your hand to do so" (Prov. 3:27). A Christlike Christian will have a warm heart and an open hand ready to meet genuine needs of all sorts as the opportunities arise.

So if we are to pursue this, we must *identify the needy*. There are plenty around who are both lazy and demanding and who may seek to pull the wool over Christians' eyes. However, the call to relieve the needy is not a freeloader's charter. Such individuals may need help of some alternative kind, taking into account that while there is sin in such an attitude, that sin has often been nurtured and encouraged by example and instruction. Our pity in such cases may be toward ignorance and impotence. However, we should not simply respond by making such men and women the objects of thoughtless, unneeded, and often wasted material care: "If anyone will not work, neither shall he eat" (2 Thess. 3:10). If a man or woman can work, he or she should work and so support himself and others. Needy people may require being taught to work and helped to work, but that ought to be the goal. Our eyes should, though, be open for the genuinely needy, remembering that we need the empathy that responds to real issues and understanding that there are kinds of poverty and need that cannot be measured on a financial scale. There are many with a material surplus who may be relationally and emotionally bereft, who may be desperately lonely or shorn of affection. There are people who are suffering and vulnerable, who are abandoned and deprived, who are oppressed and bereaved. There are those who, perhaps, wish that they could get out of their rut but have no sense of the route or perhaps even any hope that there may be such a way of escape. Shame on us if we are not willing to stoop down and get our hands dirty and have our ease disrupted for the sake of the needy! There are lonely old retirees shunted off into loveless environments, women being abused and trafficked, children being neglected and maltreated, orphans needing families and homes and friends, sick and housebound men and women of all ages, those troubled and trapped by sins and sorrows, widows and widowers vulnerable and isolated, people with mental illnesses who are bewildered and distressed. There is no lack of genuine need on any number of levels and in a variety of spheres, and in societies in which God is being forgotten, all the latent carelessness and cruelty of men will be increasingly evident. As the remnants of past godliness leach out of certain cultures, it will be increasingly clear that men who have no thought of God have no regard for those made in God's image.

Perhaps you say, "I do not know anyone like that." Perhaps, my friend, you are living too high. If you stoop like Christ you will have no difficulty finding and identifying the needy. Our problem is not so much that they are absent, but more that we cannot or will not find them or are afraid of ministering to them. To the warm heart we must add the open eye, ready to see appropriate objects of compassion accurately and quickly, both among the people of God and in the world at large.

And so we must *consider the opportunities*. Again, this is not a matter of having vast discretionary funding at our disposal. The greater issue is that warm heart, that open eye, and then those willing feet and ready hands. Consider again that without a purposeful plan we are likely to fail, or at least fall short. Once the genuine needs are carefully and thoughtfully identified, we must think about how we might address those needs. There are individual and corporate dynamics. How do we do this as a church or as a family or as a group of friends, as men or women in the church? How might we do it as neighbors, colleagues, or individual church members? We need to move beyond the vague grandeur of "Something must be done," and get to the point at which we are willing to say and act upon "I will do something," or "We will address this."

But for this we must *make the sacrifices*. Such a practical commitment will always be costly:

Let nothing be done through selfish ambition or conceit, but in lowliness of mind let each esteem others better than himself. Let each of you look out not only for his own interests, but also for the interests of others.

Let this mind be in you which was also in Christ Jesus, who, being in the form of God, did not consider it robbery to be equal with God, but made Himself of no reputation, taking the form of a bondservant, and coming in the likeness of men. And being found in appearance as a man, He humbled Himself and became obedient to the point of death, even the death of the cross. (Phil. 2:3–8)

If we are to follow in the footsteps of Jesus Christ, it will cost us time, money, energy, and attention. It may in some instances cost us security, safety, health—even life. Christians can live like those people in a crowded room whose eyes are always wandering around to see if anyone has entered who can offer something better than the boring or demanding person in front of us. The right spirit we are speaking of will require real investment of ourselves, and Christians ought to be ready givers. We need proactively to carve out the hours and the energies in our schedules that we will give to others. Without neglecting our families, we must recognize that we must not be so illegitimately dominated by any priority that we neglect other opportunities. The particular loving labors of a husband or wife or parent or child may well involve a sacrifice from other family members that allows that one to get involved in that work somewhere else. As churches we may need to consider that such sacrifice is going to cost us manpower and man-hours.

But do not allow these warnings to fool you into thinking that only grand gestures are required. Do not imagine that unless you can do something great you can do nothing at all. Not all sacrifices need to be dramatic. A husband may sacrificially love his wife by a thousand small daily deaths to himself and never need to take a bullet for her. His love is no less real. It is the principle worked out in practice that we must consider. This is not a matter of extravagant gestures, but of faithful service: the heart, hand, and home opened to those who have bodies and souls requiring care, protection, and provision.

Neither should believers forget to *support the deacons*. In a healthy, scripturally ordered congregation these church officers will be taking the lead in ministries of mercy. This is one of their primary responsibilities. If we take Acts 6 as containing in it the seeds of the diaconal office, those protodeacons were appointed so that the apostles could devote themselves continually to prayer and the ministry of the word (v. 4). They were being distracted from those primary concerns by the care of the widows. We should not read this as the suggestion that such care was insignificant and could therefore be relegated to a bunch of nobodies while the apostles got on with the real work. Rather, the apostles had clear priorities from which they could not afford to be taken away. In order that other legitimate duties be properly carried out, the church was called to appoint "seven men of good reputation, full of the Holy Spirit and wisdom" (v. 3) to watch over these concerns, a suggestion that was warmly received (v. 5). In ministries of mercy and other such practical matters, then, the deacons ought to be spearheads for the congregation as a whole, planning, considering, assessing, galvanizing, demonstrating, and coordinating. If they are to carry out their work adequately, they need the hearts, eyes, heads, feet, hands, and funds of those on whose behalf (under God) they will be acting. The deacons of the churches ought to embrace and exemplify this pilgrim duty, taking responsibility for leading here, and other members of the church ought to be ready to offer themselves and assist and follow wherever they themselves are made able.

We must recognize, too, that in all these things there will be many discouragements. That is why we must do all that lies in our power to *maintain the pace*. Remember the two warnings to the church at Thessalonica and the congregations of Galatia: we must not grow weary in doing good (2 Thess. 3:13; Gal. 6:9–10). The fact that Paul says this twice, directing it both to a single congregation and to a number of churches, suggests quite clearly that this can easily become a problem for believers. It is easy to slacken our pace, and there are many reasons why that might be so. It may be that failures have discouraged us or that disappointments have undermined our determination. We may become sick of thanklessness and even abuse or aggression in those we are seeking to love. We may despair of being taken advantage of yet again or despond because our investments seem only to be disregarded or wasted. In the face of such obstacles we cannot afford to give up, as John Brown explains:

Have we never been, are we not now, "weary in well-doing"? Are we "doing good to all, as we have opportunity, especially to the household of faith"? If we press these questions honestly home, deep self-humiliation will be the result. But let us not, however, despair. The more languid we are, the greater is the necessity for earnest prayer and increased exertion. The less good we have done in the past, the more diligent should we be in doing good in the future. The season of doing good will soon close for ever. "What our hand findeth to do, let us do it with our might." The season of reward will soon come to those who, "by a patient continuance in well-doing, are seeking for glory, honour, and immortality." "Be steadfast, immoveable, always abounding in the work of the Lord, forasmuch as your labour is not in vain in the Lord."[17]

Is it not at just such points that the example of our Lord encourages us to sustain our endeavors? The Servant of the Lord cried out,

"I have labored in vain,
I have spent my strength for nothing and in vain;
Yet surely my just reward is with the LORD,
And my work with my God." (Isa. 49:4)

What discouragements and disappointments, griefs and distresses might have assaulted His soul! What thanklessness, abuse, aggression, and disregard He experienced! And yet He loved to the end. It is He who loved us and demonstrated His love even to the point of death who ought to carry us on. Or think of the apostle Paul, who also found—although in a slightly different sphere—that the more he loved, the less he was loved (2 Cor. 12:15).

Beggars put a mark outside Charles Spurgeon's house to let others know that the owner of the home was a soft touch and could be relied upon to impart something to those who asked. What mark would be left outside your house? Perhaps you pride yourself on being what you like to call a wise steward, a careful man of whom no one ever takes advantage. You have found a thousand reasons to hold back good "just in case" and might well be known as someone with a tight heart and a closed fist. If we live as true believers, there may be times when our good is spoken evil of, our generosity is abused,

---

17. Brown, *Galatians*, 350.

and we are cheated. No one is called to be foolish, but we should not be ashamed to be thought fools for Christ's sake. Do you have the reputation of being a soft touch or a hard soul? Is your church known as being a warm or a cold people toward those in need?

Would you not rather risk mirroring God than Satan? Would you rather be taken advantage of from time to time for the sake of Christ than often deprive the genuinely needy in the name of wisdom? Is it not better to risk occasional abuse and waste than risk a growing hardness and coldness in our souls? The Lord is looking on the heart.

But it might not all be one-way traffic, and many of us also need to learn to *accept the kindnesses* offered to us with humility and grace. If you are a Christian, you can anticipate being a recipient of the kindnesses shown first to the household of faith. To be sure, there is a proper dignity in men and women that must be respected by those who serve: the condescending tone of voice, patrician air, and dismissive attitude—even the implied sneer—must never creep into our works of mercy. The medicine may be bitter enough without us using a jagged spoon. At the same time, some of us are too proud to allow others to help us or minister to us. It may be that we feel that to be in need demeans us. But who is there who is not in constant need? Maybe we need to adjust our expectations! It may be that we are simply too stiff-necked to admit we need the care of others.

Some of us may have been accustomed to serve, and we dislike that we now need to be served. It is not unlike the proverbial inability of doctors to submit willingly and graciously to medical care when they need it, or, indeed, that some preachers seem willing and perhaps able to feed others' souls but seem incapable of being fed themselves without complaining about the spiritual flavors. Indeed, the most vigorous and generous souls in health and strength may become bitter and resentful in times of need, and so we need to recognize that there will be seasons in which we can give and seasons in which we must receive. Perhaps someone who has always been lively and cheerful in caring for others has an accident or is struck down with an unexpected illness. The tables are turned, and that one now needs to learn how to be blessed by others. Perhaps someone has been sustained in good health for years, given time and opportunity to care for others, but as age creeps on she is less and less able to do what she once did and more and more in need of others to minister to her. She may dislike the shift in what may be perceived as a balance of power.

Whatever the reason for it, a spirit that resists the kindnesses being offered by others deprives those who would serve of their reward (Mark 9:41). Generally speaking, there will be enough changes in life, enough peaks and troughs in experience, enough seasons in our pilgrimage for all to minister and be ministered to sooner or later. We need one another; we are all more or less dependent. We are each fields for sowing as well as workers hoping to reap. None of us will go through life solely as givers. As we help others, so we must be ready to be helped by others. We must be willing to let others do for us what we would—I hope—be willing to do for them if the tables were turned. Let not the cheerful givers become awkward receivers.

Finally, let us always *remember the purpose*. We do what we do to glorify our God and King: "Let your light so shine before men, that they may see your good works and glorify your Father in heaven" (Matt. 5:16). We are not doing this for ourselves. We are not here to serve our own reputations nor to put everyone in our debt. Our labors do not even, in that sense, terminate ultimately on the people whom we are serving.

The source of mercy is the Lord Himself, and we live as we do so that others may trace these streams of goodness back to the fountain. Christ's people are zealous for good works to show that they are His people, to make clear His character, to display His lovingkindness and tender mercies in every sphere, and—Lord willing—to lead men from the lesser and temporal to the greater and eternal mercies.

Many of the people of this generation do not know what God is like. They do not see Him, they do not know Him, they do not understand Him, they have no regard for Him. What is one of the first ways that they might gain an insight into the character of God? It is when the church of Christ glorifies its Head in the blessings they bring to others. We want the world to conclude that if this is the way God's people act, how much more good and gracious God Himself must be. If we give freely, readily, willingly, and generously, how much more does the God who has made us His own and is forming us into the image of His Son? Such a spirit glorifies God, not just as the one who works such grace in His people but by pointing men and women, boys and girls, back to Him as the gracious God of mercy and compassion. We show them what He is like, and—by His Spirit's work in their hearts—we pray that they will be drawn to Him. I trust that you are living in this way for this reason and that you will see the God-intended outcome: "By this My Father is glorified, that you bear much fruit; so you will be My disciples" (John 15:8).

9

APPRECIATE THE BEAUTY

What sense and nuance does the phrase *world-weary* hold for you? We live in a world that was made by a perfect designer. When He had completed His work, the divine Creator assessed all that He had made, up to and including mankind, to be "very good" (Gen. 1:31). It was into this world that sin entered, and sin has been wrecking and ruining the world ever since. Much of our emphasis so far has been on the realities of sin and its effects—the effects of the fall include a measure of marring that goodness and beauty the Lord embedded in His creation. Perhaps, under the relentless barrage of painful truth, you find yourself inclining to a sinful world-weariness, a sweeping cynicism. You may have wondered, in effect, "Who will show us any good?" (Ps. 4:6).

Some may be constitutionally inclined to melancholy. Such people see the gleam of silver and immediately conclude it is the lining of the dark cloud lurking near every such glimmer that will shortly make its appearance and overshadow us. In extremes, we can even fall prey to a kind of paranoia, suspecting that something horrible is skulking around every next corner. We may live our lives waiting for that something to pounce. Perhaps some past situation or some series of events has made you negative, trapping you in sustained bitterness of spirit. Our perceptions may have been twisted to the point at which we are perpetually miserable, persuaded that there is little or no goodness of any sort in the world, resenting the bad deal that we got in this life. It may be that you feel vindicated in this—perversely satisfied, even—by what we have considered so far. Everything we have said, in your mind, only confirms your deepest suspicions about the unremitting grimness of life. The result of these things may be that you are substantially robbed of the capacity to behold anything else. All the joy has been sucked out of your life, and you are now dry and sour, blind to any goodness and beauty that remain in the world the Lord God made. If that is what world-weariness means to you, then you need to repent of it.

There is a legitimate world-weariness in true saints, expressed in poetry like this:

> Weary of earth, and laden with my sin,
> I look to heaven and long to enter in.[1]

This may be the tiredness that comes with the protracted battle, the longing for rest after struggle, the desire for home after exile. But has that mutated into a thankless, godless world-weariness? Is there a boredom that grips us, an apathy that possesses us, an *ennui* that dulls us, a cynicism that poisons us? Do we refuse to recognize or even acknowledge God's gracious hand toward us as we make our way through the world? Subject to such a spirit, nothing excites us, nothing interests us, nothing enthuses us about life in God's world. This is sinful. Even where it does not—as it so often does—begin to color our perceptions of everything, including our participation in the pilgrimage, it fails to take full account of who and where we are. We have said that the world is to be considered in its various spheres and senses, not just in the moral-ethical sense but also in its creative and extensive senses. Such a crippled spirit takes little or no account of the fact that God made the world very good, has not utterly abandoned it, and intends to restore it. Such a perverse outlook refuses to understand that men made in the image of God, though thoroughly wrecked by sin, retain some vestige of that created dignity, a sense of living before God, having the work of the law written in their hearts, their consciences also bearing witness, and between themselves their thoughts accusing or else excusing them (Rom. 2:15). This is from where we derive the basic human judgments of right and wrong, pure and foul, delightful and despicable. If we lose sight of any prospect of the goodness of the Lord in the land of the living (Ps. 27:13), if we abandon a proper range of perspective, then we will be in danger of falling into the traps of isolation and inattention,

---

1. Samuel J. Stone, "Weary of Earth and Laden with My Sin."

neglecting the blessings scattered about us and the opportunities lying before us as we make our way in the world. Perhaps we have even stopped expecting such blessings and have given up looking for such opportunities.

It is not my intention here to deal with the issue of beauty and the arts in the church, either more generally or as an aspect of our worship when gathered. Such questions are not entirely irrelevant in a culture in which we now have "pastors of the arts" serving congregations. Such titles raise the issues of whether people can be or ought to be pastored by means of the arts, or—indeed—whether the arts themselves need pastoring. Frankly, I am not persuaded that the arts are a proper priority for the church as the body of Christ or the proper sphere of her activity, although I trust that individual Christians will not neglect them, dismiss them, or be consumed by them. I hope that here we can at least consider something of our relationship to the beauties and goodnesses of this present world as Christians. Followers of the Way must ensure that as we prioritize eternity we do not neglect time and space as the arena in which we enjoy so many of God's blessings to us. We must consider a Christlike attitude to this present world as we walk through it. If we fail to do this, we will fail to glorify God in our pilgrimage. We must cultivate an eye for the goodness of God, or what will we do with words like these?

> Rejoice in the LORD, O you righteous!
> For praise from the upright is beautiful.
> Praise the LORD with the harp;
> Make melody to Him with an instrument of ten strings.
> Sing to Him a new song;
> Play skillfully with a shout of joy.
>
> For the word of the LORD is right,
> And all His work is done in truth.
> He loves righteousness and justice;
> The earth is full of the goodness of the LORD. (Ps. 33:1–5)

We are to "rejoice in the LORD" and recognize that "the earth is full of the goodness of the LORD." How do we respond to such a charge and such a declaration? Shall we deny it, as if to say, "I don't know what world that fellow is talking about, but it's not the one I live in!"? We live in a world that is still full of God's goodness, and we need eyes to see and hearts to appreciate it if we are to please and honor Him. Again, this is a Christlike way to live.

Appreciate the Beauty: Scriptural Framework
Rich in Good Works

> Command those who are rich in this present age not to be haughty, nor to trust in uncertain riches but in the living God, who gives us richly all things to enjoy. Let them do good, that they be rich in good works, ready to give, willing to share, storing up for themselves a good foundation for the time to come, that they may lay hold on eternal life. (1 Tim. 6:17–19)

Scripture speaks to all kinds and classes of men, sometimes generically to mankind as mankind, sometimes to men and women as they belong to a specific group, sometimes even to specific individuals. Here Paul speaks *to the rich* in this present age, reminding us that pastors and preachers have particular messages to particular persons. Many of us in the modern world might consider ourselves relatively rich or relatively poor on a wider scale. However, geographically and historically, most of us are far closer to absolute wealth than we are to absolute poverty. If you are reading this book in some readily available paper or electronic format, you probably belong to the wealthier group. There is, then, something here for most of us and something very definite for the large majority of us.

The apostle speaks *against pride*, calling us away from the haughtiness and high-mindedness to which the rich are prone. His warning suggests that it is all too easy to become conceited on account of our wealth, puffed up because of our blessings (which are, properly considered, a matter of gift and not entitlement). Paul seems conscious that it is a somewhat effortless thing for the rich to presume that their material blessings are, in some way, a register of their innate worth or worthiness. Such an outlook suggests that we have a right to look down on others, that our will is weightier, our opinion counts for more, our persons have more dignity than those who lack what we enjoy. Paul says to those who are rich (or, at least, richer), "Do not succumb to such a wicked outlook."

So he speaks *concerning trust*, for self-reliance and wealth-reliance are both tragic errors. We should not overwork to be rich and set our eyes on things that are not. Riches are uncertain: they "certainly make themselves wings; they fly away like an eagle toward heaven" (Prov. 23:5). Worldly wealth is a poor foundation upon which to build our lives. The wise man is neither self-reliant nor wealth-reliant but God-reliant in principle and in practice, for the Lord lives and abides forever. Please note, however, that Paul is not teaching us here to despise riches. He is warning us not to depend on them. Paul never makes the kind of bald statement often mistakenly attributed to him that money in and of itself is the root of all evil, absolutely and finally considered. He is clear that "the love of money is a root of all kinds of evil, for which some have strayed from the faith in their greediness, and pierced themselves through with many sorrows" (1 Tim. 6:10). An inordinate desire for money is the problem, not money itself. There is nothing inherently wrong with enjoying the gifts as long as we do not overlook the Giver—it is He whom we trust, tracing up the streams to the fountain.

And therefore Paul brings before us *God's goodness*, for it is He who gives us all things richly to enjoy. We should not depend upon our riches, but we certainly should not despise them. When you trust and delight in the Giver, you are free to enjoy the gifts because your worship is already centered where it belongs. From a large heart and with an open hand the Lord dispenses His tender mercies, showing great generosity in the grant and abundant kindness in the purpose of the good things He bestows. The Lord has given us all things *richly*: He does not hold back His kindnesses toward us, and many of His children receive those kindnesses in things material as well as things spiritual. It is right that we should gratefully enjoy them. Paul is utterly unambiguous: God's blessings are to be enjoyed, though not indulged in. We should revel in God's gifts and rejoice over them, considering them an expression of His particular fatherly care to multitudes of His children.

Notice too how God's generosity becomes a pattern for our own dealing with others. Paul does not want the rich to lose sight of heaven even while they are blessed on earth: "Let them do good, that they be rich in good works, ready to give, willing to share, storing up for themselves a good foundation for the time to come, that they may lay hold on eternal life" (1 Tim. 6:18–19). We must use what we are given in time, never losing sight of the consequences of our actions for eternity. One of the ways to enjoy our present blessings is to employ those good things on earth so as to secure lasting blessings in heaven, relieving suffering with an eye on the glory to come. This is a godlike, Christlike attitude. The richer you are in yourself, the richer in good works you can be. You can be ready to give as God is Himself; willing to share as the Christ is in dispensing riches to those around Him. There are going to be blessings in heaven for those who use their riches well on earth. The more you have, the more opportunities you have been given to do good, and so to secure lasting treasures.

Gifts from Above

> Every good gift and every perfect gift is from above, and comes down from the Father of lights, with whom there is no variation or shadow of turning. (James 1:17)

James is making the point that God is the author of all good and of good only, for, according to verse 13, no one should say that he is being tempted by God, "for God cannot be tempted by evil, nor does He Himself tempt anyone." The sense may be that every act of good giving and every good gift—both the matter and the manner of God's donations to His people—are in keeping with the divine character. James again uses universal language, highlighting the greater gifts—"of His own will He brought us forth by the word of truth, that we might be a kind of firstfruits of His creatures" (James 1:18)—and encompassing all the lesser. Have you ever received any good thing in any good way? It is God's gracious heart and hand toward you. If you enjoy *any* good gift, graciously bestowed, it has come down to you from the Father of lights, as Matthew Henry points out:

> We must own God as the author of all the powers and perfections that are in the creature, and the giver of all the benefits which we have in and by those powers and perfections: but none of their darknesses, their imperfections, or their ill actions are to be charged on the Father of lights; from him proceeds every good and perfect gift, both pertaining to this life and that which is to come.[2]

---

2. Henry, *Commentary*, 6:783.

The name "Father of lights" is, perhaps, intended to highlight God's creative power: "By the word of the LORD the heavens were made, and all the host of them by the breath of His mouth" (Ps. 33:6). It remind us of His intentions from the beginning: "Then God saw everything that He had made, and indeed it was very good. So the evening and the morning were the sixth day" (Gen. 1:31). The name points us to the God who—in all the brightness of His unchanging goodness, grace, and glory—has granted us His mercies. God's uncreated stability is the source of every blessing. James offers regeneration as the starting point of our experience, not least because the renewed heart is the only one that is tuned to appreciate all God's mercies—every act of good giving and every good gift. Only the heart that has been turned back to God in repentance and faith by the Spirit's illumination, discerning Him as He is in all the fullness of His mercy, can testify of God's goodness in this way.

Get Good and Do Good

What profit has the worker from that in which he labors? I have seen the God-given task with which the sons of men are to be occupied. He has made everything beautiful in its time. Also he has put eternity in their hearts, except that no one can find out the work that God does from beginning to end.

I know that nothing is better for them than to rejoice, and to do good in their lives, and also that every man should eat and drink and enjoy the good of all his labor—it is the gift of God. (Eccl. 3:9–13)

This text does not reflect an unmitigated pessimism, but rather offers an accurate perspective on life. It opens with *a penetrating question*: "What profit has the worker from that in which he labors?" It is a question that we are all, at times, inclined to ask, even or especially those who are not converted: "What is the point?" No one is immune. Julius Caesar was perhaps the greatest of the Roman emperors and became a model to those who followed him. It is said that this great emperor—the absolute ruler of the whole Roman Empire—once looked out over his city of Rome, and asked, "Is this all?" Whatever power is ascribed to us or assumed by us, whatever we accumulate in life, it lies outside of our strength to make things happen as we wish.

The writer goes on to speak of *a God-given task*, a reminder of our limitations as the sons of men, as creatures dependent on and accountable to God. Life here is a probation of sorts, and our labor does not produce satisfaction with the world, but weariness in it. There may be a reflection here both of our mandate as God's vice-gerents and our battle in a world under a curse (cf. Gen. 1:28; 3:17–19). Only when we see our work as God's appointed stewardship do we find in it a measure of significance. We ought to embrace our callings as being responsible to the One who is training us, testing us, conditioning us as His children. We bring glory to His name when we embrace our God-given task and find the dignity and significance of work that may be despised in the eyes of men.

Then we are told of *a bestowed beauty*, for by God's appointment everything that He has made finds its proper time and place and accomplishes His sovereign purposes, for only providence can untangle all the knots of this life. Look at the back of this tapestry and you see a mess; turn to the front and you see God's pattern woven into the fabric.

Then there is *an astounding grant*. Why do we ask questions about the point and value of life? Why do we wrestle with such concerns? It is because the Lord, making man in His own image, has put a sense of eternity in the human soul, giving us such an appetite for something beyond this life that we live in search of significance and substance. Is this all? Of course not! It was never intended to be all. A man or woman made to reflect God's glory is always going to long for meaning, pursue a sense of purpose and accomplishment, and feel that he or she was made for something of value—that life ought to have a point. Eternity demands an answer to that question and allows us to answer it. Here arises the cry of the human soul for something of substance and significance in a world that so often seems to offer neither.

So what is our problem? In part, *an acknowledged ignorance*, for "no one can find out the work that God does from beginning to end." Although all these things are so, I cannot always see it. There is so much that is hidden from us, and unaided human wisdom cannot discern the hand and intent of God in all that He does. We cannot trace the lines providence weaves that may never seem ordered to us until we look back on them with the hindsight of heaven.

All this leads us to *a wise conclusion*: "I know that nothing is better for them than to rejoice, and to do good in their lives, and also that every man should eat and drink and enjoy the good of all his labor—it is the gift of God" (Eccl. 3:12–13). We should rejoice, get good and do good, and enjoy God's gift. That is emphatically not the same as saying, "Let us eat and drink, for tomorrow we die!" (Isa. 22:13; 1 Cor. 15:32). It is not the conclusion that there really is no point or profit after all. It is a call to walk the path appointed for us and to enjoy God's blessings as we go—to get good and to do good. You may not always know precisely where you are, but it is still possible to enjoy the journey. These words must be placed firmly in the context of the God who is governing all things, working out all things in accordance with a gracious and righteous purpose. Where you cannot see the end of your road in advance, you can at least travel along it with a trustful gladness: a man "must either live a life of measureless frustration, or he must live his life in the fear of God."[3] This is not a life of measureless frustration and final pointlessness. God has given the lives of His children purpose and point, even if we cannot always see the patterns woven into them; God makes everything beautiful in its time.

The Joy of Jesus Christ

And the Lord said, "To what then shall I liken the men of this generation, and what are they like? They are like children sitting in the marketplace and calling to one another, saying:

'We played the flute for you,
And you did not dance;
We mourned to you,
And you did not weep.'

For John the Baptist came neither eating bread nor drinking wine, and you say, 'He has a demon.' The Son of Man has come eating and drinking, and you say, 'Look, a glutton and a winebibber, a friend of tax collectors and sinners!' But wisdom is justified by all her children." (Luke 7:31–35)

Consider the incidental details that add such color to this episode as the Lord Christ asks the Pharisees about John the Baptist and then

---

3. Stuart Olyott, *A Life Worth Living and a Lord Worth Loving: Ecclesiastes and Song of Solomon* (Darlington, U.K.: Evangelical Press, 1983), 29.

compares "the men of this generation" to "children sitting in the marketplace." It is very clear that Jesus observed the world and that He took a genuine interest and pleasure in watching what occurred in it, even down to children playing in the marketplace. Some of these children that Christ watched wanted to play at weddings; others wanted to play at funerals. But some were party poopers. They did not want to play either of those games. Indeed, if they could not play their game by their rules, they would probably stomp off home in a fit of pique.

This is an activity that many of us might consider to be beneath us, let alone the Lord, but He looks and learns. The Man of Sorrows was not morose or miserable. He exposed those who went through the world with a jaundiced eye, looking for faults in everyone and everything. The Pharisees, full of spiritual sourness, were just such— they found no joy in the world. Christ makes the point that neither John in his asceticism nor Jesus in His enjoyment could please the Pharisees, and they became the religious equivalent of the selfish brat who, because he cannot make everyone play according to his rules, kicks the ball as far away as possible or picks it up if it is his and runs home.

Note further what it was with which they took issue in Christ Jesus: they can see no beauty in anything, least of all in Christ's enjoyment of the good things of His Father's world. They criticized Him because of His lack of asceticism, for His readiness in eating and drinking, for His lack of shame in enjoying life's blessings even when He was being censured for doing so. His was not a life of sinful indulgence, but neither did He live in a state of unnatural restraint (and I am not suggesting that John the Baptist sinned because of the regime under which he, as a prophet, was operating). Christ's was a spirit of holy enjoyment and genuine thankfulness even as He sought to bring blessings to others. He condemns the Pharisees, in part, because they do not know how to be happy over the blessings they receive. Perhaps Robert Law overstates his case slightly, but there is much truth in his assessment of Christ's perspective. He begins by acknowledging that, to Christ, "this world was an imperfect world, on which the powers of evil had a terrible grasp, of which the Evil One might even be said to be the ruler; yet not so that it was not throughout God's world, with God's hand everywhere upon it,

God's presence everywhere in it." Christ's view of this present world was a properly and profoundly realistic one. However, says Law,

> While no one has spoken so sternly as Jesus of the necessity that may be laid upon us to be content with less than the full natural enjoyment of the world, and for the sake of ultimate salvation accept a life that is temporarily curtailed and maimed, He never holds this up as the ideal. Neither in the life nor the teaching of Jesus is there a trace of the ascetic principle that the physical is the necessary, lifelong foe of the spiritual. The world is God's world; and men are God's children for whom this world is made.
>
> Jesus, because He was the Perfect Man, the Son of God, could not be an ascetic. Nor could He hold up an ascetic ideal to others; for He came to lift up men to His own plane, to give them that loving consciousness of God which makes all things sacred, that purity to which all things are pure, that potency of spiritual life which converts all things to its own uses.[4]

Christ was a social being, as much in His humanity as in His divinity. He lived among people and sought to bless them and enjoyed their company. Something of our Savior's warmth can be seen in the way in which He called children to Himself and they came readily and willingly. How many miserable and bitter old sourpusses do you know whose company naturally delights and attracts children? The righteous man's spreading branches and green leaves provide welcome shade for many to find shelter. Christ loved society in the best sense, and the Pharisees loathed it: "The Son of Man has come eating and drinking, and you say, 'Look, a glutton and a winebibber, a friend of tax collectors and sinners!' But wisdom is justified by all her children" (Luke 7:34–35). Friendship with sinners and tax collectors did not involve condoning their sin, but it did require genuine benevolence toward them. Such wisdom receives its full vindication in the fruit it bears. We see again how our Lord enjoyed social blessings and natural beauties in Matthew 6:28–29: "So why do you worry about clothing? Consider the lilies of the field, how they grow: they neither toil nor spin; and yet I say to you that even Solomon in all his glory was not arrayed like one of these." Our Savior walked this

---

4. Robert Law, *The Emotions of Christ* (Stoke-on-Trent, U.K.: Tentmaker Publications, 1995), 20.

world with His eyes open, drinking in the beauties of the created order. He saw God's hand in creation, He recognized God's care of creation, even at its most transient. Remember Psalm 103:15–16:

> As a flower of the field, so he flourishes.
> For the wind passes over it, and it is gone,
> And its place remembers it no more.

The uncultivated flowers of the field so outshone Solomon's splendor that his royal garments could not compare in grandeur to one lily—and there is no question here but that Solomon's royal robes were truly glorious, which tells us that clothing can be properly magnificent also.

Our Savior was not blind to this. The Lord has filled this globe with things that are good and beautiful—perhaps all the more so because of the backdrop of sin and misery against which they are placed. It is the Lord who makes all these beautiful things and the incarnate God who appreciates their beauty. It is a mark of His care for creation and His goodness to His creatures and ought to be appreciated as such.

Pursuing the Praiseworthy

> Finally, brethren, whatever things are true, whatever things are noble, whatever things are just, whatever things are pure, whatever things are lovely, whatever things are of good report, if there is any virtue and if there is anything praiseworthy—meditate on these things. (Phil. 4:8)

Here we receive instruction from the apostle as to what saints should actively pursue, the substance of what we should imbibe and ingest in the mind and heart. Here are the things that we should embrace and in which we can and should engage. We must take into account the fact that culture is not morally neutral. The stuff of this world is more or less loaded with moral and ethical baggage both by those who send it out and those who drink it in. Because of this, the saints are to seek out and dwell on what is true rather than what is false, what is noble rather than what is base, what is just rather than what is corrupt, what is pure rather than what is filthy, what is lovely rather than what is ugly, what is admirable rather than what is despicable—all those things that are morally excellent and worthy of praise when assessed by the divine standard. Paul says, "Look out for such things and make them the objects of your meditation and delight."

Such a command from the apostle clearly implies, firstly, that such things can be found in the world that the Lord God has made. They exist! They are not figments of some wistful but forlorn imagination, but present and real blessings. Secondly, they can be readily discerned by the spiritually sensitive child of God, living as a pilgrim in this world. They may not always lie on the surface, but they are not so scarce as to be only occasional delights. Thirdly, the saints can genuinely appreciate and delight in all such things in their proper place and proportion. The healthy Christian has a heart calibrated to seek, find, and enjoy the genuinely good things in the world that God has made and to enjoy them as marks of His favor and indications of His presence with them as they make their way through the world. Here is the promise that follows: "The things which you learned and received and heard and saw in me, these do, and the God of peace will be with you" (Phil. 4:9).

Appreciate the Beauty: Summary Thoughts

There is a goodness and beauty in the world our God has made. We cannot and should not deny that its goodness has in measure faded and its beauty has been broken:

> For the earnest expectation of the creation eagerly waits for the revealing of the sons of God. For the creation was subjected to futility, not willingly, but because of Him who subjected it in hope; because the creation itself also will be delivered from the bondage of corruption into the glorious liberty of the children of God. For we know that the whole creation groans and labors with birth pangs together until now. (Rom. 8:19–22)

Nevertheless, a faded goodness is goodness still, and a broken beauty may retain enough of its loveliness to excite the heart of the sensitive man or woman. There is still goodness and beauty to enjoy and to appreciate as children of God in a fallen world, and not just in anticipation (although the present blessings ought to sweeten our appetite for future glories). Our heavenly Father has blessed us with many good things to enjoy. There is no inherent holiness—no

necessary Christlikeness—in crass denial, willful blindness, or careless ingratitude, still less in resentment and complaint. The creation
itself may be crying out for redemption, but there is still much to see
that declares the goodness and glory of the Lord:

> The heavens declare the glory of God;
> And the firmament shows His handiwork.
> Day unto day utters speech,
> And night unto night reveals knowledge.
> There is no speech nor language
> Where their voice is not heard.
> Their line has gone out through all the earth,
> And their words to the end of the world. (Ps. 19:1–4a)

Look up and out and see the handiwork of the holy and just One
in everything around you! That body of yours, which will crumble
to dust before being gloriously remade, testifies to divine skill and
wisdom. Even the unaided eye of human wisdom should be able to
trace something of this in the creation at large: "Since the creation of
the world His invisible attributes are clearly seen, being understood
by the things that are made, even His eternal power and Godhead"
(Rom. 1:20). For those with eyes to see, the goodness and glory of the
Lord are everywhere displayed in His creation. Who should have better eyes to see a Father's handiwork than His own beloved children?

To be sure, we must be alert to the underlying hostility of a sinful world in rebellion. We must recognize the dangers of living in
this present evil age. We must ensure that this passing world does
not blind us to enduring eternity. But, at the same time, we must
not allow ourselves to live as if we were not really here. We are still
stewards of creation, still fighting to carry out in measure, in our current environment, the mandate given at the beginning: "Be fruitful
and multiply; fill the earth and subdue it; have dominion over the
fish of the sea, over the birds of the air, and over every living thing
that moves on the earth" (Gen. 1:28). We are to engage, enjoy, and
enthuse about the good things God has given to us, from the salvation we possess through His Son, with whom He has freely given us
all things, to all the good things we have been freely given.

We ought to deny neither the glory of God in creation nor the
gleams of God's image in men and women as they inhabit and

interact with God's world. Whether in the arts (for example, music, literature, drawing, and painting) or in the sciences (design, physics, engineering, or anything else), or any combination of the two, properly interpreted, the glory of God can be seen. Why does that piece of haunting music make the tears trickle down your cheeks? Why do the histories of great men lift up your soul and prompt you to more noble endeavors? Why do the arching beams of bridges and buildings draw out your admiration? Why does the beauty of the painting thrill your heart? Why do the intricacies of the physical realm dazzle your mind? When you gaze on the mountain peaks and consider the hosts of heaven, is it not God's being and doing that is impressed upon you? He has put eternity in your heart! The more you enjoy time, the more you will look forward to eternity, for these blessings are the present tokens of God's goodness toward us.

Even in the Old Testament God's people were not Philistines. Consider what happened when the Lord wanted a tabernacle that would reflect something of the glory of the eternal dwelling. Moses said,

> "See, the LORD has called by name Bezalel the son of Uri, the son of Hur, of the tribe of Judah; and He has filled him with the Spirit of God, in wisdom and understanding, in knowledge and all manner of workmanship, to design artistic works, to work in gold and silver and bronze, in cutting jewels for setting, in carving wood, and to work in all manner of artistic workmanship.
>
> "And He has put in his heart the ability to teach, in him and Aholiab the son of Ahisamach, of the tribe of Dan. He has filled them with skill to do all manner of work of the engraver and the designer and the tapestry maker, in blue, purple, and scarlet thread, and fine linen, and of the weaver—those who do every work and those who design artistic works.
>
> "And Bezalel and Aholiab, and every gifted artisan in whom the LORD has put wisdom and understanding, to know how to do all manner of work for the service of the sanctuary, shall do according to all that the LORD has commanded."
>
> Then Moses called Bezalel and Aholiab, and every gifted artisan in whose heart the LORD had put wisdom, everyone whose heart was stirred, to come and do the work. (Ex. 35:30–36:2)

My point here is not about worship. Considered in that regard, these were childish things compared with the spiritual splendors that we now enjoy. But it was God who filled these men with His Spirit, who gave them wisdom and understanding, who made them designers and craftsmen of things beautiful and intricate, stirring up the hearts of gifted artisans. How can there be any shame in such godlike labor?

The best gifts (the eternal blessings) should open our eyes to present good gifts (the temporal mercies), for Joseph Addison teaches us to sing,

> When *all* Thy mercies, O my God,
> My rising soul surveys,
> Transported with the view, I'm lost
> In wonder, love and praise.[5]

If such sentiments—even if not the precise words—never rise from your heart, then you are living a half life, and the half you have is not Christlike. Only when your soul knows how to recognize and rejoice in God's goodness do you gladly walk in the footsteps of the Christ who ate and drank and observed and enjoyed people and things in the world made by God, things with goodness shining from them and beauty inscribed into them. Spurgeon says,

> "These are my Father's works, and therefore they are mine." If there be anything in life that can yield fitting enjoyment for an immortal Spirit, it belongs to the Christian. Ours is not the religion of the cloister and the cell. "Religion never was designed to make our pleasures less." We are men among men, walking among them though not of them, and feeling that in the world there is a beauty and a joy, a sweetness and a love, which are all our own, ours by a special propriety, and in a higher sense than ever can be the case with the transgressor who tramples under foot the laws of nature, or the rebel who refuses to do homage to the Great God and our Redeemer. Ours then are all things to enjoy. Not that we can ever find the pith and substance of our joy in the creature. The Creator is the well-head from which we must draw. Yet in the relationships of life the Christian finds a sanctified enjoyment; in the society of God's people, he feels that all things are his, and he thus has a gracious pleasure. Do not imagine that we who fear God are thereby deprived of

---

5. Joseph Addison, "When All Thy Mercies, O My God" (emphasis added).

enjoyments. There are silly sports and sensual gratifications that we do not resort to, nor could we relish them, for they clash with our conscience, and would rather entail misery than excite mirth in our breasts; but all that can contribute real joy to the heart belongs to the Christian as a heritage to-day and forever.[6]

If there is anything of beauty, value, virtue, and praiseworthiness in this world, it belongs to the child of God in a distinctive sense. It is to be enjoyed as a reflection of the heart of God toward us.

Appreciate the Beauty: Specific Counsels

If we are to appreciate the beauty, we must first *remember the fall*. Recalling the fact of sin and the reality of ruin might seem counterintuitive, but we must put all this into its biblical proportion and balance. It is too easy for us to swing from one extreme to another, and we must not allow the things spoken here to cause us to forget the fact of our own sin as those living in a fallen world. Our desires need to be recalibrated, our appetites need to be healthily recovered, and our discernment needs to be well honed. I am not seeking to undo what I have just set out to do, simply to remind you that these are not "either–or" matters but "both–and" truths. We do not live in a neutral environment, and we are the objects of enemy assaults. Even in our moments of greatest relaxation and ease and peace here, we "use this world as not misusing it. For the form of this world is passing away" (1 Cor. 7:31). But this ruined world is still the world that God made and sustains. There is enough of God in it to bring glory and honor to His great name when it is seen and appreciated for what it is. We must remember eternity and look forward to it, even while we do not forget time and space and the blessings in them that we already enjoy.

Then, with our eyes fully open, we must *follow the Lord*. If we are to navigate this world well in this regard, let us remember whose people we are and in whose footsteps we are treading. Our Master knew whose world this is, and He appreciated and enjoyed every

---

6. C. H. Spurgeon, "Things to Come! A Heritage of the Saints," in *C. H. Spurgeon's Sermons beyond Volume 63: An Authentic Supplement to the Metropolitan Tabernacle Pulpit*, comp. Terence Peter Crosby (Leominster, U.K.: DayOne Publications, 2009), 338.

glimmer of His Father's creative and redemptive goodness, every demonstration of His Father's loving care. The Redeemer could recognize the shades of beauty still painted onto the canvas of creation, could hear the notes of divine care and compassion that sound through the cosmos, could delight in those demonstrations of divine order and purity, those things truly attractive and engaging. God is not absent from the world that He has made. Paul could even say on Mars Hill that "He is not far from each one of us; for in Him we live and move and have our being, as also some of your own poets have said, 'For we are also His offspring'" (Acts 17:27–28). For saints, there is a sweeter and deeper level to climb to: God is not just paternal in the creative sense, but our Father in the adoptive sense. He has brought us into His family so that we may enjoy His goodness. His heart is for us, His eye is upon us, and His hand is blessing us. As in all else, we must learn to see, feel, and act in accordance with the pattern our Lord and Savior has left for us.

Furthermore, we need to learn to *observe the good*. We may need to train ourselves to do this if we have lost the habit or never developed it. We cannot afford to be either willfully or ignorantly blind to what is good and beautiful in the world: "The earth is full of the goodness of the LORD" (Ps. 33:5). If you cannot see it, that is not God's fault! The problem lies with your sour eyes and your dry soul. And if you fail here, you will struggle to obey God's commands to be content and thankful. You will go through the world in a huff, resenting the husband or wife, the job or car, the church or family that the Lord saw fit to bestow upon you. Nothing will seem good, cause you joy, or inspire gratitude in your soul if you simply cannot see the good. As the eye is drawn to the black mark on the white sheet, so our eyes are too often magnetized by what is marred and blind to the beauty, simply missing the shining brightness of so much of God's creation. There is beauty that alleviates the ugliness. We must learn to look for the true, the noble, the just, the pure, the lovely, and the admirable—all those things that are virtuous and praiseworthy in God's estimation. We must pursue those good gifts given to be enjoyed by hearts that know Him and that discern in what measure to appreciate those gifts, hearts increasingly equipped to sieve out what is distasteful to God and abhorrent to His Spirit and to search out what is pleasing to and reflective of God. We must keep our eyes open for glimmers of God's image in man and the demonstration of His goodness in the world. I am not suggesting that this sets us in pursuit of saccharine sweetness and sickening sentimentality—that would be nauseating. Instead, it prompts a proper appreciation of God's character—His wisdom, power, and mercy—and His delight in making it manifest in the world He created.

In addition, we must *trace the streams* to their fountainhead in the triune God. Every benefit must be followed back to the Benefactor, every gift acknowledged to the Giver. We must never dip our eyes so low that we cannot see the source of our blessings, never dull our minds to the point at which we lose sight of His stated purposes of good, never stop our mouths from expressions of faith and praise, even in the midst of troubles. Let us note it well that every blessing granted to any man is from God: "He makes His sun rise on the evil and on the good, and sends rain on the just and on the unjust" (Matt. 5:45). Common grace and saving grace are both His work. Every good thing that His undeserving creatures receive from His hand ought to be noted. As Christians, everything we have—from the "indescribable gift" (2 Cor. 9:15) down—is a gift: "And what do you have that you did not receive?" (1 Cor. 4:7). Furthermore, it is a token of His love and a demonstration of His goodness. This can be hard to believe, but we must believe it to be so: if you are a child of God and there were a better state and condition for you to be in than the one you are now in, you would already be in it. That is because all good is dispensed from the heart and by the hand of our loving Father in heaven. Every circumstance and situation—both troubles and joys—has been formed and fashioned by God to bring you to a pitch of Christlike maturity by His means and in His time. Why are we so blind to this? Why so full of complaints? Oh, my soul, berate yourself for your ingratitude and not your God for His supposed carelessness and cruelties, for such ugliness never mars His holy heart!

So let us *enjoy the blessings*. Do we feel guilty because we have been shown kindness? Perhaps so, but why should we, if we handle our blessings righteously? Are we tempted to downplay the goodness we have received, to pretend it is not there? This is nonsense! We do not need to become ascetics. Perhaps you have met people crippled by this spirit. I have known those who feel guilty when they are full and so they will not eat; who feel guilty when they are comfortable and so buy broken furniture. They could see no middle ground between sinful indulgence and self-inflicted unpleasantness, no happy medium between wastefulness and wantonness on the one hand and a cultivated wilderness on the other. That is not Christianity—that is masochism! There is no holiness in misery for its own sake. All good things have been given to us to enjoy and to employ. That person whose imagined holiness consists in an extravagant and excessive self-imposed austerity often robs him or her of the ability to bless others—if you eat cardboard and sit on rocks on principle then you may rarely be in a position to give real hospitality, for example.

I am far from criticizing the Christian who lives wisely and reasonably within his means as a way of investing in the kingdom of God. That is just what we ought to do. But our good gifts are given to be gratefully gathered and received, not overlooked, dabbled in, wasted, or even neglected out of some strange notion that holiness is aided by sourness. Let every good gift be enjoyed by those to whom it is given, and let us prove godlike in our response to them and employment of them. The gifts granted to us are enjoyed most and employed best when they are being shared with and passed on to others. Asceticism and cynicism do not become children of God.

In all this, we must not forget to *bow the knee* and worship. Perhaps you have too quickly forgotten where every good and every perfect gift comes from. Perhaps you have not even properly acknowledged the unmerited goodness of God toward you. Though not all enjoy gifts of the same degree, every reader has received his or her life, breath, and all things from the hand of the living God (Acts 17:25). Do you have a home? A family? Any food in your belly? Any clothes on your back? And, for almost all of us, how many more comforts and kindnesses? Should our song not catch something of this spirit?

> Come, Thou fount of every blessing,
> Tune my heart to sing Thy grace;
> Streams of mercy, never ceasing,
> Call for songs of loudest praise.[7]

Do our prayers as believers testify to the blessings we have received? Do we spontaneously and cheerfully pour forth our gratitude,

---

7. Robert Robinson, "Come, Thou Fount of Every Blessing."

publicly and privately, or does it need constantly to be prompted or dragged out of us by a sense of guilt or obligation? Such things ought not to be! But how many of us manage to concoct a catalog of complaints, a weighty sense of our deprivations, all the while overlooking the cataract of kindnesses that we receive moment by moment, drinking at streams of mercy all the while asserting that we live in a dry land? What of the great kindness, the grand demonstration of divine goodness—the sending of God's own Son to suffer and to die in the place of the wretched? How many live and—to their eternal sorrow and our penetrating grief—die without any sense of the mercies held out to all in Christ Jesus?

If some things should move all men to gratitude, how much more should the saints be characterized by grateful worship? Not only has Christ been offered to us, but we have been given hearts to receive Him. And now

> All things are ours; the gift of God,
> The purchase of a Saviour's blood;
> While the good Spirit shows us how
> To use and to improve them too.[8]

We ought to be cheerfully thankful for the least common grace and abundantly, extravagantly grateful for every shining strand of saving grace, for all the multiplied and manifold goodness purchased by the blood of our great God and Savior, Jesus Christ. We should give thanks for eyes to see, ears to hear, and hearts to feel the blessings graciously bestowed upon us: "For who makes you differ from another? And what do you have that you did not receive? Now if you did indeed receive it, why do you boast as if you had not received it?" (1 Cor. 4:7).

But also—and we will explore this more fully in the coming pages—we must *anticipate the destiny,* for these blessings are the first-fruits, the tokens of more to come. Christ's death is the grand pledge of everything else: "He who did not spare His own Son, but delivered Him up for us all, how shall He not with Him also freely give us all things?" (Rom. 8:32). We possess the first things; we are entitled to the best things; we will receive all things. There is a sense in which

---

8. Isaac Watts, "How Vast the Treasure We Possess!"

we cannot be more entitled to more blessings than we already are, but we can enter into them and experience them and enjoy them more completely—we can be more happy, but we cannot be more secure. It is that experience of full and final happiness to which the pilgrim is looking forward. We must learn to put time and eternity in their proper places, to see them in their proper perspective, and to value them in their proper proportion. We must use the blessings of time to carve out bright prospects for eternity. God has given a significance to everything you have—your time, your money, your energy, your brain and your body, your home and your things. Do not underestimate those temporal mercies, for they are given to be employed and enjoyed here. But do not overestimate them—they are not given to govern us, to swallow us up and choke our affections, but to point us to the things that await us, for the blessings still stored up and yet to be poured out: "Therefore let no one boast in men. For all things are yours: whether Paul or Apollos or Cephas, or the world or life or death, or things present or things to come—all are yours. And you are Christ's, and Christ is God's" (1 Cor. 3:21–23).

10

ANTICIPATE THE DESTINY

"Some people are so heavenly-minded that they are of no earthly use." That is how the saying goes. It is one of those completely nonsensical and entirely flawed pieces of common wisdom. If anything, the great danger for the saints is that they will fail to be heavenly-minded people and so have nothing of any real and lasting value to sustain them in or enable them to contribute to life on the earth in its present form.

As we have seen, there is a danger that we, in all sincerity, overlook or even despise the present blessings of goodness and beauty that God Almighty is bestowing on us as we make our way through this world. We must understand that these blessings are given to be genuinely enjoyed, and we can and should enjoy them. At the same time, there is another danger—perhaps a greater one—for the people of God. All Christians must take care that their eyes and their hearts are not to be fixed on this life, "for where your treasure is, there your heart will be also" (Matt. 6:21). It is easy for our hearts to be taken up with the beauties and goodness that belong primarily or entirely to this world, which sometimes results in our wavering in our journey to the heavenly city.

One of the battles that a pilgrim must fight is an unhealthy attachment to this present world. It presses in upon us. The strange thing is that an attachment to or even an obsession with the stuff of this life can happen particularly if we have much of it or if we do not have much of it at all. These challenges in two directions are summarized in Proverbs 30:8–9:

> Give me neither poverty nor riches—
> Feed me with the food allotted to me;

Lest I be full and deny You,
And say, "Who is the LORD?"
Or lest I be poor and steal,
And profane the name of my God.

This is a prayer that we might enjoy a competent portion—just our daily bread, if you will—rather than struggle with smothering excess or biting lack. If we are blessed with a great deal, we can put too much emphasis on the things of this world and so lose sight of God altogether. The things of this world demand all our attention and swallow up our souls. If we are deprived of much, we can presume that the answer to our problems is having more, and, in grasping after the things that belong to this world, we might profane the Lord's name.

In addition, many believers struggle to hold in scriptural balance what is sometimes described in terms of a distinction, even a tension, between what is "already" and what is "not yet." This language recognizes that there are good things that belong in nature or character to the coming age that are *already* given to the saints while at the same time acknowledging that those good things are *not yet* all given or entirely given. For example, you catch something of this in John's language in his statement that "now we are children of God; and it has not yet been revealed what we shall be, but we know that when He is revealed, we shall be like Him, for we shall see Him as He is" (1 John 3:2).

It is possible to lose sight of a real and substantive heaven—heaven as it really is. When this happens, it is frighteningly easy for us to get taken up with the things of this world. For far too many Christians, heaven is entirely ethereal, perhaps just a great white space or a line that stretches ever onward into a void. There is nothing personal and nothing concrete about their expectations, and so there is little that is attractive about the prospect of glory. Indeed, this can be a challenge for preachers. I distinctly remember a conference in which a preacher was asked to preach on heaven. By the time he had finished, I am not sure that anyone in the congregation really wanted to go there. He had made the whole prospect seem unappetizing to the point of repugnant. How he managed that with such a magnificent topic remains beyond my comprehension! In the same way, perhaps we sing a good number of hymns and songs about going to be with

Christ when we die. It may also be that we sing considerably fewer about our expectation of a new heaven and a new earth in which we will live with resurrection bodies. We sing more about our immediate prospects after death than about our ultimate prospects as the resurrected people of the living God. Where we do not have these grand biblical notions about the future hope of the saints, some of us will push off the hope of heaven because we do not understand it, are even scared of it, or simply do not really know what to expect. Perhaps this is the reason why so many today are trying to get hold of what actually belongs to the experience of glory in all its fullness and to drag forward into the here and now what the Lord in His wisdom has reserved for the future.

There are two tendencies, then, against which we fight. One is the tendency to push away the "not yet," losing sight of it or losing our appetite for it because we do not understand it well enough and see it plainly enough. The other is the tendency to bring forward the "not yet," as if those things that belong to heaven alone—perfect harmony and absolute peace and justice, for example—can be secured while we live on earth. We must recognize that we live between the times and therefore fix our eyes on glory while remembering that it will arrive in God's good time.

If we are pilgrims, then an accurate and sincere expectation of glory will recalibrate our souls and concentrate our eyes and our minds on the things that are of first importance (because they are lasting) while here on earth, even as we recognize the other good things that God has given to us for our temporary stay here. And so we must anticipate the destiny that God has set before us and assured us that we will receive.

Anticipate the Destiny: Scriptural Framework

The Saints' Inheritance

Blessed are the meek, for they shall inherit the earth. (Matt. 5:5)

Christ promises true and lasting happiness to the meek in their inheritance of the earth. Who are these meek people? Is this a description of people who are spinelessly quiescent, the human embodiment of a particularly worn doormat? Not remotely! The language of meekness refers to a Christian's confident submission in relation to his God and a gracious gentleness in relation to his fellow men. The meek man is not ambitious, not grasping after position and reputation, not always seeking applause and prominence. He is not combative and quick to resent a slight, but rather hard to provoke and easily pacified. Such a spirit does not aggressively compete for carnal good on the world's terms, but rather lives easily now in anticipation of blessings to come. The reason for his meekness is that he is not competing with gritted teeth and a desperate glint in his eye for some small and shabby part of this passing world. Rather, he recognizes that he is going to inherit the earth. As a result he can rest easy in his soul and in his relations now because he anticipates his best things to come. Such a believer is confident that Christ has conquered all His and our enemies and has won back the earth for the saints:

> For yet a little while and the wicked shall be no more;
> Indeed, you will look carefully for his place,
> But it shall be no more.
> But the meek shall inherit the earth,
> And shall delight themselves in the abundance of peace.
>   (Ps. 37:10–11)

He anticipates the time when—having already been made "kings and priests to our God"—"we shall reign on the earth" (Rev. 5:10). If we are Christians, we are looking forward to the inheritance that we shall share with Jesus Christ. We are "heirs of God and joint heirs with Christ." We expect to inherit all that Christ has secured with the Christ who secured it, as those who, having suffered with Him, shall then be glorified together with Him (Rom. 8:17). The meek one—the one who is poor in spirit, who recognizes his sin and trusts in God, who realizes that he is not living for the here and now—does not need to embrace the creed of "nature, red in tooth and claw,"[1] fighting against all comers for every inch of territory. He knows that he will receive his blessings in due time and that all this will come to pass when the Lord returns in His glory.

Those who are meek will inherit the earth, and it is, without a shadow of a doubt, this earth that we will inherit. It is here that we

---

1. Alfred, Lord Tennyson, *In Memoriam A. H. H*, canto 56.

shall reign as kings and priests. This world, in the creative sense, is the inheritance of the saints. To grasp this, we must turn to Romans 8.

The Creation Liberated

> For the earnest expectation of the creation eagerly waits for the revealing of the sons of God. For the creation was subjected to futility, not willingly, but because of Him who subjected it in hope; because the creation itself also will be delivered from the bondage of corruption into the glorious liberty of the children of God. For we know that the whole creation groans and labors with birth pangs together until now. (Rom. 8:19–22)

Paul laments that the whole creation is subject to decay and death. All this can be traced back to Adam's fall. As a result of Adam's sin and though retaining some vestiges and glimmerings of the original design, the creation of God is now marked—how grievously!—by impurity, deformity, and infirmity. Paul gives this world a personality (this is a literary device, and not an admission of some kind of pantheism or the attribution of sentience to the world considered as a created whole) and considers it as chained, longing for deliverance.

There is a sense in which we can say that things were not meant to be this way. This world was not designed for vanity and corruption, and yet that is its present lot. As a result, the creation is sighing for restoration, crying out to be delivered.

Think of a phenomenal sports car, the sort of vehicle that—even without an engineering bone in your body—you can consider in its sleek lines and instinctively recognize that this thing is designed to move. You could sit in the seat and put your foot down, and every element of this machine will cooperate in speeding the whole construct along a straight, wide, open road. How would you feel if you saw that sports car rusting on a patch of grass in front of someone's home? How do think that the car would feel if it had character and personality? Would it not be saying, "I was made to drive! I was designed to go fast! I was not made to rust and corrupt. I was made to act as intended, to excel in accordance with my design, to express fully my capacity." Imagine creation as if it had its own character and personality, designed to bring glory to God, for all its elements to cooperate in bringing praise to the Lord who made it. It has been subjected unwillingly to futility, and yet it hopes—it is sighing for restoration because of its present corruption. The whole creation groans and labors with birth pains together until now.

Elsewhere we read of wars and earthquakes and troubles in the earth. This creation is subject to what we might call cosmic contractions in anticipation of the not-far-distant and inevitable rebirth alongside the glorified saints, sharing with them in the blessings of Christ's return. One day this world will sigh, not with sorrow, but with joy and relief because its Lord will come again, and it will share with His people in the restoration of all things. What a wonderful prospect! All nature—animate and inanimate—will rejoice at Christ's coming:

> Say among the nations, "The LORD reigns;
> The world also is firmly established,
> It shall not be moved;
> He shall judge the peoples righteously."
>
> Let the heavens rejoice, and let the earth be glad;
> Let the sea roar, and all its fullness;
> Let the field be joyful, and all that is in it.
> Then all the trees of the woods will rejoice before the LORD.
> For He is coming, for He is coming to judge the earth.
> He shall judge the world with righteousness,
> And the peoples with His truth. (Ps. 96:10–13; cf. Ps. 98:7–9)

I do not know what trees and seas, mountains and skies, and fields and forests sound like when they rejoice. But we will when they do, when Jesus Christ comes to judge the world with righteousness. How do you begin to imagine what this creation will sound like, what song it will sing when it breaks out in joy because its Lord, Creator, and Redeemer returns to strip off all the rot and corruption and to make it what it ought to be once more, restoring it to the perfection of harmony?

This World Dissolved

> Therefore, since all these things will be dissolved, what manner of persons ought you to be in holy conduct and godliness, looking for and hastening the coming of the day of God, because of which the heavens will be dissolved, being on fire, and the elements will melt with fervent heat? Nevertheless we, according

to His promise, look for new heavens and a new earth in which righteousness dwells. (2 Peter 3:11–13)

Peter first issues a stark reminder—even a warning—that this whole world will be dissolved, loosed from the bonds that have held it fast. If this is going to happen, what kind of people ought the children of God to be? Holy behavior is required of them. They are to live as those who are conditioned primarily not by this present world but by the passing of this world. We must be characterized by holiness.

As believers do this, Peter suggests that such behavior will hasten the day they anticipate. Their prayers, practices, and pursuits are all serving, in various ways, to bring about the end, perhaps through their active participation in the various purposes of God that must be brought to pass before the end comes. They are praying, "Come, Lord Jesus, come quickly." Their gospel preaching in all the world is bringing in God's elect, and so bringing ever closer the end of all things.

Then, that awful day is assured. God will arrive in the person of His Son, Jesus Christ, robed in the majesty of His glorified humanity, seated on the throne of His glory, with all His holy angels with Him. That glorious advent will secure the dissolution of all things, as there is a melting in the fervent heat that accompanies His bright arrival. Christ will fold up the world He made like an old, threadbare garment (Heb. 1:10–12).

But this is not the end. There is also a glorious promise ahead. The Lord has undertaken that there will be a new heaven and a new earth in which righteousness dwells, sin having been exterminated and excluded. The end of all things is not the end of material matter, but is the true beginning of material matter as God intends it to be for all eternity. Peter's point in all this is that all our present existence must find its primary influences in our future expectations and our glorious prospects as the people of God.

Time and Eternity

For our light affliction, which is but for a moment, is working for us a far more exceeding and eternal weight of glory, while we do not look at the things which are seen, but at the things which are not seen. For the things which are seen are temporary, but the things which are not seen are eternal. (2 Cor. 4:17–18)

Paul's *light* afflictions—which ones are those? Perhaps the near-constant torments and regular brushes with death! The sufferings that the apostle Paul underwent were quite monstrous, and he is not shy of cataloging them, even if he spares us a detailed description. At the beginning of this letter to the Corinthians he speaks "of our trouble which came to us in Asia: that we were burdened beyond measure, above strength, so that we despaired even of life" (2 Cor. 1:8). A little earlier in this passage, he acknowledges that "we are hard-pressed on every side, yet not crushed; we are perplexed, but not in despair; persecuted, but not forsaken; struck down, but not destroyed—always carrying about in the body the dying of the Lord Jesus, that the life of Jesus also may be manifested in our body" (2 Cor. 4:8–10). Perhaps best known is the register of ministerial pains and persecutions he provides later in this epistle:

> Are they ministers of Christ?—I speak as a fool—I am more: in labors more abundant, in stripes above measure, in prisons more frequently, in deaths often. From the Jews five times I received forty stripes minus one. Three times I was beaten with rods; once I was stoned; three times I was shipwrecked; a night and a day I have been in the deep; in journeys often, in perils of waters, in perils of robbers, in perils of my own countrymen, in perils of the Gentiles, in perils in the city, in perils in the wilderness, in perils in the sea, in perils among false brethren; in weariness and toil, in sleeplessness often, in hunger and thirst, in fastings often, in cold and nakedness—besides the other things, what comes upon me daily: my deep concern for all the churches. (2 Cor. 11:23–28)

After such surveys and summaries we might ask, "How can you describe such afflictions as light and momentary?" For most of us, they probably seem unbearably oppressive and agonizingly prolonged. But Paul has compared and contrasted them with the "far more exceeding and eternal weight of glory," considering that these sufferings for Christ's sake are securing future blessings that far outweigh them. In themselves, how heavy they feel! By comparison with the glories they are securing, they are barely worthy of being weighed in the same balance.

What produces such a perspective? By the world's standards, Paul is a disappointment of magnificent proportions, a complete failure. He is the golden boy who lost it all. He is the man who had climbed to the top of the tree, then fell fast and hit hard.

However, he knows—as the saints should know and grasp—that what is worthwhile and truly lasting are not those things that are seen but the things that are not seen. The things we see, for all their apparent substance and permanence, are temporary. The things that are not seen, for all their sometimes seeming distance and insubstantiality, are eternal. It is faith only that perceives these things accurately, faith that sees what the eye of flesh cannot discern and says, "That will last!" God's promise "indicates the removal of those things that are being shaken, as of things that are made, that the things which cannot be shaken may remain" (Heb. 12:27). The same faith that perceives this accurately will choose correspondingly and wisely.

The Earnest of Our Inheritance

In Him you also trusted, after you heard the word of truth, the gospel of your salvation; in whom also, having believed, you were sealed with the Holy Spirit of promise, who is the guarantee of our inheritance until the redemption of the purchased possession, to the praise of His glory. (Eph. 1:13–14)

God's saints have His stamp upon them. They are marked out as His people for the purposes of confirmation and protection by the Holy Spirit who has been given to them. The Spirit is the already bestowed down payment on what is to come. To use the older but accurate language, He is the "earnest" of our inheritance—that guarantee of what still lies ahead, a guarantee that is part of and of the same nature as the inheritance considered as a whole. For example, if you owed someone one hundred dollars and offered your watch as collateral, a sort of guarantee, you would still owe that person one hundred dollars and, having paid the whole sum, you would ask for your watch back. But suppose you said to that person, "I will give you ten dollars," you would then have only ninety dollars left to pay. The point is, you have given that person an earnest of the whole, a down payment that is the same in nature as the entirety that will eventually come. That is how the Spirit is described here.

In that sense, the believer's "already" experience is a properly Spiritual one (the capital *S* is deliberate), even as we anticipate a

Spirit-governed "not yet." Having the Holy Spirit already, the full inheritance is already guaranteed. It is certain, but it is future: by Him we have been "sealed for the day of redemption" (Eph. 4:30). Our expectation is of a life entirely characterized, completely influenced, and fully governed by the Spirit of God, as communicated in Paul's first letter to the Corinthians. Our body "is sown a natural body, it is raised a spiritual body. There is a natural body, and there is a spiritual body.... As was the man of dust, so also are those who are made of dust; and as is the heavenly Man, so also are those who are heavenly. And as we have borne the image of the man of dust, we shall also bear the image of the heavenly Man" (1 Cor. 15:44, 48–49). When we read these words, perhaps we are in the bad habit of contrasting what is spiritual with what is physical or material. That is the wrong contrast. We are to contrast what is spiritual with what is natural. What kind of body will we have in the resurrection? A spiritual body—a physical entity, a material reality, but spiritual rather than natural. This mortal will put on immortality; this corruption will put on incorruption. There will be a flesh-and-blood person who is entirely characterized by and under the influence of the Holy Spirit.

Our present experience of salvation is of the same nature as our coming experience. The Spirit who has now taken up residence in our hearts—giving us assurance, working likeness to Christ and the realities of our adoption as sons—is the same Spirit by whom we shall enter into all the blessings that are stored up for us. What we possess now, with the Spirit indwelling these bodies retaining the image of the man of dust, is a sweet and splendid foretaste of the banquet that is spread for the people of God in the new heaven and the new earth in which righteousness dwells.

The Spirit's work in us now is real and radical, but it is—relatively speaking—at present a work more in the bud, though genuine and enduring. That work is going to bloom eternally in Christ Jesus at His coming again, when we shall bear the image of the heavenly Man in the fullest and most complete sense.

Holy Indifference

> But this I say, brethren, the time is short, so that from now on even those who have wives should be as though they had none, those who weep as though they did not weep, those who rejoice

as though they did not rejoice, those who buy as though they did not possess, and those who use this world as not misusing it. For the form of this world is passing away. (1 Cor. 7:29–31)

Paul is concluding a section in which he is giving counsels about a time of "present distress" (1 Cor. 7:26). It seems that, at this point, he broadens out his applications and presses home the principles of the present distress to the whole way of living in the last days. By comparing the present distress with coming woes, Paul is drawing out a general rule that the temporal nature of things in the world should provide a relativizing key to life in this world, a register by means of which things assume their proper proportion. Relations and afflictions, enjoyments and employments—all must be weighed in the scale of eternity.

Paul encourages us to cultivate a disposition that Matthew Henry calls a "holy indifferency."[2] Notice that it is not an absolute and sinful indifference, as if we are not to care at all about these things. Instead it is a righteous holding of the things of this world with a light grip, enjoying them but not depending upon them. Here is marriage, sorrow, rejoicing, buying—but these things are not to be treated as if they are the be-all and end-all of our existence, the sum and substance of life on earth. All must be held lightly because they cannot be finally retained. We cannot guarantee them for good or for ill. The world is to be used for a holy purpose, not misused or abused for sinful pleasure. This is all of a piece with Paul's counsels to the rich: "Command those who are rich in this present age not to be haughty, nor to trust in uncertain riches but in the living God, who gives us richly all things to enjoy. Let them do good, that they be rich in good works, ready to give, willing to share, storing up for themselves a good foundation for the time to come, that they may lay hold on eternal life" (1 Tim. 6:17–19). Here is the same appreciation for good things with the same conviction about the best things, a balance that keeps us from a God-dishonoring dependence on even the good things of this world and enables us to hold them with a light grasp.

Why do we hold these things lightly? Because time is short and the form of all these things is passing away. This is already true, and it is why we acknowledge, "Change and decay in all around I

---

2. Henry, *Commentary*, 6:436.

see."[3] But it will soon prove absolutely true when the great change is ushered in.

The traveler who stays in a hotel room for a couple of nights does not put down roots in that place. She does not get emotionally attached to the bed. She does not organize the little fridge in the corner for her convenience. She may appreciate the good things available, but they are not home, and so she treats them with a grateful but reasonable lack of deep affection. She is only lodging there, not staying there. It is only a temporary stopping point. The furniture and the provisions are relatively, but not absolutely, precious. When her time there is done, she is going to leave and go home. So the saints are conscious that they are in what may be a fairly well-appointed hotel room, but it is not home, and so they entertain a holy indifference toward these things.

The End of Rebellion

> And the world is passing away, and the lust of it; but he who
> does the will of God abides forever. (1 John 2:17)

John draws a direct contrast between the love of the world and the love of God. He is speaking of the world primarily in the ethical sense. The world, considered as the fallen creation in its opposition to God, together with all the lusts that are characteristic of that world are transitory. The world, together with all the lusts it stirs up in the hearts of men and women, is passing away, and nothing of it will be left behind.

We must remember how John uses the idea of the world. He is not telling us that there will no longer be anything substantial, as if creation will be uncreated and a void left behind. John is not describing here the end of material things, but rather the termination of all spiritual and ethical opposition to God and His rule. Rebellion against God is going to come to an end. The Holy One is going to draw a line under the antagonism toward His rule and put the earth into the form and pattern He intends for it. The earth has been won back by the death of Christ. The present age and its passing pleasures are doomed; they must fade and fail because Christ came and

---

3. Henry Francis Lyte, "Abide with Me."

conquered. There is no lasting fruit and no enduring future in world-liness. Who will be standing when the end comes? "The one who does the will of God." Only the obedient and the fruit of their obedi-ence will endure when all that opposes God and is contrary to Him is swept away.

An Eternal Reward

> By faith Moses, when he became of age, refused to be called the son of Pharaoh's daughter, choosing rather to suffer afflic-tion with the people of God than to enjoy the passing pleasures of sin, esteeming the reproach of Christ greater riches than the treasures in Egypt; for he looked to the reward. (Heb. 11:24–26)

Here is the keynote of all that we have been addressing: *faith*. It was by faith that Moses endured. Faith is "the substance of things hoped for, the evidence of things not seen" (Heb. 11:1). The writer to the Hebrews records the mature judgment of someone who had tasted the best and faced the worst that the world had to offer. Moses was not a fifteen-year-old in the first flush of strength or a twenty-five-year-old just coming into his maturity. He was forty, perhaps even eighty, when he made and confirmed these decisions. He had expe-rienced the highs and the lows of life; he knew the nature of its joys and its sorrows.

He had seen the misery of Israel and the beauty of Egypt. In the light of that experience he reached a conclusion and made his decision. He weighed time and its afflictions against eternity and its glories and then chose to reject the present world's highest honors, greatest riches, and sweetest pleasures in order to secure an eternal reward, even though it would cost great reproaches and afflictions in the present age. If you were to take heaven out of the equation, then Moses is one of the maddest men who ever walked the planet. But, in truth, Moses chose wisely and well, enduring as one who could see the invisible God. That is the very essence of a Christlike faith. Remember how the Lord Jesus lived and died, "who for the joy that was set before Him endured the cross, despising the shame, and has sat down at the right hand of the throne of God" (Heb. 12:2).

Moses set out to secure an eternal reward. He judged that the reproach of Christ was of greater riches than the treasures in Egypt for he looked to that reward associated with it. In the words of P. E. Hughes, "The man of faith chooses the way of obedience and suffering, not by constraint, but willingly and joyfully, knowing that the goal is a glorious one."[4]

Anticipate the Destiny: Summary Thoughts

We are passing through a passing world. Both its deepest sorrows and its sweetest joys are, in themselves, temporary. This world will never finally and fully reflect the glory of God until Christ returns and all is made new. It may seem laudable, then, on one level, to set out to make poverty history, as the slogan goes, and we have spoken of what it means to alleviate the suffering of the needy in a legitimate way. But the final eradication of such things will not happen until Christ comes again.

There are certain expectations that some believers seem to have, as if—by their own labors—they can create heaven on earth. Some seem to imagine that they can bring forward and establish certain things that the Lord God has reserved for the coming of Jesus Christ. You want to make poverty history? Then you must ignore the plain statement of the Lord that "the poor you have with you always" (John 12:8).

Only at Christ's return will suffering cease forever. Only then will every tear be wiped from the eyes of God's people. Only then will pain and sighing pass away. Only then will grieving come to a final end, when God in His glory is made known, when the New Jerusalem descends from heaven and all is made well in the world, with the beauty of creation fully restored in a new heaven and a new earth in which righteousness dwells.

This is the Christian hope, and it is an abounding hope! This is not a message of hopelessness, but hopefulness because Christ's church knows that this present world is not eternal. There is a heavenly, abiding city to which we are traveling, a place that is real—touchable and tasteable and inhabitable—located in a world of joy and love. It is not a world of nothingness and a realm of mist, but a place of substantial, sweet, and enduring reality—the world to come is the place

---

4. Philip Edgcumbe Hughes, *A Commentary on the Epistle to the Hebrews* (Grand Rapids: Eerdmans, 1993), 497.

where realness really begins! We anticipate a city that has foundations, whose builder and maker is God (Heb. 11:10). We are looking forward to a place of peace and plenty. Our lasting inheritance and highest and purest blessings are there, where Christ reigns absolute.

It is not death that brings us there, but life—resurrection life. This is one of the reasons why John sees under the altar the souls of those who had been slain for the word of God and for the testimony which they held and hears them crying with a loud voice, saying, "How long, O Lord, holy and true, until You judge and avenge our blood on those who dwell on the earth?" (Rev. 6:10). This is why Paul, who desires to depart and be with Christ, must also say that "we who are in this tent groan, being burdened, not because we want to be unclothed, but further clothed, that mortality may be swallowed up by life" (2 Cor. 5:4). What we are looking toward, the ultimate terminus of the Christian hope, is the resurrection life in and with Christ Jesus:

> Now this I say, brethren, that flesh and blood cannot inherit the kingdom of God; nor does corruption inherit incorruption. Behold, I tell you a mystery: We shall not all sleep, but we shall all be changed—in a moment, in the twinkling of an eye, at the last trumpet. For the trumpet will sound, and the dead will be raised incorruptible, and we shall be changed. For this corruptible must put on incorruption, and this mortal must put on immortality. So when this corruptible has put on incorruption, and this mortal has put on immortality, then shall be brought to pass the saying that is written: "Death is swallowed up in victory."
>
> "O Death, where is your sting?
>
> O Hades, where is your victory?"
>
> The sting of death is sin, and the strength of sin is the law. But thanks be to God, who gives us the victory through our Lord Jesus Christ. Therefore, my beloved brethren, be steadfast, immovable, always abounding in the work of the Lord, knowing that your labor is not in vain in the Lord. (1 Cor. 15:50–58)

This is the end point to which we look and for which we long—a restored humanity! Then body and soul will be glorified together and we shall be as God intends us to be, in the presence of Christ the Savior in all His glory.

This makes us righteous realists here: "Set your mind on things above, not on things on the earth. For you died, and your life is hidden with Christ in God. When Christ who is our life appears, then you also will appear with Him in glory" (Col. 3:2–4). We know what is true and real, and so we refuse to adjust our principles and practices to fit the values and demands of a passing world. Amid all the imperfections and sufferings, we look to our glorious hope, acknowledging that we know a little but that we have barely begun to guess the whole: "Beloved, now we are children of God; and it has not yet been revealed what we shall be, but we know that when He is revealed, we shall be like Him, for we shall see Him as He is" (1 John 3:2).

As pilgrims, we appreciate the blessings of time. Without the perspective described here, we will not fully grasp that the earth is not our enemy but is sighing with us for redemption. This body is not our captor, holding us against our will, despite our mutually fallen condition. We are looking forward to a day when this corruption will put on incorruption and when our humanity blooms into the full glory of its Christlike prospects. Such convictions point us forward to what is real and lasting.

Therefore, the pilgrim subordinates time to eternity, anticipating the cosmic regeneration at Christ's coming and so living always with an eye to the world to come. We understand that we cannot always preempt that world, however much we might long to do so, neither should we turn our backs upon it, as if the best life is now. The prospect of life in heaven should make all the difference to our present life on earth. Our eyes are fixed on the future: "For our citizenship is in heaven, from which we also eagerly wait for the Savior, the Lord Jesus Christ, who will transform our lowly body that it may be conformed to His glorious body, according to the working by which He is able even to subdue all things to Himself. Therefore, my beloved and longed-for brethren, my joy and crown, so stand fast in the Lord, beloved" (Phil. 3:20–4:1). Let us note again that Christian hope does not lie in the present but passing acts of men, but in the present and coming rule of Christ. If we build our hopes here, we are doomed to failure. Consider the lesson that Bunyan's pilgrim learned in the House of the Interpreter when that teacher of truth led him into a room where two children sat on their chairs.

The name of the elder was Passion, and the name of the other Patience. Passion seemed to be much discontented, but Patience was very quiet. Then Christian asked, "What is the reason of the discontent of Passion?" The Interpreter answered, "The governor of them would have him stay for his best things till the beginning of the next year, but he will have all now; but Patience is willing to wait."

Christian watches as someone pours a bag of treasure at the feet of Passion, in which he revels while reviling Patience. But it is not long before he has wasted it all and has nothing left but rags. Christian then asks the Interpreter for an explanation:

> These two lads are figures: Passion, of the men of this world; and Patience, of the men of that which is to come; for, as here thou seest, passion will have all now, this year, that is to say, in this world; so are the men of this world: they must have all their good things now, they cannot stay till next year, that is, until the next world, for their portion of good. That proverb, "A bird in the hand is worth two in the bush," is of more authority with them than are all the Divine testimonies of the good of the world to come. But as thou sawest that he had quickly lavished all away, and had presently left him nothing but rags; so will it be with all such men at the end of this world.

Christian understands then that "Patience has the best wisdom, and that upon many accounts," namely that he is willing to wait for the best things and that he will possess and enjoy the glory of those things when Passion has nothing left in which to boast. The Interpreter adds his insights:

> Nay, you may add another, to wit, the glory of the next world will never wear out; but these are suddenly gone. Therefore Passion had not so much reason to laugh at Patience, because he had his good things first, as Patience will have to laugh at Passion, because he had his best things last; for first must give place to last, because last must have his time to come; but last gives place to nothing, for there is not another to succeed. He, therefore, that hath his portion first, must needs have a time to spend it; but he that hath his portion last, must have it lastingly; therefore it is said of Dives, "Thou in thy lifetime receivedst thy good things, and likewise Lazarus evil things; but now he is comforted, and thou art tormented."

Christian draws the plain and potent conclusion: "It is not best to covet things that are now, but to wait for things to come." The Interpreter concurs:

> You say the truth: "For the things that are seen are temporal; but the things that are not seen are eternal." But though this be so, yet since things present, and our fleshly appetite, are such near neighbors one to another; and again, because things to come and carnal sense, are such strangers one to another; therefore it is, that the first of these so suddenly fall into amity, and that distance is so continued between the second.[5]

Do you not find that the things of this world and the appetites of our bodies walk arm in arm with each other while the things to come and our "carnal sense" have barely a nodding acquaintance? And yet it is not best to covet things that are now, but to wait for things to come. Is yours the passion that wants all now, or the patience that waits for the best with the confidence that you will enjoy it when passion's gains have passed away?

Anticipate the Destiny: Specific Counsels

How, then, shall we put passion down and build patience up? How do we so lay hold on things to come that they impress themselves upon our souls and have a lasting impact on our lives?

First, we must *believe the truth*. I know it may seem obvious and simple, and in a sense it is. At the same time, it is so easy to nod in agreement with such a statement and yet never take it to heart. Do we acknowledge these things as orthodox truth without ever really hearing and heeding it? Faith must operate here. Faith must consider what is seen and tell the soul, "This is passing away." Faith must gaze upon what is not seen and communicate to the soul, "That is eternal." Faith must lift its eyes to the risen and reigning Christ and proclaim with anticipation to the soul, "He is returning!" Faith must survey afflictions for Christ's sake and assure the soul, "These things count for almost nothing." Faith must contemplate the future and state to the soul, "That is glory!" Faith lays hold of the concreteness of heaven. It is the place where saints will dwell with glorified bodies

---

5. Bunyan, *Pilgrim's Progress*, 3:99.

and sinless souls, praising God together before the God-man, Jesus Christ. We must hold that, know that, and live in accordance with it. Faith likes to climb the tower of God's truth and gaze into the distance, where it can see things that others cannot discern. May the Spirit of Christ help us in this!

Then, we must also *embrace the implications* of this. You may know the phrase "the proof of the pudding is in the eating." The sense is that the test of the matter comes in its experience or application. So it is in our attitude to this world and the world to come. Many people will readily confess that this world and the lust of it are passing away, yet go on living as if this world were everything. Our petty empires are to be won and maintained in this world: its pleasures must be pursued, its wealth treasured, its values embraced. It is as true here as in anything else that faith that does not work is dead. Faith that makes no difference to life may be many things, but it is not faith by any biblical assessment. Faith in what God has spoken about all these things must show itself in the principal and practical and ever-increasing priority of eternity over time, and therefore in the calculation of all that belongs to time in the light of eternity. Faith recognizes that one empire has already been established, is being advanced, and will soon be made manifest. Faith therefore invests in that empire of God. Without this, the pressure of the present will overwhelm us and the passing world will swallow us up. When we believe the Scriptures, the age to come conditions our attitudes and affections and activities in the age that now is.

Therefore we must *choose the best*. This world is full of fool's gold—"the lust of the flesh, the lust of the eyes, and the pride of life" (1 John 2:16). Fool's gold does glitter. That is why it is so enticing. It is dangled before us in order to draw out our hearts and win our affections. If we reject it plainly and purposefully, we will face waves of antagonism and very likely afflictions. The people who love the things of this world will not understand why we turn our backs upon those things if and when it is required of us. They may even hate us for it. But we must remember that the best and the worst of this world will pass away, and only the kingdom of Christ will stand. John Calvin said, "A moment is long, if we look around us on this side and on that; but, when we have once raised our minds heavenward, a thousand years begin to appear to us to be like a moment."[6] Here he echoes the language of 2 Peter 3. When we grasp these things, our perspective becomes, in measure, godlike. What now seems to last for ages and ages assumes the proportion of a passing second. Such a conviction recalibrates our perspective on time. Faith chooses eternity over time, future blessings over present indulgences, lasting joys ahead rather than passing pleasures now. Indeed, it weighs up present passing afflictions in the light of coming and enduring happiness and so rejects fading morsels and eternal torments. Have you made that choice? Have you chosen eternity with the Lord God over time and its passing pleasures? Where is your heart, and where is your hope?

So schooled in truth, so fixed in faith, we are able to *endure the worst*. Again, this is much easier to say than to do. Christian endurance and perseverance are not the same as stoicism, fatalism, or resignation. The flawed attitude shrugs when trouble comes, confessing that there is nothing much we can do to avoid it, and we might as well grin (or not) and bear it. Such an attitude reveals an impassivity with regard to the world, an indifference to circumstances. This is the Christianity that tends to see providence as an impersonal but irresistible force rather than the superintending care of a loving heavenly Father. By contrast, the healthy believer entertains a lively and enduring hope. This hope puts in the balance all the sufferings and afflictions we endure as saints and considers that they are working a far more exceeding weight of glory. The saint can choose afflictions for the sake of Christ in the light of the coming reward. Most of us are native cowards, and given the choice between afflictions and reliefs, we would choose the reliefs of affliction rather than reproaches with afflictions. But looking to the reward will give us strength and courage. How can we count our afflictions to be light things? By remembering that they last for a moment and by comparing them to the blessings to come. This was the faith and hope of Moses, who made his choice and suffered his afflictions as one who considered the reproach of Christ to be of incalculable value and who looked to the reward. That is the prospect which sweetens our

---

6. John Calvin, *Commentary on the Second Epistle to the Corinthians*, vol. 20 of *Calvin's Commentaries* (repr., Grand Rapids: Baker, 1996), 214.

sufferings and alleviates our afflictions as we put them in the context of the rest and joy to come.

So we should *ponder the future*. These realities will never capture our hearts until we consider them and dwell upon them. Time, at its best and at its worst, presses in upon our consciousness. It fills our view and demands our attention. We sometimes speak of the tyranny of the urgent—there is also the tyranny of the present, the dominance of the immediate. This moment demands our all. We are called to live in the here and now. We must deliberately meditate on all these things of eternity, consciously assessing and reevaluating the things that call for our hearts, stepping away from the howling demands of the moment to consider the truth and how it ought to work out in our lives. We must do this until the future glory is imprinted upon our souls. We must ensure that the truth conditions our meditation and that our meditation then conditions our living. This is not an exercise in the use of our imagination, but the chewing over of our substantial hopes. There are some vain volumes written about heaven that are patently unscriptural nonsense, which is doubtless why they sell so well. These stories are little more than fairy tales. We must lay hold of the truth. Christ is coming, the world will be restored, Jerusalem will be a praise, and all creation will sing.

So we must *treasure the promises*. We must lock on to the divine assurances against our doubts and fears, our trials and temptations. Satan will whisper, as he did at the beginning, "Has God really said…?" Yes, God has spoken! Christ heard that whisper in the wilderness and responded, "Thus says the Lord." We must pit our "Thus says the Lord!" against the whispers, lies, and howls of Satan. We must take and dwell upon the present spiritual realities that we enjoy as the earnest of our inheritance, looking forward to the day when we enter into the fullness of that inheritance.

Therefore we should *pursue the reward*. This is not to sneak in the carnal, but to cultivate the sensible! It would be childish to demand shiny rocks today when a few days' patience will provide us with heaps of diamonds (ignoring for a moment that, in the context of the present discussion, diamonds are no more than shiny rocks!). The wise man would dismiss the shiny rocks and wait for the diamonds. The former are nothing; the latter are worth waiting for. Are we waiting for the diamonds? Are we waiting for and working for our rewards? We must keep our heavenly blessings in sight and live so as to obtain them: "Do you not know that those who run in a race all run, but one receives the prize? Run in such a way that you may obtain it. And everyone who competes for the prize is temperate in all things. Now they do it to obtain a perishable crown, but we for an imperishable crown. Therefore I run thus: not with uncertainty. Thus I fight: not as one who beats the air" (1 Cor. 9:24–26).

Is that how you live in the light of heaven? The games to which Paul is referring (the ones that would be most familiar to the Corinthians) awarded crowns made of celery, a clear affront to any right-thinking man. By comparison, how should we run to obtain a golden crown woven of heavenly light? Do you not want a good spot in the heavenly choir to sing the praises of your dearest Lord? If you do, you must labor for it! Our labors do not secure our salvation, but flow from it. In flowing from salvation, they do then secure a reward in heaven. Every Christian will be in glory, but God has rewards for those who serve Him well. It is grace upon grace upon grace! Our good works are given by God, appointed beforehand that we should walk in them. Our opportunity to pursue them is our obligation to take them. And the wonder is, we shall be rewarded for doing so! We will obtain blessings in accordance with the life that we live as children of God. Paul ran like a man who wanted to win; he fought like a man who intended to defeat his foes. He strove to lay hold of that for which Christ had laid hold of him.

With such a spirit capturing our hearts and characterizing our lives, we should *await the blessings*. The meek will inherit the earth—it is not yet, but it will come to pass. The sons of God will be revealed, though now they are dismissed and despised. The ones who do the will of God will abide forever, even if their lives are sneered at here. The saints will sit down with Christ in His kingdom, though here they are made as the filth of the world, "the offscouring of all things until now" (1 Cor. 4:13). Then there will be heaven on earth, for heaven will come down to earth, and earth will be remade. The saints can walk through this wilderness world assured of all these things to come.

With this in view, let there be in every one of God's people a composed but eager expectation. Biblical realism says that we cannot make earth to be heaven, but the confidence of the saints grants a heaven on earth until heaven comes to earth:

> "Eye has not seen, nor ear heard,
> Nor have entered into the heart of man
> The things which God has prepared for those who love Him."
>   (1 Cor. 2:9)

This is not an easy perspective to maintain, "for now we see in a mirror, dimly, but then face to face. Now I know in part, but then I shall know just as I also am known" (1 Cor. 13:12). And with that anticipation, we wait for those consummating acts of God:

> "For behold, I create new heavens and a new earth;
> And the former shall not be remembered or come to mind.
> But be glad and rejoice forever in what I create;
> For behold, I create Jerusalem as a rejoicing,
> And her people a joy.
> I will rejoice in Jerusalem,
> And joy in My people;
> The voice of weeping shall no longer be heard in her,
> Nor the voice of crying." (Isa. 65:17–19)

Is it not astounding to you that you are looking forward to a day when the only thing that will put your joy in the shade is the joy of your God, as Christ welcomes His people into His heaven? His prayer has been answered: they are with Him where He is. He will see the travail of His soul and be entirely and divinely satisfied. With such blessings to anticipate, we should constantly be proving that the most heavenly-minded people are of the most earthly use.

11

CULTIVATE THE IDENTITY

If someone had to make a judgment about the Lord Jesus Christ from observing you and your life, what conclusions would he draw? What would he be entitled or obliged to think about the Lord Christ from the way that you believe and behave in professed relation to Him?

One of the principles on which we have been proceeding is that our identity ought to drive our activity. Our character underpins our calling. If we are to honor Christ, it will only come to pass if we are what God has called us to be and then live as God has called us to live. As pilgrims, our Savior has called us to a holy separation from and a holy engagement with the world in its creative, extensive, and ethical senses. We cannot afford to lapse into isolation, emulation, or inattention. We are passing through a passing world: we have work to do as we travel and a glorious destiny ahead of us.

Our task is to bring glory to our God and King; our hope is to be in His presence. We can do this only if we have accurate and clear notions of who we are. The only way to maintain our righteous acts is to maintain a sense of our being in relation to God in Christ, and therein lies the challenge. Satan knows that if he can rob us of our sense of who we are then he can cut the nerve of what we do. Our witness and usefulness will be compromised. Like it or not, men and women in the world are going to judge our Savior by His professing people. As a result, alongside of all that we have considered so far, the saints must go on cultivating their identity in the face of all the pressures to fade and to trim. If we forget who we are, we will no longer know what we should do.

Cultivate the Identity: Scriptural Framework

Salt and Light

> "You are the salt of the earth; but if the salt loses its flavor, how shall it be seasoned? It is then good for nothing but to be thrown out and trampled underfoot by men.
>
> "You are the light of the world. A city that is set on a hill cannot be hidden. Nor do they light a lamp and put it under a basket, but on a lampstand, and it gives light to all who are in the house. Let your light so shine before men, that they may see your good works and glorify your Father in heaven." (Matt. 5:13–16)

We have already considered this text when assessing the call to do good works that bring glory to God, but let us now put it more firmly in its context. It comes at the end of the Beatitudes, that section of Christ's teaching that has been called the law of the kingdom, and sets out the anticipated consequences of it. As a result of what Christ has taught us, His people are to be salt and light in the world. If we are going to be a means of bringing blessing to our fellow men and, in doing so, to be a means of bringing glory to our saving God, it is vital that we retain and manifest our saintly character. Our very distinctiveness in and difference from the world is the source of all the good that we accomplish. We cannot afford either to cut ourselves off from our fellows nor sink indistinguishably into the mass of them.

For this reason Matthew Poole tells us that "in our Christian course we are not to trouble ourselves with what men say of us, and do unto us, but only to attend to our duty of holiness, and an exemplary life, which is what our Saviour presseth plainly."[1] As salt, we promote preservation and purification as opposed to putrefaction and dissolution. In other words, we keep back the moral rot around us and give life flavor and savor. Where Christians are present there ought to be a reining in of ungodliness on account of our character. The people whom we deal with ought to have a sense that in us they find men and women who know what life is really about, who have a sense of its purpose and sweetness.

As light we provide illumination and direction in the face of confusion and indecision. As Christ, so His saints. John writes of our Lord: "In Him was life, and the life was the light of men.... That was

---

1. Poole, *Commentary on the Holy Bible*, 3:21.

the true Light which gives light to every man coming into the world....
[Jesus said], 'I am the light of the world. He who follows Me shall not
walk in darkness, but have the light of life'" (John 1:4, 9; 8:12). Christ
is, preeminently, the light of the world. But it is also written of God's
people that they "are all sons of light and sons of the day. We are not
of the night nor of darkness" (1 Thess. 5:5). Paul says again that "you
were once darkness, but now you are light in the Lord," commanding, "Walk as children of light" (Eph. 5:8). We are to reflect something
of the light of God in Christ. We are lit to bring gospel radiance, called
to be illustrious and conspicuous. We must *not* hide our light. That
defeats the whole object! By definition, the city on the hill is prominent, highly visible, especially if lit up at night in an environment not
afflicted with light pollution. Perhaps Jerusalem is in mind, visible
from a distance by day or by night as people travel to it.

So it is with the church. The world's eye is upon us and—like it or
not—the Lord Christ is measured by us:

> It is said of John, (by our Saviour,) he was a *burning and shining
> light*: so is every true minister of the gospel, yea, and every true
> Christian; not only a burning light, burning with love to God
> and zeal to God, and love to and zeal for the souls of others; but
> also a shining light, communicating his light to others, both by
> instruction and a holy conversation. Others' pretended candles
> were never of God's lighting.[2]

We must retain our flavor and display our brightness as saints.
A savorless church is a worthless church; a dull and hidden church
is a failing church. Thus powerless and pointless, we would fail to
glorify our God.

We live with the constant danger of losing our distinctiveness.
That is why our Lord issues this stirring warning that it is possible
for us to lose our character and a telling exhortation not to allow that
to happen.

The Upward Path

> But the path of the just is like the shining sun, that shines ever
> brighter unto the perfect day. (Prov. 4:18)

---

2. Poole, *Commentary on the Holy Bible*, 3:22.

The common course of a Christian's life is pure and clear and grow-ing. Righteous men advance in knowledge and righteousness "until all be perfected and swallowed up in glory."[3] We are to "grow in the grace and knowledge of our Lord and Savior Jesus Christ" (2 Peter 3:18). Our shining ought not to be static—not merely a matter of main-tenance, but of progress.

As the saints, we are heading toward a consummation of all our hopes and desires, and our holiness and happiness ought to be increasing. Perhaps we know what it is to experience an extended spell of gloomy weather and then to wake up one morning to find light flooding into our eyes. Then, as the sun rises into the cloudless sky, it comes to its noonday heat and brightness. So it is with the saints. Theirs is a real and sweet light, but it increases only as they advance in their lives as followers of Jesus Christ.

Our trajectory as saints ought to be upward. We ought to be more aware of sin, but also more antagonistic toward it and aggressive against it, more dependent on and vigorous in grace, growing in likeness to our Redeemer. Our advance may at times be slow, but it is to be both sure and evident.

A Call to Purity

Therefore
> "Come out from among them
> And be separate, says the Lord.
> Do not touch what is unclean,
> And I will receive you."
> "I will be a Father to you,
> And you shall be My sons and daughters,
> Says the LORD Almighty."

Therefore, having these promises, beloved, let us cleanse our-selves from all filthiness of the flesh and spirit, perfecting holiness in the fear of God. (2 Cor. 6:17–7:1)

This command comes at the end of a series of exhortations to purity. The saints are to consider themselves as the temple of God, indwelt by the Lord. What are the implications of that? What ought to be the result of a people in whom the Holy Spirit has taken up residence?

---

3. Poole, *Commentary on the Holy Bible*, 2:221.

Conscious of and cultivating such character, we ought to leave utterly behind all spiritual uncleanness. If we are the temple of the Spirit of holiness, then we should avoid all spiritual taint as we would respond to an open vial containing the pathogen of some profoundly contagious disease. In some parts of our disease-conscious modern world, it is not unusual for a preacher to cough in the pulpit and then to be amused at finding people at the door unwilling to shake his hand for fear of infection or offering some kind of cleansing wipe or spray to purify him! We almost instinctively shy away from contagion—diseases that spread at a touch are the nightmare visions of books and films. We do not often willingly expose ourselves to those kinds of dangers. The Christian is supposed to show some measure of that in his own experience with regard to spiritual uncleanness.

We must not push this beyond its scriptural limits, lest we fall back into the trap of spiritual isolation. We have noted before that in 1 Corinthians 5:10 Paul tells the church that when he wrote to them not to keep company with sexually immoral people he certainly did not mean with the sexually immoral people of this world or with the covetous, extortioners, or idolaters, since then they would need to go out of the world. In similar fashion, in 1 Corinthians 7:12–13, a married believer is neither required nor at liberty to divorce his or her unbelieving spouse, on the assumption that the spouse is willing to remain married to the believer. That bond is not ours to break. So, with regard to the spiritually sick around us, we should minister to them even as we take all reasonable precautions to avoid being infected by them, trusting in God and using His appointed means to keep us in the way of life.

We are called into a divinely established covenant in which our part is cheerful, committed, conscientious obedience. There is no lasting communion with God as Father without genuine faith, sincere repentance, and cultivated godliness. The Lord says, "Come out from among them and be separate. Do not touch what is unclean, and I will receive you. I will be a Father to you, and you shall be My sons and daughters." If we have been called as sons and are being treated as sons, then we ought to act like sons and manifest a likeness to our heavenly Father. In this way we will enjoy true and deepening fellowship with the Father.

Given such associations and with such assurances, all ungodliness ought to be put off our whole humanity. We are to cleanse ourselves from all filthiness of the flesh and spirit. Every part of our humanity needs to be actively scrubbed clean and then kept clean. Alongside of this, all holiness is to be perfected in the fear of the Lord—we are to bring godliness to the highest possible pitch of completeness and maturity. We are conscious of the fact that we have been redeemed by the God who has called us to be holy just as He Himself is holy. Godly motives ought to draw the saints to godly lives. We die to sin, and we live to righteousness. We feel the weight of all the language of the New Testament calling us to put off what belongs to the old man and to put on what belongs to the existence of a man made new in Christ Jesus. All impurity is to be avoided, all purity to be pursued.

Shining Lights

> Do all things without complaining and disputing, that you may
> become blameless and harmless, children of God without fault
> in the midst of a crooked and perverse generation, among whom
> you shine as lights in the world. (Phil. 2:14–15)

We are to labor toward godliness, applying ourselves to the pursuit of holiness in accordance with the divine design and reliant on the divine power. We are here working out our own salvation with fear and trembling, for it is God who works in us both to will and to do for His good pleasure.

Paul calls every Christian to sustained and strenuous effort after godliness. He calls for *complete obedience* in all things, characterized in everything by *sweet peacefulness* rather than a critical spirit, whether manifested in silence or speech. All carping, grumbling, complaining, and murmuring is to be absent from the heart and mouth of the saint. Why? So that we become what we ought to be. Our lives should be marked, now and increasingly, by *evident blamelessness*, in which we are not able to be censured by those who are about us for anything that is genuinely unholy. No one should be able to point his finger at us and say, "There is wickedness!" "There is cruelty!" "There is vindictiveness!"

In all this, we are cultivating a *heavenly childlikeness*, showing ourselves sons of God and reflecting His character and the character of

Christ, to whose image we are being conformed. We carry all this out in an atmosphere of *oppressive perverseness*, the crooked and twisted morality of a world opposed to God, who

> "have corrupted themselves;
> They are not His children,
> Because of their blemish:
> A perverse and crooked generation." (Deut. 32:5)

In the face of such, we are to shine with a *genuine brightness*. When people think of us, our convictions and actions, they should—even if they do not or will not frame it in this language—think of us as standing out like stars lighting up a dark sky. The light of Christ should shine out of our souls as we hold fast to the Word of God and hold forth His truth.

Living Sacrifices

> I beseech you therefore, brethren, by the mercies of God, that you present your bodies a living sacrifice, holy, acceptable to God, which is your reasonable service. And do not be conformed to this world, but be transformed by the renewing of your mind, that you may prove what is that good and acceptable and perfect will of God. (Rom. 12:1–2)

Can we doubt, reading this, that true religion is genuinely practical? Paul brings *holy pressure* to bear on the Roman believers. He uses gospel entreaties: God has loved you, given His Son for you, and saved you in order that you might know God as your God. Paul builds up all the force of God's saving goodness to call us to a willing surrender to the Lord in accordance with those rich mercies toward us. He therefore issues a call to *holy living*, exhorting the saints to be living sacrifices, giving their whole selves—all that they are and all that they have—as undefiled offerings to the God of salvation. This is a clear-thinking and determined act on the part of all Christians, laying themselves out for Him. What He commands us, we will do; where He sends us, we will go; what He requires, we will give; what He bestows, we will receive. We willingly put ourselves in His hands: all we are and have is God's to take and to do with as He pleases, for His own glory.

For this we must be marked by *holy resistance*, not being conformed to the world. We are not to be marked by the standards,
patterns, and expectations of an ungodly world. The sense is that
the pressure will be on you to make yourself like everyone else. You
are to stand up and stand out against that, breaking definitively with
those standards and patterns and actively resisting the pressure that
would squeeze you back into those forms. This will lead to a *holy
change*, being transformed by the renewing of your mind. This is the
same language as in 2 Corinthians 3:18, where the apostle speaks
of our "being transformed into the same image from glory to glory,
just as by the Spirit of the Lord." There is to be an intelligently and
deliberately cultivated metamorphosis in our lives. We set out to
reflect the character of God in Christ. It is a change that is reliant
upon grace, which employs the appointed tools and uses the available means so that we become like Jesus Christ. All this is governed
by a *holy will*, as we seek to find out what is acceptable to the Lord
and act in accordance with that standard (Eph. 5:10). In this way we
experience in ourselves and demonstrate to others the excellence of
the divine will. By such a life we show that this will of God is good
(of benefit to us) and acceptable (being pleasing to God) and perfect
(needing no supplements). Nothing in God's revealed will is lacking
for us to know how we may conduct ourselves to the praise of His
glorious grace.

Cultivate the Identity: Summary Thoughts

Because this world is not neutral, the saints cannot afford to be static.
We cannot hope to stand fast by standing still. The tide of this world
is against us, and we will not hold or advance without real endeavor.
If you do not swim with all your might—and it must be against the
current all the way—you will sink into indistinctness and ultimately
be swept away. Perhaps you know what it is to be in some great city
at rush hour, with hordes of people all streaming in a given direction. Have you ever been walking in what can so easily feel like the
wrong way because you are going in the opposite direction of almost
everyone else? You are trying to cross some concourse, and everyone
else is rushing the other way: this man bumps you and that woman
trips you with her suitcase, and here comes a sort of human wall

that you cannot avoid. You are rocking and dodging and avoiding obstacles and spotting gaps. Sometimes your consistent and persistent attempts to move in the right direction barely result in any forward movement. It is as much as you can do simply to keep your place in the face of the wave of the world. That, friend, is your life as a Christian. Pilgrims march against the mass of fallen humanity in the world. You must fight to hold your place, let alone to make progress along the pilgrim way.

The church of Christ is salt and light, and if we are to live up to that reality we must attain and maintain our distinctive character, laboring to retain our flavor and luminescence against all that would erase, erode, and extinguish them. We face constant pressure to conform to patterns of sin, to neglect our character, to forget our identity, or to so indulge in the world that we can be safely assimilated, even subsumed. But our holiness as the children of God, even in the midst of a crooked and perverse generation, ought to be increasing. Our distinctiveness is to be ever more apparent as we make our way through the world. Our sense of being citizens of heaven, and the evidence for it, should grow as we go.

Indeed, in some measure that sense becomes more painful as we travel. The more like Christ we become, the more conscious we will be that this present world is not our home, and our desires for rest will increase. The Welsh have a word, *hiraeth*, which is used, for example, to describe the Welshman or woman who is away from the homeland and therefore experiences a deep sense of incompleteness tinged with longing. It is even used when in Wales to speak of a wistful desire for a sort of idealized country. Christians should suffer from a holy *hiraeth*, a sort of heavenly homesickness that ought to become more painful the longer they are absent from the place where an increasingly holy person truly belongs.

This growth in grace and this appetite for glory do not simply happen as we sit around and wait for them. Such progress never really occurs in the life of a casual Christian. Spiritual advance never comes easily. There is no drifting in the right direction—there is only determined driving. Do you want to bring glory to God in the earth? Then Paul calls you to obedience, to work out your own salvation with fear and trembling, for it is God who works in you both to will and to do for His good pleasure (Phil. 2:12–13). Every child of God is to pursue and perfect holiness in the fear of the Lord (2 Cor. 7:1), striving to lay hold of that for which Christ has laid hold of us. In such a spirit, Paul himself could say, "I do not count myself to have apprehended; but one thing I do, forgetting those things which are behind and reaching forward to those things which are ahead, I press toward the goal for the prize of the upward call of God in Christ Jesus" (Phil. 3:13–14).

We must wear the uniform of Christlikeness and raise the banner of the Lamb without shame. Only in this way can we glorify God and do good to men. Our usefulness hinges on our distinctiveness. In one sense, we simply need to be what we are. However, as we have seen, that is telling the soldier to be himself on the battlefield, and that means fighting. It means telling the doctor to be himself in the hospital, and that means caring and doing good. It means telling the pilgrim to be himself on the heavenly way, and that means moving ever onward and upward. Now and increasingly we must cling to and cultivate the identity that forms and drives our activity in the face of all pressures and temptations to the contrary. Unless we do that we will lose our distinctiveness, bring no glory to our God, bring little lasting blessing to the lost, and ultimately, perhaps, be swept away on the tide and swallowed up by the murky deeps. Our identity forms and drives our activity and so must be protected and promoted against every pressure and temptation that bubbles up from within and that presses in from without—pressures and temptations to give up and sink down, to switch off the light and abandon our saltiness, to give up on godliness.

Cultivate the Identity: Specific Counsels

As ever, we must ask the question, how do we go about this? It is all well and good to call believers to such a life, but how is it pursued, and what is realistically involved in its cultivation?

If we are to do this, we must first *recognize the pressures*. You must not simply recognize, generically, that there is pressure. You must consider, specifically, what are the particular pressures that you face as you make your way along the path to let go of your distinctiveness as a child of God in this world. Satan has two main approaches: force and fraud. Either he will seek to batter you into submission, or he will trick you and cheat you. He will set out to oppress you, to restrain you, to divert you, to divide your attention, and to deaden your soul. He has not the least shred of love for you and has no qualms about doing all the cruel harm he can. If you are still holding fast, he will show himself a master of deceit. He will lull you, influence and restrain you, dull you and dampen you (if he can) without your ever being aware of it. As his power and permission allow, he will bring people into your orbit who scare you or entice you. He will make use of circumstances to restrict you or to burden you. He will introduce things that drive you out of the way or deaden you in it. He will make the most of trials to wound and cripple you. He will lay out obstacles that hinder and obstruct you. He will dangle before you pleasures that distract and consume you. If he cannot make you slide downhill, he will at the very least seek to hold you back. He will preach a thousand sermons against the truth that you believe. You will hear maybe one or two true sermons each week, perhaps a few more if you are keen, but you will be subjected to thousands of sermons as you turn on your television, flip open a magazine, open a website, read a book, listen to the radio, or speak with your friends, and few of them will do any good to your soul.

By these means Satan will do all he can to elevate time over eternity, self over God, the world over the church, ease over labor, the broad path in all its apparent beauty and ease over the narrow way in all its trouble. He will make the cross of Christ repugnant and despicable in your eyes rather than that in which you boast. Do you see it and feel it? Will you not pause a moment and consider what pressures you face to lose your identity? What sermons are you hearing, and what messages are you receiving? Which are the temptations and trials that will catch about your ankles as you seek to make your way to Zion? What are the particular pressures that you face from Satan at which particular points in your pilgrim path, seeking to hinder your progress in godly distinctiveness in this world? Who are the people who hinder your standing for Christ, the friends or family members who make you fall silent or push you to places and activities that should be no part of a saint's life? What are the programs or websites that kill your sense of God and your taste for heaven? If we are to stand, we need to work out where these pressures that either introduce ungodliness or undermine godliness are coming from. If you cannot—or will not—recognize them, then they will walk up to you and catch you off guard. They may still sometimes execute a surprise assault, but at least make them sneak up on you rather than stroll up to you!

However, as much as we must contend against such threats individually, we must also contend against them corporately. There are teachings and practices in our societies that are also pressing in upon the church as a whole. The church is browbeaten: we feel ourselves obliged not to stand out, not to be righteously aggressive in our witness, not to be distinctive in our profession of Christ. We are told that we take it all too seriously. We are fanatical about it. We drag into the public sphere what ought to remain private. We are old-fashioned. We are narrow-minded. Why do we reject the wisdom of the world—its scientists, philosophers, specialists, and politicians? Why can't we just be like them? Why can't we just fit in with everybody else? The answer is because we are the people of the living God. We must note where these pressures are coming in upon us and take our stand at that point.

While we must avoid these snares, we must also, more positively, *copy the model*—"Be holy, for I am holy" (1 Peter 1:16). In the face of all the pressures that would drive us from God and godliness, we must fix our eyes upon Him. We must follow Christ Himself—this is the mark assigned to us as the people of God. This is what He calls us to do:

> "Whoever desires to come after Me, let him deny himself, and take up his cross, and follow Me. For whoever desires to save his life will lose it, but whoever loses his life for My sake and the gospel's will save it. For what will it profit a man if he gains the whole world, and loses his own soul? Or what will a man give in exchange for his soul? For whoever is ashamed of Me and My words in this adulterous and sinful generation, of him the Son of Man also will be ashamed when He comes in the glory of His Father with the holy angels." (Mark 8:34–38)

It is what faithful teachers call us to do: "Therefore we also, since we are surrounded by so great a cloud of witnesses, let us lay aside every weight, and the sin which so easily ensnares us, and let us run with endurance the race that is set before us, looking unto Jesus, the author and finisher of our faith, who for the joy that was set before

Him endured the cross, despising the shame, and has sat down at the right hand of the throne of God" (Heb. 12:1–2).

Christ Himself shows us what it means to live godly in the world. Through the Scriptures and through the history of the church there are a cloud of witnesses, a great stream of faithful disciples. They have shown us, often in the most awful of circumstances in which it is either easy to drift away or difficult to hold the line, what it means to walk in godliness. We must follow hard after God, follow hard after Christ, and follow hard after those who have already followed Christ faithfully: "Therefore I urge you, imitate me.... Imitate me, just as I also imitate Christ" (1 Cor. 4:16; 11:1).

We cannot bring the savor of Christ with us unless we are being conformed to Christ, becoming more and more like our Lord. We want men and women to breathe the spiritual perfume of our lives and say, "Ah, someone different has been here, someone who has brought something fresh and sweet! There is something of heaven in this. This person has restrained the wickedness around him. He has brought peacefulness and gentleness." We are to cultivate godliness—that is, moral likeness to God—and pursue holiness, without which no one will see the Lord. We must reflect the light, take our stand as belonging to God and being like God. This is the standard that we need to establish for ourselves against the low level of the world.

If we are to do this, we must *heed the teaching*. As hinted above, one of the primary responsibilities of God's gospel ministers is to cultivate and encourage this character, this sense of things, among God's people. So, for example, consider these passages:

> Him we preach, warning every man and teaching every man in all wisdom, that we may present every man perfect in Christ Jesus. To this end I also labor, striving according to His working which works in me mightily. (Col. 1:28–29)

> You are witnesses, and God also, how devoutly and justly and blamelessly we behaved ourselves among you who believe; as you know how we exhorted, and comforted, and charged every one of you, as a father does his own children, that you would walk worthy of God who calls you into His own kingdom and glory....

For what is our hope, or joy, or crown of rejoicing? Is it not even you in the presence of our Lord Jesus Christ at His coming? For you are our glory and joy. (1 Thess. 2:10–12, 19–20)

For what thanks can we render to God for you, for all the joy with which we rejoice for your sake before our God, night and day praying exceedingly that we may see your face and perfect what is lacking in your faith?

Now may our God and Father Himself, and our Lord Jesus Christ, direct our way to you. And may the Lord make you increase and abound in love to one another and to all, just as we do to you, so that He may establish your hearts blameless in holiness before our God and Father at the coming of our Lord Jesus Christ with all His saints. (1 Thess. 3:9–13)

Do all things without complaining and disputing, that you may become blameless and harmless, children of God without fault in the midst of a crooked and perverse generation, among whom you shine as lights in the world, holding fast the word of life, so that I may rejoice in the day of Christ that I have not run in vain or labored in vain. (Phil. 2:14–16)

We have looked at some of these texts before, but can you see in them now the earnest pleading of the man of God appointed for the purpose of putting the saints in mind of these things? Do you hear faithful preachers and read righteous writers so as to cultivate your pilgrim identity? Do you merely listen to them, or do you really hear and heed them? You may know the story in the Bible about the time when Paul was preaching in Troas, how "on the first day of the week, when the disciples came together to break bread, Paul, ready to depart the next day, spoke to them and continued his message until midnight." The Scriptures describe how the room was hot, perhaps airless, with many lamps to chase away the deepening gloom. In a window sat a certain young man named Eutychus, who was sinking into a deep sleep and was overcome by weariness as Paul continued speaking (Acts 20:5–9). This story gets turned a hundred different ways. Apparently it gives us lessons on proper ventilation, which is not unreasonable. Apparently it warns us against sleepy hearing, though often ignoring the possible circumstances of Eutychus. Apparently it advises against long preaching, even though Luke does not tell us when Paul started his sermon. But surely, if nothing else, it shows us the appetite of Eutychus for the Word of God from a man gifted by God to explain and apply that truth, showing him how to live godly in this age. Surely it shows us the readiness of the man of God to make that truth known. If we hear and see a thousand false sermons during the week, and many of us have, perhaps, only one opportunity on the Lord's Day to hear the Lord speaking to us through His appointed faithful servants, will we not make the most of that opportunity? Do we long to know and feel the impress of divine truth? These are not light matters! We are fighting against a rising tide of ungodliness, and unless we make the most of God's appointed means, we will be swept away. A church without the Word of God at its heart is a pointless exercise in regular social gatherings.

Remember, too, that there is a world of difference between simply being under the sound of faithful preaching and actually profiting from it. We are to lay aside all filthiness and overflow of wickedness and receive with meekness the implanted word, which is able to save our souls, being doers of the word, and not hearers only, deceiving ourselves (James 1:21–22). This truth of God both brings us into the kingdom and brings us on in the kingdom. Hear Peter as he pleads for its full effects in the lives of the saints:

> Since you have purified your souls in obeying the truth through the Spirit in sincere love of the brethren, love one another fervently with a pure heart, having been born again, not of corruptible seed but incorruptible, through the word of God which lives and abides forever, because
> "All flesh is as grass,
> And all the glory of man as the flower of the grass.
> The grass withers,
> And its flower falls away,
> But the word of the LORD endures forever."
> Now this is the word which by the gospel was preached to you.
> Therefore, laying aside all malice, all deceit, hypocrisy, envy, and all evil speaking, as newborn babes, desire the pure milk of the word, that you may grow thereby, if indeed you have tasted that the Lord is gracious. (1 Peter 1:22–2:3)

This book has been without value to you if it makes no difference in your convictions and actions. What has changed as you study

God's Word, as you hear your pastor, as you read this book? I have heard tragic complaints about certain books and preachers: "Too much Bible!" Too much Bible? To be sure, the Bible must be explained and applied, but there cannot be too much truth. This is one source of sweetness that never overwhelms us. The reason a faithful preacher always carries you back to the Scriptures is because by this, and this alone, can he legitimately direct your steps and righteously bind your conscience. His opinion as a mere man is largely worthless; it is the truth he proclaims that sets us free and sends us on. So we must turn from every exposure to the Word of God and ask, "What must I do or not do, or do differently, or do increasingly as a result of the truth that I have heard?"

Furthermore, we must *value the church*. This goes hand in glove with heeding the teaching, for Christ has provided a safe environment in which this process of maturing under teaching occurs. There is a place where Christlikeness is nurtured and disciples formed. A healthy local expression of the body of Christ provides an atmosphere designed and intended by God for this very purpose, clearly implied in Christ's words to His people: "All authority has been given to Me in heaven and on earth. Go therefore and make disciples of all the nations, baptizing them in the name of the Father and of the Son and of the Holy Spirit, teaching them to observe all things that I have commanded you; and lo, I am with you always, even to the end of the age" (Matt. 28:18–20). Christ is formed in believers not in isolation from one another, but in company with one another. This whole sequence presumes the existence of the church as the place in which souls are nurtured. Read Titus 2:1, where Paul speaks "the things which are proper for sound doctrine." He spells out the roles and relationships that are to characterize older and younger men and older and younger women, teaching each other, engaging with one another, encouraging and exhorting one another. It is in the church that we stand fast and hold fast together:

> Brethren, join in following my example, and note those who so walk, as you have us for a pattern. For many walk, of whom I have told you often, and now tell you even weeping, that they are the enemies of the cross of Christ: whose end is destruction, whose god is their belly, and whose glory is in their shame— who set their mind on earthly things. For our citizenship is in

heaven, from which we also eagerly wait for the Savior, the Lord Jesus Christ, who will transform our lowly body that it may be conformed to His glorious body, according to the working by which He is able even to subdue all things to Himself. Therefore, my beloved and longed-for brethren, my joy and crown, so stand fast in the Lord, beloved. (Phil. 3:17–4:1)

Can you see that Christ has not sent us out alone but in company, and that for our own good and the good of others? When Paul tells the saints in Ephesus to be strong in the Lord and in the power of His might, putting on the whole armor of God, that they might be able to stand against the wiles of the devil (Eph. 6:10–11), he is not giving a command to one lonely little soldier about to be overwhelmed by the massed forces of darkness. He speaks to a cohort of men and women united to Christ and to each other, standing shoulder to shoulder with a shield wall against all the spiritual hosts of wickedness. It is the isolated Christian who is exposed and endangered. If you cut yourself off from the body of Christ, you will be in terrible trouble. The church is the hospital in which we are healed and made strong, the training ground on which our spiritual skills are honed, the family home in which we are loved and nurtured, the earthly fold of the flock where the soul is fed, character is cultivated, trouble confronted, and the needy instructed. Paul knows how much we need one another: "Now we exhort you, brethren, warn those who are unruly, comfort the fainthearted, uphold the weak, be patient with all" (1 Thess. 5:14). Do you know how much you need your brothers? We fight alongside and for one another. We advance best together.

As we advance, we must *embrace the distinctiveness* of our calling and *despise the shame* that comes with being saints. Let us be unashamedly different. We do not need to be unnecessarily weird. Our holiness will be quite weird enough, for the world will "think it strange that you do not run with them in the same flood of dissipation, speaking evil of you" (1 Peter 4:4). It will be strange enough that you do not give your weekends to wickedness and head out on a drunken debauch with so many others. It will be weird enough that you are faithful to your wife or to your husband. It will be weird enough that you believe that marriage is and cannot really be anything but a matter of one man exclusively joined to one woman. It will be weird enough that you do not eat whatever you want, sleep with whomever you want, wear whatever you want, and simply live by the law of your own appetite, without regard for God and His Word. Living before God will mark you out.

We cannot and must not pursue a policy of appeasement with the world. In 1938, British Prime Minister Neville Chamberlain returned from a meeting in Munich. He assured the waiting crowds with these words: "This morning I had another talk with the German Chancellor, Herr Hitler, and here is the paper which bears his name upon it as well as mine." Later that day he quoted the agreement that had been signed and said, "I believe it is peace for our time," before advising people to go home and get a nice, quiet sleep. Less than a year later the Nazi armies invaded Poland and Europe, and then the world was plunged into war. Chamberlain negotiated with a madman and returned home with a promise of peace not worth the paper it was written on. But how many Christians pursue a policy of appeasement with the world, the flesh, and the devil? Perhaps we imagine that if we leave sin alone, sin will leave us alone. Have we forgotten the counsel of John Owen, that you must be killing sin, or sin will be killing you? If you are Christ's, then the sinful world will hate you just as it hated Him. We might as well get used to the idea and then get on with the business of living for God in Christ Jesus.

The instinct of the ungodly will be to deride and dismiss, even to assault, such holy characters. When John Bunyan is writing about the experience of pilgrims in Vanity Fair, he offers this affirmation: "Christianity and the customs of our town of Vanity, were diametrically opposite, and could not be reconciled."[4] We should note that this is not a phrase put directly in the mouth of Christian or Hopeful. Bunyan puts it in the mouth of the false witness, Envy, who reports it of Faithful. Envy then rages that, in these words, "he doth at once not only condemn all our laudable doings, but us in the doing of them."[5] Bunyan knows that the fallen world recognizes that what we are and what they are, are diametrically opposed and cannot be reconciled, and that this is a standing condemnation of the world's carnality. Why, then, does the church of Christ so often seem to bend over backward to persuade the world that there can be peace between

---

4. Bunyan, *Pilgrim's Progress*, 3:130.
5. Bunyan, *Pilgrim's Progress*, 3:130.

us? We whine that if they will just give us a bit of room, we can figure out our differences and learn how to fit in without causing any
trouble. The world wants the church to fit in because the church's
difference from the world exposes and rebukes sin. Saltiness exposes
flavorlessness and counteracts rottenness; light penetrates darkness.
The tragedy is that too often we accept the world's demands, hiding
our light and withdrawing our savor, becoming cowed and embarrassed. After all, it is the easiest path. But note the stirring charge
of Sinclair Ferguson: "Be willing to pay whatever price needs to be
paid in terms of the world's response. It is important, if our lives are
to make a moral impact on others, that we live as Christians among
them and take our stand right from the very start."[6] How often do
we go into a new environment and fudge and hedge, trying to make
sure that no one finds out too early that we are one of those born-
again Christians? We want to earn our credibility first, find our feet
before we face the music. Once people like us, once they get on with
us, once they are comfortable around us, little by little we let the cat
out of the bag and hope that it does not upset the pigeons.

As Christians, we do not need to be kooky and abrasive, but
why are we so slow to plant our flag and stand as a follower of Jesus
Christ? Christians do not belong in the world, in that sense, and
never will belong. We do not fit in, and that, actually, is not our problem, but theirs. Listen to the apostle Peter again and more fully as he
sets out the tension of godliness against godlessness and its resolution: "In regard to these [characteristic sins of the world], they think
it strange that you do not run with them in the same flood of dissipation, speaking evil of you. They will give an account to Him who is
ready to judge the living and the dead" (1 Peter 4:4–5). If the world
cannot stomach your saltiness and turns away from your brightness,
it is they who will answer to God for their disposition.

So let us *pursue the way*. Christ has freed us to be what we are
called and constituted to be. We have been given liberty to live as
saints. Let us stop worrying what people think about us, hiding our
light under a basket and trimming our sails. Let us stop hoping that
no one finds out we are serious Christians. Let us stop being ashamed

---

6. Sinclair B. Ferguson, *The Sermon on the Mount: Kingdom Life in a Fallen World*
(Edinburgh: Banner of Truth, 1987), 57.

of the Christ who laid down His life to save us from our sins. Let us stop being embarrassed and afraid and start standing up for Jesus of Nazareth as soldiers of the cross. You know the challenges here and the warnings against drifting, but I hope that you also know the blessings that lie ahead. If we want the glory to come, we must embrace the suffering here. Why should we shamble along the way? Why should we drag our feet when we are called to strengthen the hands that hang down and the feeble knees and make straight paths for our feet so that what is lame may not be dislocated, but rather be healed? We are to

> pursue peace with all people, and holiness, without which no one will see the Lord: looking carefully lest anyone fall short of the grace of God; lest any root of bitterness springing up cause trouble, and by this many become defiled; lest there be any fornicator or profane person like Esau, who for one morsel of food sold his birthright. For you know that afterward, when he wanted to inherit the blessing, he was rejected, for he found no place for repentance, though he sought it diligently with tears. (Heb. 12:14–17)

We are to run in the way of God's commandments, for He shall enlarge our hearts (Ps. 119:32). We are not to count ourselves as having already apprehended, but rather—with a single-minded sense of purpose—to forget those things which are behind and reach forward to those things which are ahead, pressing toward the goal for the prize of the upward call of God in Christ Jesus. This is spiritual maturity—a genuinely apostolic attitude (Phil. 3:13–15). Ours ought to be a life marked out by ardent pursuit of and evident advance in full-orbed scriptural godliness.

Perhaps you have had the childhood experience of turning up on the door of an aunt or uncle or grandparent. There you were, and they had not seen you for months, or perhaps a year or so. You knock, the door swings open, then follows the squeal of what I hope would be delight and surprise: "My, how you've grown!" In the time that has elapsed since the last meeting, there has been demonstrable development. Would anyone say that of you spiritually? Would a few minutes or hours in your company for the first time in a year or so prompt a discerning saint to remark on your spiritual growth? Would an older saint smile at you and say with approval, "My, haven't you grown!" Do you carry more of Christ in you and about you, do you manifest a more complete maturity, do you look and sound more like a citizen of heaven than used to be the case? Have you had the sincere comfort and encouragement that some true friend sees you are more like Jesus now than you were the last time you met? It should be that more of the savor of Christ hangs about you, more of the light of the gospel shines from you, more clarity and maturity are evident. You sound and act more and more like a citizen of heaven and a child of God.

If we desire this, let us *seek the blessing.* Understand that this is not just the pursuit of being different for its own sake. This is never to be mere kookiness or awkwardness—there is already enough of that in the professing Christian scene. This distinctive identity, the result of a heavenly calling and conduct and destiny earnestly cultivated, is so that God is honored and men are blessed as we make our way through the world. This light is to *shine* and bring good to men and glory to God! We must be readily and cheerfully conspicuous as godly men and women. We do most good not when we are most worldly but most otherworldly, not closest to the edge of carnality but clearest in our likeness to Jesus Christ our Savior. What we need is so to behold God in His greatness, goodness, graciousness, and glory that we will stop being afraid and that we will be happily, readily, willingly, and cheerfully God's people, Christ's disciples, walking in the light. So let us pray for courage to cultivate this identity and that—in consequence—our Lord would be glorified in all things.

12

SERVE THE KING

"My kingdom is not of this world" (John 18:36). So spoke our King when He stood befor Pontius Pilate. So speaking, He established a fundamental reality that should determine the perspectives and pursuits of all His people, those who belong to a kingdom that is not of this world. Christ is King, and allegiance to the King is the controlling factor in our relationship to the world in all its various aspects. The saints are a people separated to the King and in service to the King. The default disposition of our own age—indeed, of every age—is willful autonomy, rebellious self-rule. For all of us by nature, our will governs our ways as much as we are able to ensure it: where I go, what I do, how I live—all goes according to how I please. "I am in charge," is the mantra of the sinful creature, though he may not put it with the brash and miserable eloquence of the poet:

> It matters not how strait the gate,
> How charged with punishments the scroll,
> I am the master of my fate:
> I am the captain of my soul.[1]

Fallen man's boast—tragically empty but still fiercely grasped—is that he is a self-determining creature and will do as he pleases.

Such a spirit is entirely contrary to God's people. For pilgrims, both the direction and the tenor of life are governed by another. We have been called out of this world to go through it to the next as servants of Jesus Christ. He is our undisputed King, and our lives are

---

1. William Ernest Henley, "Invictus."

governed by Him who loved us and gave Himself for us (Gal. 2:20).
The Christian pilgrim bows the knee to Christ alone in everything.

Serve the King: Scriptural Framework
Bond Slaves of Christ

> So he, trembling and astonished, said, "Lord, what do You want
> me to do?"
> Then the Lord said to him, "Arise and go into the city, and
> you will be told what you must do." (Acts 9:6)

Here are the definitive and determinative question and answer for
any true disciple. When the rebel comes face-to-face with the risen
Christ, everything changes, entirely and eternally. Up until this
point, Paul had effectively been living with his fist raised in the face
of God. He had watched over the coats of the men who stoned Stephen, who had himself looked into the face of the ascended Jesus as
he died. And now Saul of Tarsus, the arch-persecutor of the saints,
sees the same face. And when he sees Christ as He is, the crucified
but risen Lord of glory, everything changes. Life is reversed. A thoroughly new disposition of the heart is manifest. From being a rebel
against Christ, he becomes a bond slave of Christ.

In the disciple's question is the language of resigning the self to
another, with absolute devotion to Christ. Here is willing surrender
and entire consecration: "What shall I do, Lord?" (Acts 22:10). Matthew Poole says that Paul makes himself "a white paper, for Christ
to write what he would upon."[2] Christ's will is absolute and central,
and it is exercised by Christ and accepted by Paul as such. The Master's answer to the question is, in effect, "Whatever I tell you to do."
In a sense, a more detailed answer at this point is not important, for
the details of obedience are not really the issue as much as the principle. It will become clear that for Paul, a very distinct tribulation
lies ahead: "I will show him how many things he must suffer for My
name's sake" (Acts 9:16).

This is the disciple's disposition: "You speak, and I will obey."
Christ's word is the final word for the disciple. It is the determining
factor in all that we do as His people. He is, indisputably, an absolute

---

2. Poole, *Commentary on the Holy Bible*, 3:413.

monarch. When we see the King as He is, gazing upon Him with the eye of faith opened, our hearts are subdued, and the only question we have left is, "Lord, what do You want me to do?"

Serving the Lord

> And whatever you do, do it heartily, as to the Lord and not to men, knowing that from the Lord you will receive the reward of the inheritance; for you serve the Lord Christ. (Col. 3:23–24)

Earlier in Colossians 3, Paul has made plain a general principle: "And whatever you do in word or deed, do all in the name of the Lord Jesus, giving thanks to God the Father through Him" (v. 17). These later verses form part of the application of that principle, speaking here to those who are slaves in the human sphere. He tells them that all the things they do (in that relationship of slaves to masters and—by extension—other, similar authority structures) must be done heartily, with vigor of spirit, as one who is serving the Lord Himself. You must look higher than whatever transaction is taking place between you and another person. It is Christ Jesus who is the great Master and ultimate Rewarder of His people, however menial and mundane our work may seem to be in itself. Our work may be hidden and may appear insignificant. Perhaps, as Christians, we sometimes wonder whether or not our vocations really make much difference to anything. Are our efforts without value?

The basic question of the disciple in Acts 9:6—"Lord, what do You want me to do?"—does not imply that the common answer is, "Be a preacher of the gospel!" We are not all missionaries in the distinctive sense in which that word is sometimes used. We are not all called to put behind us homes and families and strike out into the great unknown for the cause of Christ, making extravagant acts of sacrifice (which, incidentally, can garner a fair amount of rather attractive applause from the watching Christian world). Volume of applause is no measure of the true worth of the act performed or the actor performing it.

What did the answer to this question mean for the slaves of Colosse? It meant doing the work that they had been given to do to the very best of their ability, conscious that they were doing it not first for the men who ordered them but for the Christ who had redeemed them. Their service was to the Lord; their relationship to Him was the key factor.

So for us, whatever the answer to that question may be, it is our relationship to Christ that governs our approach to our calling. Our work in the world, whatever it may be, must be done heartily rather than tamely, limply, and halfheartedly. So "whatever you do in word or deed, do all in the name of the Lord Jesus, giving thanks to God the Father through Him" (Col. 3:17). Tasks assigned will be completed—done thoroughly, finished entirely, and accomplished cheerfully. Heart service to the Lord God renders all we do worthwhile. It leaves nothing in the realm of the mundane. The most menial tasks so considered glow with a heavenly light. It is as the work is done to the Lord that the reward is granted, regardless of whether or not or how much it is appreciated and rewarded by men on earth. These slaves labored "not with eyeservice, as men-pleasers, but as bondservants of Christ, doing the will of God from the heart" (Eph. 6:6). They worked not because the eye of man was upon them, but with the eye of God over them.

What did that mean in practice? According to R. Kent Hughes, this sense of the nobility of the slave's labors and the corresponding spirit in which they were carried out meant that "Christian slaves invariably brought higher prices in the slave market."[3] What a testimony that would have been! You could pull to his feet a man with a chain around his neck and proclaim to the crowd, "This man is a follower of Jesus the Nazarene! As a result, the price is 20 percent higher for this specimen!" And people would pay that price, perhaps even with a cruel eagerness to take advantage of the disposition that marked such men and women. They knew that a Christian slave would be a diligent, faithful, and honest worker, even if they did not understand that this was because he was living before his God rather than before men.

Does anybody want to hire you because you are a Christian? Do true believers have the reputation that, for the same wage as anyone else and in the equivalent position, your diligence and productivity, your reliability and timeliness, and your vigor and commitment will

---

3. R. Kent Hughes, *Colossians and Philemon: The Supremacy of Christ* (Wheaton, Ill.: Crossway, 1989), 131.

be exemplary? Do you force people to say, perhaps, "I do not like Christians, but I want more of them in my company"?

In the nineteenth century, the British army in India was adorned with a man called Henry Havelock, a faithful Christian man who sought to call his officers and men to Christ and to train them in godliness. His reputation, as well as that of his men, spread and was somewhat cemented in Burma in late 1825. With an outpost under assault, it was discovered that the men of the next company on the roster were largely drunk. The commander in chief, Sir Archibald Campbell, to whom Havelock was then deputy assistant adjutant-general, cursed vigorously and roared, "Then call out Havelock's saints—they are always sober and can be depended on and Havelock himself is always ready."[4] Later, in the 1830s, another officer called Colonel Sale, dealing with slanders about Havelock and his Baptists, lost his temper with the accusers, thumped his desk, and exclaimed, "Baptists! Baptists! I know nothing about Baptists! But I know that I wish the whole regiment were Baptists. Their names are never in the defaulters' roll and they are never in the congee-house."[5] These men, known to be true Christians and often disdained as such, were nevertheless esteemed for their excellence, sobriety, diligence, and reliability in their calling.

What a testimony it would be today if you could credibly put the word *Christian* on your job application and know that you would immediately be shifted toward the top of the list on the basis of what that meant for your disposition in the work that you did! What a testimony it would be if your presence in a workplace meant that your bosses were asking if anyone else in your church wanted a job! That is often the testimony of those who serve their King above all.

Pleasing God

> For we do not preach ourselves, but Christ Jesus the Lord, and ourselves your bondservants for Jesus' sake. (2 Cor. 4:5)

---

4. John Pollock, *The Way to Glory: Major-General Sir Henry Havelock: The Christian Soldier* (Fearn, Ross-shire, U.K.: Christian Focus, 1996), 32.

5. John Clark Marshman, *Memoirs of Major-General Sir Henry Havelock, K.C.B.* (London: Longmans, Green, and Co., 1885), 41. A *congee-house* is Indian army slang for the cells.

> For do I now persuade men, or God? Or do I seek to please men? For if I still pleased men, I would not be a bondservant of Christ. (Gal. 1:10)

God's gospel ministers are here specifically called to pursue this spirit of service, but in doing so they are to exemplify it and to promote it. We labor at Christ's command, speaking of His person and His work. We speak for Christ. We do not preach ourselves—our preferences or pursuits. Ministers of the gospel do not accommodate themselves to human will and wisdom, either their own or that of others. They are not men-pleasers but God-pleasers. They do not set out to tickle the ears of men who want to hear only what delights them and demands nothing of them. According to John Eadie, "No one can serve Him who makes it his study to be popular with men."[6] Another preacher whose words we have noted repeatedly, John Brown, is equally blunt: Paul's "great object was to please God; and this object he must prosecute, however much men might be displeased."[7]

That is why we seek to turn others to Jesus Christ and serve the church in the way that we do. Ministers, then, are the bondservants of the saints for Christ's sake, with their love for Christ forming and informing their desire for the blessing of men, as Charles Hodge notes: "A regard for the glory of Christ is a far higher motive than regard for the good of men; and the former is the only true source of the latter."[8]

The minister's intention is to turn the eye, the heart, the hand, and the foot to Christ alone, so that others cease to be men-pleasers and become God-pleasers. We want others to live with a Godward eye rather than being slaves to human opinion, pandering to the whims of creatures. All the ministry of a faithful pastor and preacher is directed by and for Christ to call sinners to bow the knee to Him and then to stir the saints to follow in His footsteps and advance His glory. The highest service any such man can render to the church is making known the will of Christ plainly and earnestly. Matthew Henry explains that the business of the apostles

---

6. Eadie, *Paul's Letter to the Galatians*, 32.

7. Brown, *Galatians*, 49.

8. Charles Hodge, *A Commentary on 1 and 2 Corinthians* (Edinburgh: Banner of Truth, 1974), 464.

was to make their Master known to the world as the Messiah, or the Christ of God, and as Jesus, the only Saviour of men, and as the rightful Lord, and to advance his honour and glory. Note, all the lines of Christian doctrine centre in Christ; and in preaching Christ we preach all we should preach. "As to ourselves," says the apostle, "we preach, or declare, that we are your servants for Jesus' sake." This was no compliment, but a real profession of a readiness to do good to their souls, and to promote their spiritual and eternal interest, and that for Jesus' sake; not for their own sake or their own advantage, but for Christ's sake, that they might imitate his great example, and advance his glory.[9]

This is why gospel ministers speak faithfully, openly, honestly, and transparently. It is why they cannot be governed by the preferences and expectations of the culture at large or even a preexisting Christian culture (real or imagined) where such cuts across the truth of God's Word. The issue for the church of Jesus Christ is not what we want, but what God desires for and requires of us. Ministers of the gospel are bound to demonstrate, by their living and preaching, that they have embraced that principle, and they are further bound to call others to pursue the same life.

Serving and Suffering

When He had called the people to Himself, with His disciples also, He said to them, "Whoever desires to come after Me, let him deny himself, and take up his cross, and follow Me. For whoever desires to save his life will lose it, but whoever loses his life for My sake and the gospel's will save it. For what will it profit a man if he gains the whole world, and loses his own soul? Or what will a man give in exchange for his soul? For whoever is ashamed of Me and My words in this adulterous and sinful generation, of him the Son of Man also will be ashamed when He comes in the glory of His Father with the holy angels." (Mark 8:34–38)

Peter was, at this point, somewhat confused and resistant to the notion of a suffering Messiah, perhaps not least because disciples were expected to follow where the Master went. He took Jesus aside

---

9. Henry, *Commentary*, 6:496.

and began to explain to Him that He had got His messianic understanding skewed somewhere along the way. "Messiahs don't suffer
and die at Jerusalem, Lord." The Lord Jesus turned around and
spoke bluntly to him.

When Jesus said "whoever desires to come after Me," He was
making a statement about what is normative and definitive for Christian disciples. When Satan urges you to stay on the broad road, he
paints all its pleasures in his brightest colors and denies its perils. He
offers immediate and enduring gratification. When Christ calls you
to the narrow way, He identifies its perils and makes plain all its sure
and certain promises. He reveals the dangers of the way and guarantees the rewards that will follow. He speaks of suffering, then glory.
He offers the cross and then the crown. In this, the disciple follows
his Lord, accommodating his will to God in Christ and embracing
the way the Master went. The true disciple of the Lord Jesus counts
the cost, recognizing that it is a great one. He identifies the prize
and presses on, persuaded that it outweighs any price he might pay
to obtain it. The cost is temporal, the prize is eternal. Therefore, he
takes up his cross, embracing the instrument of death, sacrificing
any imagined or real lesser goods for the true and lasting greater
good, owning Christ alone as his Lord and Master. "True it is," said
Bishop Hooper, the night before he suffered martyrdom, "that *life
is sweet,* and *death is bitter,* but *eternal death is more bitter,* and *eternal
life is more sweet.*"[10] The disciple serves the Lord Jesus without fear
or shame, willing to suffer in His service rather than deny Him to
escape such suffering.

What is at stake? "Whoever is ashamed of Me and My words in
this adulterous and sinful generation, of him the Son of Man also
will be ashamed when He comes in the glory of His Father with the
holy angels" (Mark 8:38). If you want nothing to do with Christ now,
He will have nothing to do with you then. If you are not prepared to
follow Him through this world, then He will not receive you when
the world ends.

---

10. Henry, *Commentary,* 5:409.

Following Christ

> "He who loves his life will lose it, and he who hates his life in this world will keep it for eternal life. If anyone serves Me, let him follow Me; and where I am, there My servant will be also. If anyone serves Me, him My Father will honor." (John 12:25–26)

This is part of a declaration that the Lord Jesus makes when certain Greeks are seeking Him out toward the end of His ministry. Christ says that unless a grain of wheat falls into the ground and dies, it cannot produce a harvest. He will produce a harvest by His death, and so He makes plain that these Greeks must go beyond seeing to serving. Matthew Henry comments, "He did not come into the world, to be a show for us to gaze at, but a king to be ruled by."[11] Christ's statement acknowledges the honor of being followed and of following. Christ will reap a great harvest of followers through His sacrificial death, and those followers will go in the same way of service and suffering. The priorities of the saints are clear. What is most important is not what is here, except insofar as it relates to what is to come. We subordinate time to eternity. "Self," says D. A. Carson, "must be displaced by another; the endless, shameless focus on self must be displaced by focus on Jesus Christ, who is the supreme revelation of God."[12] We do this because the life of this world is nothing compared to the life of the world to come. God's present and eternal favor is to be our preeminent concern. Therefore the disciple serves, follows, and imitates Christ in all of life, enjoying His presence and anticipating the fulfillment of all His promises. Honor from God is the thing desired and pursued.

Faith and obedience are the leading marks of real followers and will always be seen in true believing Christians. Their knowledge may be small, and their infirmities great; their grace may be weak, and their hope dim. But they believe what Christ says and strive to do what Christ commands. And of such Christ declares, "They serve Me; they are Mine."[13]

---

11. Henry, *Commentary*, 5:869.
12. D. A. Carson, *The Gospel According to John* (Leicester, U.K.: Apollos, 1991), 439.
13. J. C. Ryle, *Expository Thoughts on John* (Edinburgh: Banner of Truth, 2012), 2:243.

"Where I am," said the Lord, "there My servant will be also." We go where He goes, as He goes, and we will find Him always present with us.

The World's Hatred

"If the world hates you, you know that it hated Me before it hated you. If you were of the world, the world would love its own. Yet because you are not of the world, but I chose you out of the world, therefore the world hates you. Remember the word that I said to you, 'A servant is not greater than his master.' If they persecuted Me, they will also persecute you. If they kept My word, they will keep yours also. But all these things they will do to you for My name's sake, because they do not know Him who sent Me." (John 15:18–21)

In an earlier conversation with His disciples, the Lord Jesus made clear that "a servant is not greater than his master; nor is he who is sent greater than he who sent him" (John 13:16). Now, once more, He presents us with a stark choice. If Christ has chosen us, the world will hate us. The former guarantees the latter. J. C. Ryle writes, "Mere churchmanship [of any denomination] and outward profession are a cheap religion, of course, and cost a man nothing. But real vital Christianity will always bring with it a cross."[14] The issue is not, then, who you are in yourself, but who you are in relation to the Lord. Our treatment by the world will be governed by our association with the Lord Jesus. Can the servant avoid what the Master suffered? Yet how often we seek the world's love over God's love. We seek by all means to avoid the world's hatred, compromising when faced with persecution or taking our ease when obedience is demanded. Whom God loves the world hates; the world always hates whom and what God loves. You cannot alter that fact. If we are faithful to the King, we cannot avoid suffering. We will be a distinctive people, and that will bring on us the sneer and the snarl of the unconverted. Nevertheless, it is all embraced readily because this comes "for My name's sake." It is because of our attachment to the King and in the demonstration of His government over us that this comes to pass. It is this that conditions our whole experience of

---

14. Ryle, *Expository Thoughts on John*, 3:88.

suffering. Christ carries us into suffering, on despite suffering, and ultimately through suffering.

The Lens of the Cross

> But God forbid that I should boast except in the cross of our Lord Jesus Christ, by whom the world has been crucified to me, and I to the world. For in Christ Jesus neither circumcision nor uncircumcision avails anything, but a new creation. (Gal. 6:14–15)

There is a triple crucifixion in this text. Christ is crucified; the world is crucified; the Christian is crucified. The first is the one that determines the others. Christ crucified hangs between the world and the church. The world and the church relate to one another through the medium of the cross. The cross puts the world in its shadow from the church's perspective, and the church in its shadow from the world's perspective. Each to the other is dead. The world sees the offensiveness and the foolishness of the cross-clingers of Christ. If we are believers, we see the hostility and hollowness of the "godless values and hopeless pleasures of the present age."[15] After all, "those who are Christ's have crucified the flesh with its passions and desires" (Gal. 5:24).

The cross of the King is determinative for the way in which believers view and are viewed in this world. The Christian looks at everything in this world through the lens of the cross. The believer says with Matthew Poole, "I care no more for the world than it careth for me; the world despiseth and contemneth me, and the doctrine of the cross which I preach and publish in it, and I contemn it, with all its vain pomp and splendour. And this I do through the *cross of Christ*, remembering how the world dealt with Christ, and how little he regarded the world: or, through the grace of Christ, who hath enabled me to it."[16]

John Brown offers a more developed but still very penetrating analysis. He begins with a reminder as to how the vast majority of people view the world, and how the apostle once viewed it:

> "The world," in the estimate formed of it by mankind in general, may be compared to a mighty prince, who has unlimited

---

15. Ryken, *Galatians*, 277.
16. Poole, *Commentary on the Holy Bible*, 3:661.

means of bestowing rewards and inflicting punishments, and whose favour, of course, it is of the highest importance to secure and retain. They conceive that happiness is to be found in present sensible things. To be rich and honourable, to have all the accommodation and pleasures of the present state, to enjoy the smiles of this potentate, is, in their estimation, to be happy. To be poor and despised, persecuted and afflicted, to be subjected to the frown of this potentate, is, in their estimation, to be miserable. This is the mode of thinking and feeling natural to man, and it was once the apostle's mode of thinking and feeling.

Then, Brown describes the seismic shift in Paul's thinking:

He once counted worldly honour, and wealth, and pleasure, and power, gain; but now, instead of viewing the world as a mighty potentate, he regarded it as a condemned malefactor nailed to a cross. He no longer looked to it for happiness; he no longer regarded it either with admiration or fear; he no longer courted its smiles; he no longer dreaded its frowns. The wealth, and honours, and pleasures of the world could not seduce him, nor all its varied evils terrify him into an abandonment of the Saviour or of his cause—make him renounce or even conceal one of his doctrines—neglect one of his ordinances, or violate one of his laws. In his estimate, to do anything inconsistent with duty to his Lord, in compliance with "the course of this world," in order to attain its richest reward, or avoid its severest punishment, would be as absurd as if to procure a favourable glance from the eye of a worthless expiring felon on a cross, a person were to subject himself to the displeasure of an accomplished and powerful sovereign, who had every claim on his affections and allegiance.[17]

For Paul, and for those who would follow in his footsteps, the world has fully and finally bowed to the cross. The world's temptations can no longer seduce us nor do its terrors compel us into any denials of our Lord, either of principle or practice.

The Volunteer Spirit

Your people shall be volunteers
In the day of Your power;

---

17. Brown, *Galatians*, 372.

In the beauties of holiness, from the womb of the morning,
You have the dew of Your youth. (Ps. 110:3)

Here we see David, as prophet, effectively carrying God's message to his Lord and Savior, the Messiah. Messiah has been enthroned by God, and David speaks concerning the establishment of His kingdom, the defeat of His enemies, and the maintenance of His rule. God is telling His Messiah what will come to pass. Here the Father speaks of Messiah's people, those who will be volunteers in the day of His power. This sovereign King has a people who are His by right of redemption, and those people have a characteristic attitude of most willing consecration. They freely—never grudgingly!—give themselves in sacrificial service to their Lord, for it is the day of His power, and He is reigning. Derek Kidner tells us that, in these words,

> The general picture emerges...of a host of volunteers rallying to their leader in a holy war.... This verse (as I see it) pictures the Messiah going forth in primal vigour, holiness and glory, at the head of a host which is as dedicated as those early Israelites who 'jeoparded their lives to the death' (Judg. 5:18). The Christian can identify such an army with the overcomers portrayed in Revelation 12:11, little as he may recognize himself and his fellows in either picture.[18]

When the cry goes up "Who will serve the Lord? Who will go for Him?" this is a people who respond with every foot stepping forward in voluntary motion in the eager hope that they will be sent. Not one takes a step back. "Lord, only speak the word, only point the finger—show me my duty, and I shall pursue it." The crowned King has a people who readily serve Him, breathing a spirit of cheerful adoration, complete obedience, and ready service.

The King's Prayer

> "Father, I desire that they also whom You gave Me may be with Me where I am, that they may behold My glory which You have given Me; for You loved Me before the foundation of the world. O righteous Father! The world has not known You, but I have known You; and these have known that You sent Me. And I

---

18. Derek Kidner, *Psalms 73–150* (Nottingham, U.K.: IVP, 2008), 428–29.

have declared to them Your name, and will declare it, that the love with which You loved Me may be in them, and I in them." (John 17:24–26)

Notice how many threads are drawn together here. We find in the prayer of our Lord a distinctive people, called out of the world to God. Christ's disciples are marked by allegiance to Christ as opposed to and despite hostility from the world. But then they are sent out into the world to call others and so to draw together a people marked by spiritual unity and destined for eternal glory. They are preserved, sanctified, united, beloved, and glorified. Christ the King considers them all, each one, and desires and designs to bring them at last to be with Him where He is. He is praying them home into glory: "Father, I want them to be with Me where I am, to see Me in My glory as the King of kings and Lord of lords." Why will you reach heaven? Because Christ wants you there. The people of the King will soon march into the presence of the King in accordance with the prayer of the King. Ryle writes:

> We do not see Christ now. We read of him, hear of him, believe in him, and rest our souls in his finished work. But even the best of us, at our best, walk by faith and not by sight, and our poor halting faith often makes us walk very feebly in the way to heaven. There shall be an end of all this state of things one day. We shall at length see Christ as he is, and know as we have been known. We shall behold him face to face, and not through a glass darkly. We shall actually be in his presence and company, and go out no more. If faith has been pleasant, much more will sight be; and if hope has been sweet, much more will certainty be.[19]

Our destiny, as those who follow the King whose kingdom is not of this world, is to be with the King in His kingdom. It will surely come to pass. Until then, we serve Him here.

Serve the King: Summary Thoughts

Your relationship to the King conditions and determines all your life, the whole existence of every one of His people: your life here, your

19. Ryle, *Expository Thoughts on John*, 3:148.

death when it comes, and your life in the world to come. It is, in a way, even broader than this, for your relationship to the King matters even if you do not acknowledge His lordship. In that sense, your relationship to this King is all that really matters. Is he your King? Do you belong to His kingdom?

As believers, who we are and what we do find their root and their fruit in Him. Still, we endure as those who see Him who is invisible (Heb. 11:27), the eyes of our faith being fixed on Christ whom, not having seen, we love. If we are His people, it is His Word and will that direct us. Our identity has its genesis and grounding and our activity its guidance and government in our union with Christ.

Our grasp of this truth situates us rightly with regard to the world, considered in all of its various s nses. Failure to grasp this sets us drifting, leaving us rootless, aimless, and fruitless. The early saints, following the apostles, recognized themselves as disciple-making disciples, followers of the crucified One. If you are a Christian, you might define yourself quite simply: "I am a slave of Jesus Christ." In the old covenant, there was a picture of this when a servant wanted to remain in a household. The servant would go over to the door of that house, and the master would put an awl through his ear and mark him out as one who longed to belong to that household forever (Ex. 21:6). In effect, that bondservant was saying, "I could be anywhere else, but I will to be here and to have you as my master." That is what a Christian does. He takes Christ willingly, cheerfully, and entirely. We are not robots or mindless automatons. We now have minds of our own, enlightened by the Holy Spirit, and that is why we serve Him. We serve because this is the wise, right, perfect way. We can say, "This is what I was designed for. This is where I find my true identity. This is where I generate all my worthwhile and purposeful activity."

Our destiny is to be conformed to the image of the King (Rom. 8:29). Our life is lived in Him, by Him, for Him, and all to the glory of God (Gal. 2:20; Rom. 11:36; 1 Cor. 10:31, respectively). Why would you live for Him? Because He died for you! What is the great end for which you were created? For the glory and honor of your God and Savior. We cling to Him in faith, not just as the way into the kingdom but as a way of life once in the kingdom. We cling to Him in love: the longer we go on, the more delightful and desirable He becomes. We cling to Him in hope: He is our abiding Helper by His Holy Spirit whom He has given to us. In dependence upon Him we live for Him. If He calls us to it, we will suffer for Him, and if He designs it for us, we will die for Him. Like Saul we ask, "Lord, what do You want me to do?" We do not know what the answer to the question must be, but that must be the question.

It is He who tells us, "These things I have spoken to you, that in Me you may have peace. In the world you will have tribulation; but be of good cheer, I have overcome the world" (John 16:33). We overcome because He is greater than the world (1 John 4:4). Our new identity and lively faith in Him are the means of our overcoming, "for whatever is born of God overcomes the world. And this is the victory that has overcome the world—our faith. Who is he who overcomes the world, but he who believes that Jesus is the Son of God?" (1 John 5:4–5).

Why are we pilgrims? Because the King has called us onto His road. What do we do when the world comes calling? We may often feel the tug of old habits. We hear the siren voices of temptation, the insistent cry of sinful appetites that we have renounced. But Christ has conquered us and has been cheerfully crowned in our hearts, and the voice of the world no longer draws and binds us as once it did.

> 'Tis to Thee we owe allegiance,
> God our Saviour and our King;
> May we render true obedience,
> Every day our tribute bring;
> And with rapture
> Of Thy love and glory sing.
>
> May we bow to Thy dominion,
> Yielding to Thy righteous sway.
> Careless of the world's opinion,
> May we all Thy will obey;
> Saviour, lead us,
> Lead us in the perfect way.[20]

We are a pilgrim people, recognizing that the kingdom of God on the earth is simultaneously a fortress and an outpost. We are

---

20. Thomas Kelly, "'Tis to Thee We Owe Allegiance."

separated by way of distinctive holiness and engaged by way of gospel passion. We are pilgrims through this wilderness world, and we are on our way home, seeking to glorify the God of our salvation every step of the way until we at last arrive. How shall we then live?

Serve the King: Specific Counsels

First, we must *know the King*. This almost goes without saying, but do you know who He is? Do you know what He has done? Paul was utterly lost until he saw Him, not after the flesh but as He truly is: the crowned Lord of glory, the risen Jesus enthroned at the right hand of God. He realized that the despised Nazarene was the incarnate God and the true Christ. He saw this One who—having accomplished a once-for-all redemption by His sacrifice of Himself—rose from the grave in triumph and ascended to the highest place, waiting until His enemies are made His footstool. He is altogether lovely and entirely glorious, a Lamb as if slain and a Lion untamed, to whom all authority has been given, worthy of the adoration and obedience of every one of His creatures. Grasp this and all else follows. One Spirit-influenced glimpse of Christ as He truly is turned the persecutor into a preacher. Once Paul did all he could to pull Christ down. Now he asks simply, "Lord, what do You want me to do?" Anyone who would be of this kingdom and would serve this King should come with the question of the Greeks at the feast: "Sir, we would see Jesus." That is the starting point. The more clear this is, the more complete all else will be.

Then we must *acknowledge the King*. By this, I do not mean an intellectual acceptance of certain data, but the heartfelt embrace of the reality of His reign, taking Him as sovereign Savior and supreme Lord. One day everyone will do it, willingly or otherwise: "Therefore God also has highly exalted Him and given Him the name which is above every name, that at the name of Jesus every knee should bow, of those in heaven, and of those on earth, and of those under the earth, and that every tongue should confess that Jesus Christ is Lord, to the glory of God the Father" (Phil. 2:9–11).

Saints do it readily now and will do it with unbounded joy in their hearts on that day. They have already made this decision and grasped this reality. They accept His person, bow to His rule, and embrace His authority. They consider that what they think and feel is to be governed by what Christ knows and says, and they find their perfect liberty in doing so. They are concerned not with what men think but with what God knows. We are not pleasers of men, but of God. The opinion and esteem of the Lord matter above those of wife or husband, sons or daughters, friends or neighbors or colleagues, authorities or enemies. The saints fear God above men (Matt. 10:28). This is, perhaps, why so many of us struggle: we live as if caught between two competing authorities, two competing fears, rather than being rightly governed by a holy fear of God that drives out the fear of man. As the old paraphrase of Psalm 34 by Nahum Tate and Nicholas Brady advises us: "Fear Him, you saints, and you shall then have nothing else to fear!" If we are Christians, we ought to have already decided that God's King rules us. The only question will be, when and how will that work out in the conflicts of this life?

Beyond that, we must *adore the King*. Perhaps someone—perhaps you—would read the words above about bowing to our supernatural Lord and say, "Wackos!" or something even less polite. It sounds preposterous to many, and it may sound extreme to some who call themselves Christians. But they do not know our King! Those who think that serving Christ is madness have not grasped who He is. They have not felt the benefits of His blood, the pardon of our sins, the peace of forgiveness, the Father's embrace of the justified, the strength of those indwelt by the Spirit. They have no sense of the inheritance of sons. They have not yet gazed on the Son of Man, the incarnate Son of God Almighty, and seen His majesty and His meekness, His grace and His glory. They have not considered the Lamb in the midst of the throne and felt that they have come to the center and pinnacle of all things. They have not understood that all of heaven is singing the praises of God and of the Lamb. They have not considered that He is worthy of all we have and are because of all He is and does. They have not become unashamed worshipers of the God-man. If this were grasped, the saints' attitude to Christ makes perfect sense. In fact, the madness lies in *not* worshiping Him. It is insane not to follow this Jesus.

And that is what we do: we *follow the King*. There are no shortcuts to the heavenly inheritance. Christ calls us to follow Him through suffering to glory, to take up the cross and to walk where He leads.

There is a refreshing, although an unsettling honesty in such a bald statement. The slave will not avoid what the Master faced. We are to own Christ Jesus as Lord indeed and so take up our own cross and follow Him. That preacher who fails accurately to represent his Lord in this is a liar and unfaithful to God and men, a destroyer of souls. If you follow Christ faithfully, there will be pains; there will be sacrifices, sorrows, and struggles. Only the compromiser and the lukewarm person will avoid them.

But the question is not about what we will suffer on the way so much as about the righteousness of the path and the promised glorious reward at its end. Are you ashamed of Christ? Then you have a problem. You can afford to be ashamed of Christ when you need Him no longer. Are you embarrassed to stand as a Christian? Some of us seem willing to do almost anything to avoid being identified as a follower of the crucified One.

There is a very telling story about a man whose father was a pilot in the American Air Force and had died in a training accident. He did not know a great deal about his father, except a few stories that had been handed down. The man tells the following tale of his father:

> One night my dad's squadron took a "mandatory" trip to a beach house somewhere along the Atlantic Coast. No wives or children were allowed to come. This was a special night in which many of the young pilots would receive their "call-signs." Shortly after my father arrived at the beach house, he realized why family members were not invited. Someone had invited strippers as entertainment for the evening. Later that night, when he confided this event to my mom, she asked him how he responded. He said that he had stayed in the corner of the beach house with his hand over his eyes. A few months after my father's crash, a pilot in the squadron gave my mom a picture that someone had taken inside the beach house that night. He told my mom that deep down "everyone respected Kelly for it, but no one had the guts to follow him." Sure enough, in the background was my father with his hand covering his eyes. As a young boy, my mom showed me that picture and explained to me the integrity and courage my dad had displayed in that moment. She then explained the necessity of walking a path of purity in my own life. My mom framed the picture and put it in my room for me as a constant reminder to always walk in

purity. The legacy of purity my father left for me has made a huge difference in my life.[21]

The man of God hid his face in his hands rather than allow sin in through the gate of his eyes. His colleagues knew why. What of us? When was the last time we were ready to hide our faces from sin, willing to be the odd one out? Or do we spend all our lives striving to ensure that our allegiance to Christ remains well hidden? Are we not, too often, cowards? The only thing that will make a difference is when we know and follow the King. If you are one who regularly buckles in the face of the world's pressure, you ought to consider afresh what is at stake: "For what will it profit a man if he gains the whole world, and loses his own soul? Or what will a man give in exchange for his soul? For whoever is ashamed of Me and My words in this adulterous and sinful generation, of him the Son of Man also will be ashamed when He comes in the glory of His Father with the holy angels" (Mark 8:36–38).

Furthermore, and taking all that into account, we must *trust the King*. This can be such a challenge to so many of us. It is often the root reason why we struggle to follow Him. We are not confident that His word is certain, that His promise is sure, that His presence is perpetual, His saints provided for, and His purposes surely accomplished. Perhaps we wonder if He is willing or able to keep us. We fear that our families will disown us, our children will be put off, our jobs threatened, our comforts compromised, our feebleness exposed. As a result, we play it safe, hedge our bets, and fudge the issues that face us. All our life long is spent weaving safety nets just in case the One who laid down His life for us might forget us or forsake us. If we know who He is, if we see Him in His glory, if we understand His power and authority, if we feel the beating of His ardent heart, what do we need to fear? "Father, I want them to be with Me, where I am." Can we not trust the One who died for us and who always lives to make intercession for us?

---

21. Grant Castleberry, "The Explosion in West, Texas and Fatherhood, The Council on Biblical Manhood and Womanhood, http://cbmw.org/men/fatherhood /the-explosion-in-west-texas-and-fatherhood/.

If, then, we trust Him, we will also *obey the King*. Settle it now in your mind and heart that—because of who Jesus Christ is in Himself and to you and because of what He has done in itself and for you, for His glory and your good—you will take Him at His word and do all that He commands. When we read that His people will be volunteers in the day of His power, could others point to us and our lives and say, "That is what that verse means"? Do we manifest the attitude, pattern, spirit, and labor of such a life? Whose approval do you seek? Whose do you need? Nothing will matter in the day of His return but His "Well done!" to His servants. Overly precious thespian types are often mocked as struggling to discern their conjured incentives when acting out a scene: "So tell me, what's my motivation?" Many overly precious Christians seem to ask the same question. What more motivation do we need? He is the King all glorious! Do it, then, not because you are cornered like a rat in a trap, but because He is worthy. The Baptist pastor and theologian Andrew Fuller says that "if we were in a proper spirit, the question with us would not so much be, What *must* I do for God? as, What *can* I do for God? A servant that heartily loves his master counts it a *privilege* to be employed by him, yea, an *honour* to be intrusted with any of his concerns."[22]

Do we live life as if it were a string of opportunities to glorify Christ? If so, we will give ourselves to this cheerfully and wholeheartedly rather than grudgingly and halfheartedly. Do it not because the elders have been on your back, because the deacons have pursued you, because the rest of the church happens to be watching, or because everyone else is doing it and you have to go with the flow or risk being exposed. And really do it—do it as to the Lord. One analyst of the modern age "mourns television's assault on exposition in which the Church historically has been dependent for teaching doctrines and creeds. [Scholar Marva J.] Dawn...believes 'television has habituated its watchers to a low information-action ratio, that people are accustomed to "learning" good ideas (even from sermons) and

---

22. Andrew Fuller, "Causes of Declension in Religion, and Means of Revival," in *The Complete Works for the Rev. Andrew Fuller*, ed. Andrew Gunton Fuller (Harrisonburg, Va.: Sprinkle Publications, 1988), 3:320.

then doing nothing about them.'"[23] Whether it is television or some other influence, have you learned to hear the Word of God without obeying it? That is a fearful, even a fatal error. Let us learn to obey. Do righteous things in a righteous way and leave the consequences with a righteous God.

Let us therefore *preach the King*. When it comes to preaching, it is Him we proclaim (Col. 1:28). This was the hallmark and keynote of apostolic preaching from the beginning: "Therefore let all the house of Israel know assuredly that God has made this Jesus, whom you crucified, both Lord and Christ" (Acts 2:36). Paul preached Christ in Thessalonica, "explaining and demonstrating that the Christ had to suffer and rise again from the dead, and saying, 'This Jesus whom I preach to you is the Christ'" (Acts 17:3). In Athens, Paul preached to them Jesus and the resurrection (Acts 17:18), concluding his more developed argument that "truly, these times of ignorance God overlooked, but now commands all men everywhere to repent, because He has appointed a day on which He will judge the world in righteousness by the Man whom He has ordained. He has given assurance of this to all by raising Him from the dead" (Acts 17:30–31). It must be the hallmark and keynote of our own preaching: the unashamed, unapologetic, unembarrassed declaration of Jesus as Lord. The ministers of the gospel have a glorious calling: "For we do not preach ourselves, but Christ Jesus the Lord, and ourselves your bondservants for Jesus' sake. For it is the God who commanded light to shine out of darkness, who has shone in our hearts to give the light of the knowledge of the glory of God in the face of Jesus Christ" (2 Cor. 4:5–6).

Finally, let us *expect the King*. If all things ended here, in this world, what a bundle of pathetic and cruel lies all this would be. If it were all about the here and now, what hollowness! "If Christ is not risen, then our preaching is empty and your faith is also empty.... If in this life only we have hope in Christ, we are of all men the most pitiable" (1 Cor. 15:14, 19). If Christ is dead, we are believing a fantasy and living a lie. "But now Christ is risen from the dead" (1 Cor. 15:20). The King is alive. He is reigning! He will return.

---

23. Arthur W. Hunt III, "The Secular C. S. Lewis: Neil Postman's Unlikely Influence on Evangelicals," *Second Nature*, May 2, 2013, http://secondnaturejournal .com/the-secular-c-s-lewis-neil-postmans-unlikely-influence-on-evangelicals/.

The night of weeping will soon give way to a morning of song. Not long now and you will see Him, and in that moment you will be like Him for you will see Him as He is. And then the world will pass away. Creatively, all will be made new, purged and pure. All that now has the impact and stain of sin upon it will be restored, and this will be the place in which righteousness dwells. Extensively, the world will be divided. The earth will be winnowed. The angels will come forth with their scythes in their hands, Christ Himself will stand with His winnowing fan in His hand, and the tares will be gathered out and burned and the wheat gathered in and brought home. Morally and ethically, all wickedness must pass away from this world and righteousness will reign. "The world may pour contempt on our religion, and laugh us and our Christianity to scorn; but when the Father honours us at the last day, before the assembly of angels and men, we shall find that his praise makes amends for all."[24] And so we live as a pilgrim people, separated to God, engaging for God, citizens of Christ's heavenly kingdom, seeking His glory every step of the way, living and dying to that end, waiting for His return, pressing on, passing through.

---

24. Ryle, *Expository Thoughts on John*, 2:244.